REDEFINING EDUCATION IN THE
TWENTY-FIRST CENTURY

REDEFINING EDUCATION IN THE TWENTY-FIRST CENTURY

Shaping Collaborative Learning in the Age of Information

By

DENNIS ADAMS

and

MARY HAMM

CHARLES C THOMAS • PUBLISHER, LTD.
Springfield • Illinois • U.S.A.

Published and Distributed Throughout the World by

CHARLES C THOMAS • PUBLISHER, LTD.
2600 South First Street
Springfield, Illinois 62704

© 2005 by CHARLES C THOMAS • PUBLISHER, LTD.

ISBN 0-398-07587-5 (hard)
ISBN 0-398-07588-3 (paper)

Library of Congress Catalog Card Number: 2005047069

Printed in the United States of America
UB-R-3

Library of Congress Cataloging-in-Publication Data

Adams, Dennis M.
    Redefining education in the twenty-first century : shaping collaborative learning in the
age of information / by Dennis Adams and Mary Hamm.
        p. cm.
    Includes bibliographical references.
    ISBN 0-398-07587-5 – ISBN 0-398-07588-3 (paper)
        1. School improvement programs–United States. 2. Educational change–United States.
3. Education–Aims and objectives–United States. 4. Education–Effect of technological
innovations on–United States. I. Hamm, Mary. II. Title.

LB2822.82.A32 2003
370'.973'0905–dc22

BK
$32.95

2005047069

PREFACE

Nothing great was ever achieved without enthusiasm.
                                        –Emerson

B road cultural, social, and educational trends challenge old assumptions and invite new dreams. There is general agreement that we need better teachers to help students learn how to navigate today's unsettling reality. Unfortunately, there is little consensus about how to get (or even keep) the best and the brightest educators. Much of the oxygen surrounding the schools debate as been consumed by structural innovations like charter schools and vouchers. Such distractions have clouded over more important issues like developing quality teachers who can deal with the characteristics of effective instruction in the technologically intensive twenty-first century.

Redefining Education in the Twenty-first Century includes topics such as teacher professional development, the cognitive nature of learning, concepts gleaned from the research on brain functioning, and the pedagogical implications of technology. It provides educators insights into current educational issues and translates this information into possible classroom applications. Written in a style that the classroom teacher will find accessible, the book also explores new instructional developments, content in the classroom, performance assessment, and possibilities for building an active meaning-centered curriculum. Concepts like collaboration and critical thinking are addressed so that they can be considered as tools for inquiry in the core curriculum.

Reinventing the schools means changing how we think about instruction in an age where the traditional boundaries between politics, technology, culture, education, and ecology are disappearing. It also means changing school culture to accommodate a world where we are all so much more interconnected. When a century or an institution changes, there is a power struggle between what we know and what we can imagine. When schools feel the pressure to change the habit of the familiar, it often clashes with day-to-day routine. There are severe penalties if we succumb to distraction and indifference.

Reflection, discussion, and cultivating the disposition for critical thinking can always inform and enrich our teaching. So can more authentic assessment structures, like portfolios. Even teaching to the "test" doesn't have to be a learning disaster with meaning-centered performance assessment. Whether its the teacher's professional teaching portfolio – or the student's work samples – these performance assessment processes are viewed as a step toward changing the nature of school assessment. This kind of fundamental change in the evaluation process can support changes in instruction, school culture, and the professional development of teachers.

There are some superb examples of high quality schools across the country. Many have been freed from at least some of the shackles of regulation and constant high-stakes testing. A few models of excellence have been around for some time without many public educators being able to trudge through a bureaucratically mandated swamp and get to them. A moat, full of administrative and statutory restrictions, often surrounds the possibilities for positive change in the public schools. Strict accountability under these conditions is not realistic. Before high assessment standards are applied, teachers and school administrators need more resources and control over their school environment.

There are no "silver bullet" solutions to America's educational problems. We must all show a great deal of respect for the complexity of the problems we set out to solve. Schools can make a difference, but they can't do it alone. We are all responsible for the dire straits and dilapidated condition that many of our schools find themselves in. Failures in leadership, lack of public will, and social policy have more to do with it than educators. For example, teachers have had little or nothing to do with the fact that America's urban environment has lost many of the psychological, moral, and material prerequisites of societal life. Cultural decay, global economic competition, and political lethargy have all contributed to the decline in the public sectors of American educational life. Even in the most favorable economic times times many communities and their schools are left behind.

Thirty years ago this country had the world's best educated work force. Not investing in our human capital is a major problem in the United States. While Germany and Japan invest about five percent of their gross national product (GNP) in their educational infrastructure the U.S. can only come up with one percent. On a more positive note, the United States has more technological capital than any country. Used intelligently, the Internet, for example, gives American teachers the opportunity to create a medium that can spark a student's imagination, enhance a teacher's freedom, and improve every school. Used in an undisciplined way it can be a colossal waste of time. It depends on how the technology connects to curriculum goals. There is no guarantee that technological marvels or anything else will help every child live out his or her potential in a more prosperous and just society. However, it is our belief that there is enough imagination, intelligence, compassion, courage, and money in this country to get the job done.

Economically the U.S. represents more than a third of the world's total GNP; our closest competitor, the Japanese, represents about 15 percent. Clearly, the United States does not have to choose between its children and its ideals. Democracy in both education and life is imperfect. It does not always turn out well; but without it things usually turn out badly. We may not be able to guarantee every child a wonderful home life, but we should be able to provide a high quality education for all of our children. This book stresses realism, idealism, hope, and curriculum possibilities for developing schools worthy of our children. Everyone's future depends on creating a better educated, freer, more efficient and more stable America.

The most powerful way to strengthen our democratic society is to strengthen our schools. You can't predict the future, but you can learn about the terrain you must operate on. Certain guidelines and basic principles will not disappear. For example, the curriculum has to be meaningful, make connections, emphasize responsibility, and reflect human values. We can also be sure that topics like professional development, authentic assessment, content standards, collaborative inquiry, and new technology will not disappear from the educational debate.

This book maps some possible routes to be taken today, and explores conceptual principles that have meaning for tomorrow's schools. As we set out to improve schooling, it is important to recognize that change is never completed because everyone is constantly learning and experiencing insights for practice, research and colleagues. About the only thing that is permanent now is change itself. The days of stationary educational goals are over; hitting moving targets is part of today's reality. You can be sure that in the twenty-first century there will always be waves of change flowing across any structure we build.

INTRODUCTION

Redefining Education in the Twenty-first Century explores issues, trends and practical ideas for teaching and learning in a new era. The book provides specific classroom activities and connects them to recent pedagogical developments that reach across the curriculum. It builds on our expanding knowledge of what works in classrooms. It goes on to suggest how new approaches to teaching and learning can transform our schools. Ideas and activities for standards-based active learning, collaborative inquiry, and communications technology are included.

All of our suggestions connect to the content standards, the research, and our experiences with workshops and classes around the country. We have found that there is frequently a disconnect between what children need to know in the Age of Information and the day-to-day life of the classroom. *Redefining Education in the Twenty-first Century* is designed to help correct that imbalance and assist educators as they develop ways of teaching students what they must know in the twenty-first century. Many of the methods in this book are widely recognized as good paths to effective instruction; a few look promising, but have not proven themselves. Whatever the approach, a shared objective is making the schools more exciting, more humane, and more intellectually rigorous places.

In today's rapidly changing world suggestions are in, blueprints are out. As we set out to improve schooling it is important to recognize that change is never completed because everyone is constantly learning and experiencing insights from practice, research, and colleagues. It is little wonder that a key element of educational reform is the ongoing professional development of millions of teachers. This book is designed to help that effort and assist educators as they strive to make schools more exciting, more humane, and more intellectually rigorous places.

It is important that on our way to the future we capitalize on what we know about how children learn best. *Redefining Education in the Twenty-first Century* offers an ideal starting point for those who need to think through the fundamental questions of what teaching and learning should be about in the world of today – and the world of tomorrow. The book is designed to help teachers become more comfortable with the interactive methods and the technological tools that are arriving at the the intersection of core subjects.

With today's world moving at Internet speed, teachers and students need time for observation, reflection, exploration, collaboration and a wide range of literacy-related activities. New circumstances, new technologies, and new approaches to teaching and learning are constantly opening up a wider range of literacy-intensive possibilities. *Redefining Education in the Twenty-first Century* is designed to deepen the collective conversation, challenge your thinking, and give you some up-to-date tools that you can use today.

Knowing is not enough; we must apply.
Willing is not enough; we must do.

– Goethe

CONTENTS

REDEFINING EDUCATION IN THE TWENTY-FIRST CENTURY

Chapter 1

INTRODUCTION: CREATING THE EDUCATIONAL FUTURE

*The future is not a result of choices among alternative
paths offered by the present, but a place that is created
– created first in the mind and will, created next in activity.
The future is not some place we are going to, but one we
are creating. The roads to the future are not found but made,
and the activity of making them changes both the maker
and the destination.*
— John Schaar

The last ten years we have seen major changes in science, technology, communications, the global economy, and the nature of human interaction. Although teaching and learning have taken on new dimensions, the schools have not changed as much as the world around them. The capacity of educators to deal with change, learn from it, and help their students manage the surrounding ambiguity is critical to educational reform and the future development of our society.

We are now entering a time where change forces and technological breakthroughs are reaching a critical mass. As the twenty-first century moves along the schools will not be permitted to live in the past. Retro can be a fashion, but it can't be the educational future. Information and communications technologies are just one of the reasons that the pace of educational renewal will have to quicken. As we move farther into the new century the advent of ever more powerful digital tools will require the schools to deal more effectively with these remarkable knowledge acquisition vehicles.

Looking ahead can be helpful, but often the most effective way forward is to look around. It has long been clear that while active learning and modern technology have great potential to enhance teaching and learning, but turning that potential into reality on a large scale depends on our educational

3

vision, teacher preparation, a well-designed curriculum, and the ability to respond to a rapidly changing world.

We need to look beyond our obsession with information technology and individuals to include the critical social networks on which these are always a part. The implicit educational power of better and more available technology has penetrated remote corners of the globe. Although many nations are more fractured than ever, people are tied to others around the world as never before. One result is a huge outflowing of information that contributes to shared cultural experiences. Another is the need to understand how interpersonal skills, communities, organizations, and institutions can contribute to making the richest possible use of technology in our work and in our everyday lives.

A more stimulating and aesthetic learning environment can be stimulated by combining new information distribution possibilities with the more personal collaborative aspects of interactive face-to-face learning. In the last seven years public school Internet access has gone from near zero to better than 90 percent. Of course, in some places that means that only a few computers are online. But the point is that networking possibilities are expanding rapidly. Today's technology supports global observation, interaction, and learning as never before.

It's a new world order. In the Age of Information the shape of a nation's future depends more than ever on the quality of its educational system. Technology is an important thing, but its not the only thing. Technology alone isn't sufficient. You have to have a pedagogical plan that recognizes the social nature of learning. Intellectually connected social and technological skills matter. But there is no AAA *TripTik* or predetermined route for education in the twenty-first century. The only certainty is that education will change along with everything else.

FACING AN UNCERTAIN FUTURE

Be careful how you interpret the world — it's like that.

We face a future where human communication, interaction, and learning are no longer bound by time, space, and form. The dilemmas faced by nuclear physicists in the last century may be somewhat analogous to those facing technologists and educators today. It has, however, become harder than ever to guess the sources from which future problems and impulses for dramatic educational and social change will come. What is clear is that change favors the prepared mind and the intellectual energy of a civilization matter. It is also clear that as schools prepare to greet the future they must be able to help students collaboratively perceive, analyze, interpret and discover a whole new range of meanings.

Fortunately, everything we know and value won't fade into oblivion. We now have e-books and interactive literature, but traditional paper books are an elegant user-friendly tool that won't go away. We can interact with people around the world, but we still need face-to-face cooperative group skills. No matter how technology gets added to the mix, children will still have to read, write, and do mathematics. Being able to evaluate information and taking an informed position on an issue will continue to be valued. The difference is that many valued attributes are going to be applied to new media and new situations.

Communication and information technology contributes to the process of inter linking all parts of the globe and to the local process of educational reform. It is not possible to solve "the change problem," but we can learn to live with it more productively and more pro actively. As the twenty-first century moves ahead change is ever more ubiquitous and relentless. This reality cries out for new definitions and people who can redefine themselves in terms of a rapidly changing environment. Continuous and active educational experiences are moving ever closer to the center of today's reality.

Educational models will be influenced by the experimental research on instruction, understandings about the social nature of learning, and advancing technological possibilities. Teachers can be sure that they will be called upon to shoulder some of the responsibility for devising a curriculum that helps produce citizens who can live and work productively in increasingly dynamically complex societies. Whether its high-tech or high-touch, there is no alternative to a high quality teacher in the classroom. It takes well-educated teachers to help students become inner and outer learners who will connect to wider and wider circles of society. But they can't do it unless everyone – from parents to the media – takes more responsibility for the education of children. Whether it is television, the Internet, or anything else – if a society doesn't exercise thought and scrutiny over a powerful communication tool – it will become more terrible and more crass and affect us in even more terrible ways.

The professionalization of teaching is one of the keys to schooling in a digital world. Professionals do have certain guidelines. But they do not follow a prepackaged script. In spite of Nietche's dictum, "dancing in chains" is not the highest art form. Teachers can usually make good use of some informed guidance. But they also need autonomy and flexibility. Accountability without control is a joke. When teachers have more voice, resources, and control over their schools than we can hold them more accountable.

The educational improvement of its people is one of the most fateful challenges facing the United States today. Every high quality educational future requires putting more resources into focused learning opportunities for teachers. Efforts are under way to move from traditional inservice training models to broader notions of professional development (Darling-Hammond, L., 1999). Perpetual staff development and school-embedded learning for teachers are bound to be important features in tomorrow's schools. The direction of teacher inservice education may be open to question, but the concept of the teacher as a life-long learner is now a given.

SOCIAL REALITIES IN THE AGE OF INFORMATION

A clear understanding of a problem prefigures its lines of solution.
　　　　　　　　　　　　　　　　　– Margaret Mead

　　You can't guarantee everyone a perfect family, you could guarantee them better social surroundings and better educational possibilities. Obviously the schools can't change things on their own. We now know that the neighborhood a child grows up in may well be as important as the school they attend. It takes a sustained societal commitment to improving education and the child's environment outside of school. The world outside the classroom is changing more rapidly than ever; some of these changes are for the good, many are for the worse.

　　Caught between the challenges of new media and a culturally diverse society educators find themselves on the edge of something new. Exactly what is still a mystery. Everyday reality intrudes into schools like never before. In today's social milieu the schools are sometimes the child's only venue for socially and intellectually stimulating work. Giving children an education sufficient for healthy and productive lives is more important than ever.

　　Millions of poor American children now live in the shadow of wealth. In our national life, the divide between the privileged and the rest of society is widening in areas ranging from housing to Internet use. Technology seems to favor those who can afford to buy it. If you have enough money to go online you can, for example, order goods without paying taxes. If you can't afford a computer and Internet access you have to pay the sales tax at the store. The so-called digital divide extends beyond race and ethnicity to include income and educational level. The more affluent your home and school the more likely you are to see the imaginative side of computers and the curriculum, and the more likely you are to succeed in school. Libraries, schools, and other institutions can help, but it is hard to learn about things like technology if you don't have easy access to it.

　　To deal with real world problems and stay relevant, teachers must have the resources to integrate the most powerful media into their day-to-day lessons. Once the pedagogical piece is in place, the technology can help. Every child should be able to use technological tools to explore material in a manner that sparks curiosity, encourages collaborative inquiry, and extends learning possibilities (Banks, J. A.,1998). Intellectual and technological tools must be mastered to achieve just about anything today. Certainly teachers, parents, and the local community are directly responsible for helping young people gain the knowledge and skills necessary for success in an increasingly complex society. But everyone – from the media to the business world – shares responsibility for setting the conditions under which schooling takes place.

ATTITUDES THAT INFLUENCE EFFECTIVE TEACHING AND LEARNING

Schools can become a community of learners by creating a caring atmosphere, attending to student interests, and promoting meaningful learning. When the school culture values academic achievement and personal commitment it helps break down barriers to learning and moves students in the direction of academic success. Students and teachers need to be active participants in their own learning. We must all take every opportunity to recognize the impact and positive influence that teachers can have on the children's' lives. A teacher's daily interactions with students is a powerful influence (Liberman, A. & Miller, L.,1999).

What does it take to start teaching? First of all, prospective teachers need the intellectual tools learned in the arts and sciences. Equally important, they must acquire the foundational skills that relate to strategic learning and pedagogical methods. Even the best college graduates flounder if they start teaching without a thorough knowledge of the characteristics of effective instruction. A related key to becoming a successful teacher involves early field work experiences in different communities and different school settings.

Effective teachers have high expectations for their students. They also respect creative potential and develop a personal connectedness with their students. In fact, the interpersonal relationships that develop over matters of content are at the heart of schooling.

Through active participation in staff development programs teachers can work in association with peers to grow professionally and personally (Arends, R., 2004; Zeichner, K., 1998). By cooperating to reach common goals teachers are more likely to appreciate and respect one another. Positive attitudes make a difference. When teachers possess a positive attitude towards their teaching they are more likely to continue their teaching career and students are more likely to achieve academic success. Schools that involve teachers in participatory decision-making and collaborative strategies for addressing school problems are most likely to reinforce a teacher's commitment to the profession. Effective staff development programs have taken this into account as they address the challenge of sustaining the long-term commitment of dedicated and committed teachers.

Experienced teachers understand that teaching is a complex undertaking that requires time. Conditions may be difficult, but effective teachers accept and enjoy the challenges of teaching. They know that they make a difference in students' lives.

Many teachers describe success in personal terms and view it as related to being personally durable and capable. Knowing the child and understanding the community are frequently mentioned as important. Most teachers who have elected to remain in their schools for more than three years feel in control of their environment and believe teaching is a rich and rewarding experience (Glickman, C., 1998).

Effective teachers are more likely to believe that :

- creating a feeling of excitement about the subject matter or skill being taught is important.
- the children can always learn more and that the teachers' effort and energy is instrumental in students' learning.
- providing children the opportunity for active participatory experiences is a powerful incentive for learning.
- it is important to reflect a strong sense of personal caring about students and adjust instruction to their needs.
- children try hardest when they are fairly certain of success, but not absolutely positive.
- children learn most from teachers who believe that the level of student effort can predict achievement.
- children learn most when their questions and learning activities are connected with big ideas, key concepts, and their intellectual curiosity (Adams, D. & Hamm, M. 1998).

Although there are many approaches to good teaching, it is our belief that effective teachers often share some of the same characteristics.

Activity: Take a few minutes and write down a few of the teaching characteristics of your favorite teacher. Share with another person, a small group, or with the whole class. What are the similarities and differences between the above list and your favorite teacher. See if you can change a point or add an important characteristic to the above list. Would you take something out? Remember, no human teacher is going to have all the "right" characteristics.

Revitalizing the Public Schools

Global competition is one thing. The future of American democracy is another. Both depend on the revitalization of the public schools. This is where the majority of American children will continue to be educated, make choices about life, and connect to youngsters from different backgrounds. It is also where images are formed of what it means to be a good person, have a good life, and live in a good society.

The interpreting and reinterpreting of the American dream of universal public education will be with us throughout the new century. Small-scale private sector experiments are fine, but to reach the majority of students, innovations must be transferred successfully to the public sector.

Large scale educational change requires a sustained public commitment. Once this is in place we must involve a widespread cadre of public school educators who are willing to implement new approaches to instruction. The goal should be nothing less than transforming all of the nation's schools into a world class system. Ideally, curriculum designs should can build on American traditions, values, and culture – while helping the schools carry out rigorous self-examinations, vigorous innovations, and a commitment to greater effectiveness.

Change won't come easily. Transforming our schools for the twenty-first century will occasionally require fighting state and district systems that are hostile to change. In a few schools students are still made to feel unwelcome, intellectually inadequate, uncomfortable, and bored. At the earliest opportunity, they drop out. Over one million students a year leave school before graduation. For some who stay, schools may offer little encouragement for those who have talents extending beyond the ability to manipulate words and numbers. In spite of the grim social realities that weigh heavily on the shoulders of some children, the right kind of educational support can make a permanent difference.

Education, Culture, and Leadership

Culture may be viewed as a coherent system of attitudes, values and institutions that influence both individual and group behavior. The idea of culture has become ever more elastic and blurred by modern communications, swift transport, and the breakdown of traditional societies. In some cultures (Japan and Germany) the future seems to be burying the past. In other cultures (Russia and the Balkans) tribal rivalries of the past seem to be burying the future. In many regions of the world the fabric of civil society is unraveling – making anarchy more common than a coherent ideology.

Cultures that nurture the human creative capacity across age groups usually do better than those that do not. When education is thought of as a continuum from prenatal care through adult life it is bound to have a more powerful effect. Any attack on American social and educational problems must fight uphill against profound social trends. Clearly we must make some drastic changes in our educational system to remain competitive internationally. Balancing an understanding of globalization with the unifying ideas of democracy and social responsibility is a desirable educational goal. Although today's era of globalization is built around telecommunications, teaching computer-related skills won't help much. Finding ways to use computers and telecommunications to improve learning will help a lot.

New technologies like computers, satellites, and the Internet are able to weave the world together as never before. Like books, wiz-bang technology can be used in smart ways to support learning, or you can do time-burning stupid things with it. As far as computers and the Internet are concerned, the important thing is figuring out how they can improve student achievement, provide greater equity, and prepare students for life in the twenty-first century.

Peer culture and the media can get in the way, but parents are a key ingredient in a child's education. Academic achievement is strongly influenced by the level of insistence on the part of parents that children take their studies seriously. In today's world many parents aren't able to help. They need assistance in learning child rearing competencies and forming social support networks. Schools often find themselves teaching the parents and the children.

Fundamental change in schools requires fundamental changes in society. The hard questions must be asked and the uncomfortable issues dealt with. For schools to make a major impact on childhood difficulties requires parallel changes in cultural beliefs, social incentives, the status of teachers, and basic notions about schooling. Limiting the focus to concerns like national testing and school choice avoids the more crucial issues of moral numbness, individualism degenerating into greed, spiritual alienation, social injustice, or the diminishing prospects for a healthy future. For too long, we have not worried enough about future generations, or met our obligations to each other.

When it comes to improving the schools it isn't just money; it's values, willingness to sacrifice, and the ability to look at children and young adults in their totality. To deal with many of the issues most important to a child's future teachers will have to educate in ways that haven't been fully conceived of yet. It may not be possible to change yesterday's mistakes, but it is possible to change the future. It takes leadership that is willing to address the issues of our time in a bold manner − to inspire, instill, trust, and carry out carefully conceived plans. Leaders don't just reflect the health or ailment of a society, they help create them.

> *They say a nation gets the politicians it deserves. In some sense this is true. Politicians are indeed a mirror of their society, and a kind of embodiment of its potential. At the same time - paradoxically − the opposite is true: society is a mirror its politicians. It is largely up to the politicians which social forces they choose to liberate and which they choose to suppress, whether they rely on the good in each citizen or the bad . . .*
>
> − Vaclav Havel, *Summer Meditations,* 1992

At the school district level long-term leadership with high expectations is important. In good districts the attitude is, "We can teach anybody to learn." At the principals' level success is often attributed to having latitude in curricular and spending decisions. Other positive factors include having tangible goals, careful teacher recruitment, and parent outreach programs.

An Era of Acceleration, Integration, and Change

Expressions of scientific knowledge in better technology is now global in its effect. Science and its technological tools have directly accounted for fundamental changes in the world economy and at the same time tied the world together by nearly instantaneous communication. From genetic engineering to the Internet, science and its associates are now in a position to direct and manipulate the world more than ever. We have only a dim glimpse of the world ahead.

Genetics, robotics, and nanotechnologies are just three of the newer technologies that pose a potential risk to the physical world. The possibility of people able to order out for private futures is one ethical problem. Machines that can self-replicate themselves is another. From the genetic shaping of individuals to digital experiences bought off the shelf it is becoming easier to create natural facts (like new species or molecules).

The dynamic and compelling force of information and communication technology is becoming more effective at creating virtual realities. These made-to-order worlds are bound to take time away from face-to-face human interaction and ordinary sensory experiences. Schools can temper some of the harsh edges of technology by becoming good role models for connecting the social aspects of learning with broader online communities. They can also enhance learning with dynamic visual representations of concepts and media production – from videos to Web sites. Along the way they will have to restructure the teaching and learning role and make sure that assessment practices are aligned with the curriculum. The optimistic and self-congratulatory high-technology industry may have to step back from their chaotic advance into an uncertain technological future and debate the issues surrounding the inherently negative possibilities of rapidly evolving technologies.

The revolution in the provision of information is one of the greatest cultural changes in history and the United States is at the center of that change. To extend the idea of what is possible is to change the way people think and the way they act. The communication revolution is more than a technological advance, it is a major factor in spreading new ways of thinking. For a jump of comparable importance you have to go back to the transformation of culture, thinking, and learning that was caused by printing. Our schools must reflect these new realities.

Technology, economics, and culture are increasingly tied together. Now we truly live in one world. The interaction of events and trends in all parts of the world would not be possible without the communications that have rapidly tied humanity together with a new immediacy and intimacy. More than ever, global change is driven by new technologies that have taken on a speed of their own. The result of fewer and fewer certainties is the demand for ever higher levels of education and competency.

The word *inertia* is often associated with attempts to change the curriculum. Teacher attitudes, the need to reeducate students, traditional ways of doing things, and assessment practices all get in the way of initiating a new curriculum while operating an old system. Test-taking and test-preparation are but one example of how efforts to improve the schools that may have the opposite effect. Increasingly teachers and students are being coerced into wasting time and effort on out-of-context tests. It would be better to spend the time with the imaginative life and stimulating information found in books. Learning to read beats learning testing skills any day.

We are still learning how to capitalize on schools' social character to contribute to healthy educational growth. Not staying up-to-date is to fall behind; therefore, one of the most important features of a successful educational system is the capacity for self-renewel and continuous change. Speed bumps on the way to new practices: teacher preparation, the need to reeducate students, assessment practices, and the fact that new arrangements have to be put in place while operating the old system.

Abundant national resources, temperate climate conditions, location, and good education levels all play a role in national development. Whatever may be said about American education and competitiveness, Americanization remains one of the main vehicles for modernity. As the country that benefits most from global economic integration it is in the national interest to make sure that economic progress is sustainable for as many people in as many countries as possible. We have the tools to make a difference. Taking responsibility for striking the right balance between globalization's humanizing aspects and its dehumanizing tenancies is another question. A certain respect for other approaches to modernity would be healthy. Parochial attitudes about being moral teachers to others in the world may be vainglorious, undesirable, and even dangerous in the years ahead. Our nation, after all, is not the only center of political enlightenment.

THE FUTURE: LEARNING IN ASSOCIATION
WITH OTHERS

Personal experience is a tempting prop that carries its own dangers of distortion. The borders of personal and social experience have changed so much in recent years that it is often hard to discern what is being experienced in this age of mass communication.

Children achieve literacy through social interaction in which they create and communicate meanings through media of all kinds. A vast array of media provides stories, legends and folklore in a way that contributes to a shared commitment to the true – or to the false. The Internet is an example of how, right or wrong, the collective unconscious is a powerful thing. Powerful twenty-first century electronic media can dispense illusions, open new perspectives, or reveal obstacles to our aspirations that would be dangerous if left in the shadows. Books and newspapers are one thing, being able to sort through today's unedited information glut is quite another.

The rise of online education and other new technologies has enormous implications for schooling. However, we must be sure that technology empowers us to reach further in the world without preventing us from building relationships with other in the classroom and in the community. While there is no substitute for face-to-face interaction with others, it is urgent that everyone have access to literacy in its most powerful forms.

The interaction of events and technological trends require new definitions and new approaches to teaching and learning. Information economies require higher levels and more frequent education for everyone. There is a convergence in knowledge producing possibilities: publishers, schools, the Internet, television, libraries, universities, and museums. Some of the newer communication technologies have the potential to enrich teaching and learning. It all depends on how it is used and whether or not students are taught to understand and encouraged to create with the most powerful media available.

Schools can build on the potential of new technology, but genuine education depends on personal interaction among people and ideas in an esthetically and intellectually stimulating environment. Virtual universities have their limits. Learning on the Internet can become dull – even when the instructor stops from time-to-time so that students can interact in chat groups. The possibility of learning in direct association with others is so strong that major universities are turning away more applicants than ever. Even high-tech companies are building "campuses" in ways that encourage their workers to learn from face-to-face interaction. In the workplace or in school, specific skill and general literacy activies completed in small face-to-face groups (using today's digital tools) can make the learning environment more lively and interesting for everyone.

Fortunately for teachers, many of the basic pedagogical principles remain fairly constant. Today and tomorrow effective teachers will be teaching for understanding and building on activities that reflect an emphasis on reasoning, collaboration and communication. Teachers who are familiar with the art and science of teaching (pedagogy) are crucial to what students learn. So it should come as no surprise to find out that integrating curricular reform with the professional development of teachers is key to successful educational reform.

Educational technology works best when it is student-centered and designed to facilitate instruction through interactive mediation processes (Becker, 2000). Clearly one of the keys to successful schooling is the creation of learning communities where students are active and collaborative participants in the construction of meaning. There are solid examples of positive educational change around the country. The challenge is to take the best practices and give teachers the resources to make it happen everywhere.

We are in the midst of educational change and an explosion of multimedia digital technology. Both are taking on a momentum of their own. Rushing headlong into the digital age does not have to be a passive or a solitary experience. We can't control change. But we can help plot the trajectory and make a contribution to the conceptualization of learning environments that reflect our hopes, dreams, and values in an increasingly interconnected world. By building on the best models, students and teachers can link arms to reach past today's obstacles.

What you know or dream you can begin.
Boldness has genius, power, and magic in it.
Engage, then the mind grows heated –
Begin it, and the work can be completed!
– Goethe

RESOURCES AND REFERENCES

Adams, D. & Hamm, M. (1997). *Collaborative Inquiry in Science, Math and Technology.* Portsmouth, NH: Heinemann.

Arends, R. (2004). *Learning to teach.* (6th ed.) New York: McGraw-Hill.

Banks, J. A. (1998). The lives and values of researchers: Implications for educating citizens in a multicultural society. *Educational Researcher, 29,* 4–17.

Becker, J. (2000). Who's wired and who's not. In *Children and Computers.* The Center on the Future of Children, David and Lucille Parkard Foundation, Los Altos, CA.

Bransford, A., Brown, L. & Cocking, R. (Eds.) (1999). *How people learn: Brain, mind, experience.* Washington, DC: National Academies Press.

Darling-Hammond, L. (1999). *Teacher quality and student achievement.* Palo Alto, CA: Center for the Study of Teaching and Learning.

Darling-Hammond, L. (1997). *The right to learn: A blueprint for creating schools that work.* San Francisco: Jossey-Bass.

Glickman, C. (1998). *Democracy in education: Revolution, change, and the real renewal of America's schools.* San Francisco: Jossey-Bass.

Hovel, V. (1992). *Summer meditations.* New York: Knopf.

Liberman, A., & Miller, L. (1999). *Teachers – Transforming their world and their work.* New York: Teachers College Press.

McLaughlin, M., (1998). Listening and learning from the field: Tales of policy implementation and situated practice. In Hargreaves, A., Lieberman, M. Fulton & D. Hopkins (Eds.) *International handbook of educational change. Part one.* Boston: Kluwer Academic Publishers.

Mostetter, F., Light, R. J., & Sachs, J. A. (1996). Sustained inquiry in education: Lessons from skill grouping and class size. *Harvard Educational Review, 66,* 797–828.

Orlich, D. C. (2000). Education reform and limits to student achievement. *Phi Delta Kappan,* Feb. 81(6) 468–472.

Zeichner, K. (1998). The nature and impact of teacher research as a professional development activity for P-12 educators. Paper written for the Office of Education Research and Improvement. Madison, WI: University of Wisconsin.

Chapter 2

EVOLVING TRENDS OF THINKING
AND LEARNING

We are on the verge of a revolution: the application of important
new brain research to teaching and learning.

– Jenson

What is the most important trend of the new millennium? Many have speculated "mind science" – the study of human thinking and learning (Bransford, Brown & Cocking, 1999). Humans are thinkers and learners. Without our ability to think and learn, we would have nothing. New questions about thinking and learning are extending our understanding and capabilities. We are in the process of trying to understand the mind's capabilities and how to learn from them. As far as learning is concerned, we must have an accurate conception of how the mind really works. Sad to say, contemporary psychology has multiple views of the mind.

In the last ten years, educators have started to gain a new source of knowledge about the mind called neuroscience. Technologies such as Magnetic Resonance Imaging (MRI) reveal new information about the workings of the brain. Opinions about the usefulness of this data vary greatly. The thing we know for sure: mind science, including the study of the brain, will be studied well into the twenty-first century.

Our ideas of the mind in the last century were dominated in the first part of the century by the behaviorist view. The cognitive perspective was prevalent in the second part of the century. These views are much more complicated. For example, cognitive science is much broader than behaviorism was. Recent developments in neuroscience are extending the field even further. Our focus in this chapter is not on a scientific study of thinking and learning, instead we are concerned how ideas of the mind have influenced educational practices and how they may affect learning in the future. We begin with a short introduction of behaviorism and cognitive science, which leads to constructivism and human development, intelligence, and the skills of thinking. We end with activities concerning multiple intelligences and brain research.

Models of Education: Behaviorism, Cognitive Science

The educational model or (views of the mind) that was developed in the twentieth century stressed the behaviorist view of learning. Behaviorism is the idea that mental processes cannot be seen, what could be observed was behavior. Learning was defined as changed behavior. Lacking the knowledge of what goes on inside the brain, the behaviorist theories measured behaviors and learned to modify them with behavior reinforcers (rewarding positive behaviors, punishing negative ones).

After World War II, psychologists moved away from behaviorism to be introduced to cognitive science. Many educators welcomed the change. Cognition is the process of knowing. Over time, cognitive science included a broad range of human activities: decision making, critical thinking, making judgments, and creativity. Cognitive science has given us constructivism – the human brain does not simply take in knowledge, but is actively involved in creating that knowledge. In the last decade, the active role of the thinker and learner has been our model of how learning takes place.

Recently a new model has emerged, technology changed the way we think, live and learn. In the last part of the twentieth century (1970–1999) terms or expressions like "accelerated learning," and "super learning" became common as the Age of Information expanded. New medical tools could scan the brain and provide us with ways to understand and view what goes on inside the brain. An exciting element of brain science developed; neuroscience, an interdisciplinary approach to questions about the brain. Today, thanks to the research efforts of neuroscientists, we have amazing insights about the brain and learning. Many traditional educational ideas are becoming obsolete. We are learning about the brain at an astonishing rate. In the next few years, we can expect new and more exact technologies to further uncover the brain's mysteries.

Learning Explosion Enrichment and the Brain

Although we don't yet have a logically connected inclusive model of how the brain works, educators do know enough to make significant changes in how we teach. For many years the term "enrichment" was used for so-called "gifted" students who could benefit from these programs. This narrow thinking is way off base. The human brain of every child contains over a trillion connections. This base of nerve cell connectivity is enhanced by enrichment activities. Just what do we mean by enrichment activities?

The brain of every child can be enriched if the learning is *challenging*, this means providing new information or experiences, but there must also be *interactive feedback* (some way to learn from the experience). Mental challenges can be as simple as introducing new content, adding hands-on materials, or journal writing. Frequently changing instructional strategies is also important; using computers, having students work in groups, allowing choice in projects, or taking field trips provides a stimulating environment.

Maximizing student feedback should not be overlooked. Feedback builds confidence, lowers stress, and increases the brain's coping abilities. Other learners can be the greatest asset in the classroom. Unfortunately, many traditional environments are still not taking advantage of these opportunities. Cooperative groups give students attitudes of feeling valued and cared for. In the process the brain releases endorphins and dopamine which helps students enjoy their work. Groups offer social and academic feedback. When students talk to each other they share specific ideas as well as behavioral insights.

Computer games, short video selections, story editing by peers, all offer specific feedback. Feedback is most effective if it takes place immediately. Group interaction is a valuable feedback tool, it involves nonverbal modeling as well as real life drama and choice.

Human development is another theme closely linked to constructivism. Jean Piaget and other psychologists proposed stages of development wherein the learner can be cast in an active creative role (Piaget, 1964, Bruner, 1973, Case, 1992). Both constructivism and developmental perspectives have called for pedagogical reform. The last fifty years has focused attention on cultivating thinking and learning skills.

A Search For Meaning: Thinking Critically and Creatively

Thinking is a quest for meaning, a purposeful search for understanding and clarity. This journey often generates new perspectives and solutions to problems. It calls for an individual to be resourceful and adventuresome. Thinking is intentional, purposeful and deliberate.

Critical and creative thinking are an integral part of education in a new century. Fostering the critical and creative imagination is one of the most important challenges teachers face today. Thinking is built on personal experiences. Thinking is also influenced by culture, emotions, home environment, and educational possibilities. Critical and creative thinking experiences generate and express new ideas and solutions. Both have a conscious and purposeful mental focus. The playful spirit of *creative thinking* may occur while daydreaming, fantasizing or just allowing an idea to get started while taking a hike along a trail. Creative thinking emphasizes art and beauty as it goes beyond the adequate to attempt elegant solutions.

Critical thinking is viewed as constructing meaning by observing, interpreting, analyzing, and manipulating information in response to a problem. Activities which support critical thinking involve clarifying and solving problems, considering alternatives, strategic planning, and analyzing the results. *Creative thinking* is more flowing, flexible, novel, and detailed. Skills developed in this area try to create unique expressions, original conceptions, and novel approaches. The ability to see things in imaginative and unusual ways overlaps with problem solving and are part of critical thinking. We try not to get tangled up in definitions because what really matters is encouraging the development of high-quality thinking.

As teachers encourage the unique ideas developed by children it is important to remember that many problems of the future will be solved by people who are flexible, open, original, and creatively productive. Good thinking means being able to choose alternative explanations and demonstrate intellectual curiosity in a manner that is flexible and novel.

Critical thinking lessons should encourage students to analyze the hidden assumptions that influence meanings and interpretations of information. Such intellectually demanding thinking helps children identify, clarify, problem-solve, and become more productive creatively. The questions explored can be as general as: "How sure are we about the knowledge of this subject?" Questions can be as specific as "How did they figure that out?" or "What does it mean?" The wording may be changed, but students are never too young to analyze the underlying assumptions that influence meaning. And they are never too young to question the explanations of findings and participate in the act of knowledge creation. Many get sidelined by what David Whyte (1994) calls "the eddies and swells of everyday experience" He cites a line of poetry from one of his students to make his point: "I turned my face for a moment and it became my life" (p. 23).

Thinking and Learning Habits

A child's reality can be solidly constructed with real-life experiences that evoke personal meaning in the learner. Science, math, the arts and language arts lessons may begin with real materials, invite interactive learning, and allow children to explore the various dimensions of thoughtfulness, subject matter, and real world applications. The goal is to help children build a new set of expectations and create a new sense of understanding.

When students make sense of something by connecting to a set of personal everyday experiences constructivists may call it "viable knowledge." Whether or not they are familiar with the academic terms, good teachers have always connected educational goals to practical problem solving and students' life experiences. Implementing such a real world base embeds thinking skills into the curriculum so that students are intensely involved in reasoning, elaboration, hypothesis formation, and problem solving. New conceptions of literacy have to move beyond disciplinary boundaries.

Developing mature thinkers who are able to acquire and use knowledge means educating minds rather than training memories. Sometimes the acquisition of enhanced thinking skills can be well structured and planned, at other times it's a chance encounter formed by a crazy collision of elements. The ability to raise thoughtful questions about what is being read, viewed, or heard is a dimension of thinking that makes a powerful contribution to the construction of meaning. When motivated to reason intelligently children come up with good decision making and elegant solutions. Out of this comes insightful creations that suggest possibilities for action. As all of these elements come together they form the core of effective thinking and learning.

Implementing new methods for teaching mathematics, science, the arts and language arts depends on teachers who purposely invite reflective thinking. This means that both prospective and practicing teachers must take courses in which they learn math and science through inquiry and learn to apply the arts and language arts concepts within a context similar to the one they will arrange for their students. When carried out over time, professional development activities have proven useful in helping teachers organize instruction to accommodate new ways of representing and imparting knowledge. The result expands horizons and organizational possibilities. When teachers actually try out standards-based interdisciplinary inquiry they can reflect on teaching practice with colleagues and add to their ever-evolving base of good instructional practice.

Creative and critical thinking are natural human processes that can be amplified by awareness and practice. Both creative and critical thinking make use of specific core thinking skills. Classroom instruction and guided practice in the development of these skills will include the following:

1. *Think critically:* Be accurate, clear, and open minded, defend a position, be sensitive to others.
2. *Practice creative thinking:* Engage in difficult problems, extend the limits of your knowledge, find new ways to look at situations outside conventional boundaries, dare to imagine, innovate, trust.
3. *Listen with understanding and empathy:* The ability to listen to another person, and try to understand their point of view is one of the highest forms of communication.
4. *Be aware of your thinking:* This includes being sensitive to feedback, planning, and evaluating your actions. Take your time, remain calm, think before you act.
5. *Be attentive:* Skills such as observing, obtaining information, forming questions, clarifying through inquiry are some of the skills that fall under this category.
6. *Pose clear questions in succinct, direct language:* This advances inquiry and arranges information so that it can be understood or communicated more effectively.
7. *Remain open to continuous learning:* Apply prior knowledge to new situations.

8. *Analyze, form hunches:* Analysis is at the heart of creative and critical thinking. Analysis includes recognizing and articulating attributes and component parts, focusing on details and structure, identifying relationships and patterns, grasping the main idea and finding errors.

9. *Use models and metaphors:* This involves such higher order thinking as making comparisons, constructing metaphors, producing analogies, providing explanations and forming mental models.

10. *Gather data, assess and evaluate ideas:* Skills of evaluation include establishing criteria and proving or verifying data.

11. *Take risks:* The pursuit of elegant solutions often times demands risk taking (breaking with established traditions). Thinking independently.

12. *Find humor:* Humor has been found to free creativity and stimulate higher thinking skills. People who initiate humor, are verbally playful when interacting with others, they thrive on finding incongruity, are able to laugh at situations and themselves.
[Costa & Kallick, 2000; Martinello & Cook, 1994; Marzano, et al, 1988]

For teachers to build a solid base of thinking skills into daily classroom lessons requires that they consciously question and reflect on the best approach. Every inquiry if explored with enthusiasm and with care will use some of these core thinking skills (Jacobs, H. Hayes, 2004).

Illuminating Learning by Teaching For Thoughtfulness

The multidimensional search for meaning is made at least a little easier when there is a supportive group climate for generating questions and investigating possibilities. Critical thinking questions may also come into play after solutions are put forward. Ask students to analyze problems they have solved. As they examine how underlying assumptions influence interpretations children can be pulled more deeply into a topic. And by evaluating their findings on the basis of logic they raise other possibilities. To have power over the story that dominates one's life in these technologically intensive times means having the power to retell it, deconstruct it, joke about it, and change it as times change. Without this power it is more difficult to think and act on new thoughts and open the doors to deep thinking.

The old view of teaching as the transmission of content has been expanded to include new intellectual tools and new ways of helping students thoughtfully construct knowledge on their own and with peers. Teachers who invite thoughtfulness understand that knowledge is to be shared or developed rather than held by the authority. They arrange instruction so that children construct concepts and develop their thinking skills. As a result everyone involved becomes an active constructor of knowledge and more capable of making thoughtful decisions in the future.

Recognizing the development of thinking skills is a good first step toward its application and assessment. Beyond specific teaching strategies the climate of the classroom and the behavior of the teacher is very important. Teachers need to model critical thinking behaviors – setting the tone, atmosphere, and environment for learning. Being able to collaborate with other teachers can make a formative contribution to how the teacher might better see and construct individual classroom reality. In collaborative problem solving teachers can help each other in the clarification of goals. They also share the products of their joint imaginations. Thus perceptions are changed, ideas flow, and practice can be meaningfully strengthened, deepened, and extended. Like their students, teachers can become active constructors of knowledge.

A curriculum that ignores the powerful ideas of its charges will miss many opportunities for illuminating knowledge. To teach content without regard for self-connected thinking prevents subject matter knowledge from being transformed in the student's mind. If the curriculum is to be viewed as enhancing *being and opening to the unfamiliar* – rather than merely imparting knowledge and skills – then reasoned decision-making is part of the process. Taking student thinking seriously is more likely to be successful in cultivating thoughtfulness and subject matter competence. Respecting unique thought patterns can also be viewed as a commitment to caring communication and openness.

Encouraging fresh ideas or opposing views is often difficult for administrators. All of us need the occasional push or encouragement to get out of a rut. Breaking out of established patterns can be done collectively or individually. But it takes those most directly involved to make it happen.

Journeys of Discovery

It is important for all of us to develop their own reflection and inquiry skills – becoming students of our own thinking. For example, when a teacher decides to participate with students in learning to think on a daily basis they nourish human possibilities. Can teachers make a difference? Absolutely. The idea is to connect willing teachers with innovative methods and materials so that they can build learning environments that are sensitive to students' growing abilities to think for themselves. By promoting thoughtful learning across the full spectrum of personalities, cultures, and ways of knowing, teachers can make a tremendous difference and perform a unique service for the future.

When the ideal and the actual are linked, the result can produce a dynamic, productive, and resilient form of learning. What we know teaching and thinking is increasingly being put into practice in model classrooms and schools (Boomer, 1992). These exemplary programs recognize that powerful inquiry can help students make personal and group discoveries that change thinking. Good critical thinking skills can turn an unexamined belief into a reasoned one.

By nurturing informed thinking and awareness we can all learn how to actively apply knowledge, solve problems, and enhance conceptual understanding across social boundaries. As children use reason and logic to change their own theories and beliefs they grow in ways that are personally meaningful. Understanding the essence of contradictory points of view means understanding some of the universal truths that speak to everyone. A diversity of new voices can add vigor to understanding the world and our place in it.

As students learn about the perspectives of other cultures – including social and historical background – they can explore where stereotypes come from. With a little homework each student can design a large graphic family tree to share. This way each student's cultural background can serve as a valuable tool for learning about themselves, their cultural background, and how their communities connect to others around the world.

With the globalization of media and business it becomes ever more important to see how events in the United States affect people in other countries – and vice versa. Helping students respect differences and see the common roots of present conditions means more than "taco day" at school. Gaining a global perspective means developing a more integrative understanding of the human community and overlapping cultural experiences. As teachers learn to thoughtfully view the world from multiple perspectives the way is cleared for them to become more sensitive to variation and more capable of reaching diverse learners.

Discovering Relationships and Inventing New Perspectives

Recognizing the fact that thinking skills are key to successful learning doesn't come as a surprise to most teachers. In science, for example, you formulate hypotheses, organize experiments, collect data, analyze, interpret the findings, and solve problems. As scholars who are doing original work in any field will tell you, the reality is far less clear-cut and tidy. There are many false starts and detours as they work through alternatives to discover relationships and invent new perspectives. What makes it satisfying for many scholars is the sheer power of searching at the frontiers of knowledge. This passion for inquiry and reaching outward into the unknown outward (for new experiences) is just as important for children.

Critical and creative thinkers tend to be reflective, think problems through, are flexible, consider original solutions and are curious. They pose and expand on new questions. The research evidence suggests that providing students with multiple perspectives and entry points into subject matter increases thinking and learning (Sears & Marshall, 1990). As each of the standards projects point out in their own way, notions about how students learn a subject needs to be pluralized. Almost any important concept can be approached from multiple entry points – emphasizing understanding and making meaningful interdisciplinary connections.

Today's schools are incorporating frameworks for literacy and learning that build on the multiple ways of thinking and representing knowledge. By organizing lessons that respect multiple entry points to knowledge teachers can enhance thoughtfulness and make the classroom a rich environment for inquiry. By fusing the personalization of learning to achieving an attainable level of literacy across the curriculum teachers can lay a powerful foundation for learning. We now have diverse models of thoughtful schooling to choose from. If many of today's dreams, possibilities, and admired efforts are going to be put into widespread practice than we all must be more courageous in helping move good practice from the educational margins and into the schools.

A child's thinking ability evolves through a dynamic of personal abilities, social values, academic subjects and out of school experiences. Although teachers are usually the ones held accountable, everyone is involved (directly or indirectly) in the education of children. Revitalizing the educational process means recognizing the incomplete models of how the world works that children bring to school with them. From birth children are busy making sense of their environment. They do this by curiously grappling with the confusing, learning ways of understanding, developing schemes for thinking, and finding meaning.

As they begin school children can tell stories, sing songs, and use their own processes of reasoning and intuiting to understand their surroundings. They have already developed a rich body of knowledge about the world around them by the time they reach first grade. This natural learning process can be extended in school when a teacher is committed to critical thinking throughout the year. It is important to pay attention and work with students' natural rhythms, but it takes learning-centered instruction to continue the process of developing mature thinkers. Cognitive science was partly responsible. as well as perspectives on multiple intelligences (Gardner, 1983).

Toward a New Vision of Intelligence (Multiple Intelligences)

Intelligence has been defined as a fresh view, intelligence can be taught, people can continue to enhance their intellectual functioning throughout their lifetimes, all of us are "gifted," and all of us are "retarded" simultaneously (Feuerstein, 1980). Learning has a lot to do with finding your own gifts. To make learning more accessible to children means respecting multiple ways of making meaning. The brain has a multiplicity of functions and voices that speak independently and distinctly for different individuals. Howard Gardner's framework for multiple entry points to knowledge has had a powerful influence on the content standards (Gardner, 1987). They clearly recognize alternate paths for learning. There are many differences, but each set of content standards is built on a belief in the uniqueness of each child and the view that this can be fused with a commitment achieving worthwhile goals.

Gardner first introduced his theory of multiple intelligences in his book *Frames of Mind.* He was critical of how the field of psychology the traditionally viewed intelligence. So he set out to stir up some controversy. He succeeded. An unexpected result was the enthusiastic response within the educational community. Teachers showed unexpected enthusiasm for exploring M.I. (multiple intelligences) theory in the classroom. It is little wonder. Lessons built on Gardner's ideas proved helpful in meeting the challenges of increasingly diversity and heterogeneous grouping.

Multiple Intelligences

1. Linguistic intelligence: the capacity to use language to express ideas, excite, convince, and convey information. Speaking, writing, and reading.
2. Logical-mathematical intelligence: the ability to explore patterns and relationships by manipulating objects or symbols in an orderly manner.
3. Musical intelligence: the capacity to think in music, the ability to perform, compose or enjoy a musical piece. Rhythm, beat, tune, melody, and singing.
4. Spatial intelligence: the ability to understand and mentally manipulate a form or object in a visual or spatial display. Maps, drawings, and media.
5. Bodily-kinesthetic intelligence: the ability to use motor skills in sports, performing arts or art productions, particularly dance or acting.
6. Interpersonal intelligence: the ability to work in groups. Interacting, sharing, leading, following, and reaching out to others.
7. Intrapersonal intelligence: the ability to understand one's inner feelings, dreams and ideas. Introspection, meditation, reflection, and self-assessment.
8. Naturalist intelligence: the ability to discriminate among living things (plants, animals) as well as a sensitivity to the natural world (Gardner, 1997).

Gardner defines intelligence as the ability to solve problems, generate new problems, and do things that are valued within one's own culture. MI theory suggests that these eight "intelligences" work together in complex ways. Most people can develop an adequate level of competency in all of them. And there are many ways to be "intelligent" within each category. But will the intelligences listed above be as central to the twenty-first century as they were to the twentieth? It is possible to take issue with Gardner's approach on several points, like not fully addressing spiritual and artistic modes of thought. But there is general agreement on a central point, *intelligence is not a single capacity that every human being possesses to a greater or lesser extent.* There *are* multiple ways of knowing and learning. And whether or not we subscribe to his theory, methods of instruction should reflect different ways of knowing.

Working out the ecology of teaching for thoughtfulness requires taking risks with such bold and explicit insights.

Suggestions for Using Multiple Intelligence Activities

1. Put Multiple Intelligence theory into action. Some possibilities:

linguistic intelligence:

write an article
develop a newscast
make a plan, describe a procedure
write a letter
conduct an interview
write a play
interpret a text or piece of writing

musical intelligence:

sing a rap song
give a musical presentation
explain music similarities
make and demonstrate a
    musical instrument
demonstrate rhythmic patterns

logical-mathematical intelligence:

design and conduct an experiment
describe patterns
make up analogies to explain . . .
solve a problem

spatial intelligence:

illustrate, draw, paint, sketch
create a slide show, videotape
chart, map or graph
create a piece of art

bodily-kinesthetic intelligence:

use creative movement
design task or puzzle cards
build or construct something
bring hands-on materials to
    demonstrate
use the body to persuade, console,
    or support others

interpersonal intelligence:

conduct a meeting
participate in a service project
teach someone
use technology to explain
advise a friend or fictional
    character

naturalist intelligence:

prepare an observation
    notebook
describe chances in the
    environment
care for pets, wildlife, gardens or
    parks
use binoculars, telescopes, or
    microscopes
photograph natural objects

intrapersonal intelligence:

write a journal entry
describe one of your values
assess your work
set and pursue a goal
reflect on or act out emotions

2. Encourage various learning styles:

Mastery style learner	concrete learner, step-by-step process, learns sequentially.
Understanding style learner	focuses on ideas and abstractions, learns through a process of questioning
Self-expressive style learner	looks for images, uses feelings and emotions
Interpersonal style learner	focuses on the concrete, prefers to learn socially; judges learning in terms of its potential use in helping others.

[The research suggests that it helps to understand your preferred learning style.]

3. Build on students' interests.

When students do research either individually or with a group, allow them to choose a project that appeals to them. Students should also choose the best way for communicating their understanding of the topic. In this way students discover more about their interests, concerns, their learning styles and intelligences.

4. Plan interesting lessons. There are many ways to plan interesting lessons.

[Lesson plan ideas presented here are influenced by ideas as diverse as those of John Goodlad, Madeline Hunter and Howard Gardner.]

Lesson Planning

1. Set the tone of the lesson. Focus student attention, relate the lesson to what students have done before. Stimulate interest.
2. Present the objectives and purpose of the lesson. What are students supposed to learn? Why is it important?
3. Provide background information. What information is available? Resources such as books, journals, videos, pictures, maps, charts, teacher lecture, class discussion, or seat work should be listed.
4. Define procedures. What are students supposed to do? This includes examples and demonstrations as well as working directions.
5. Monitor students' understanding. During the lesson, the teacher should check students' understanding and adjust the lesson if necessary. Teachers should invite questions and ask for clarification. A continuous feedback process should be in place.

6. Provide guided practice experiences. Students should have a chance to use the new knowledge presented under direct teacher supervision.
7. It is equally important that students get opportunities for independent practice where students can use their new knowledge and skills.
8. Evaluate and assess students' work – is necessary to show that students have demonstrated an understanding of significant concepts. Paper and pencil tests do not adequately measure students' critical and creative thinking. Observing students' behavior and their interaction with the teacher and peers are often more effective and revealing. Portfolios represent the cutting edge of more authentic and meaningful assessment. They are powerful assessment tools that require students to select, collect and reflect on what they are creating and accomplishing.

A Sample M.I. Lesson Plan

The following is a sample M.I (multiple intelligence) lesson developed by a preservice teacher at San Francisco State University.

Lesson Title: How Neuron's Work

Students should develop understandings of personal health, changes in environments, and local challenges in science and technology. The human body and the brain are fascinating areas of study. The brain, like the rest of the body is composed of cells; but brain cells are different from other cells (Sprenger, 1999). This lesson focuses on the science standards of inquiry, life science, science and technology, and personal and social perspectives.

Lesson Goals: The basic goal is to provide a dynamic experience with each of the 8 "intelligences," map out a group on construction paper.

Procedures:
1. Divide the class into groups. Assign each group an intelligence.
2. Allow students time to prepare an activity which addresses their intelligence. Each small group will give a three-minute presentation (with large map) to the entire class.

Objective: To introduce students to the terminology of the brain and how the brain functions, specifically the function of neurons.

Grade Level: With modifications, K–8.

Materials: paper, pens, markers, copy of the picture of the brain, the neuron, songs about the brain, model of the brain (recipe follows)

Brain "Recipe"
1. 5 cups of instant potato flakes, 5 cups of hot water, 2 cups sand, pour into a 1 gallon ziplock bag

2. Combine all ingredients, mix thoroughly. It should weigh about 3 pounds and have the consistency of a real brain.

Background Information: No one understands exactly how the brain works. But scientists know the answer lies within the billions of tiny cells, called NEURONS or nerve cells, which make up the brain. All the body's feelings and thoughts are caused by the electrical and chemical signals passing from one neuron to the next. A neuron looks like a tiny octopus, but with many more tentacles (some have several thousand). Neurons carry signals throughout the brain which allows the brain to move, hear, see, taste, smell, remember, feel, and think.

Procedure:
1. Make a model of the brain to show to the class. The teacher displays the brain and says "The smell of a flower, the memory of a walk in the park, the pain of stepping on a nail – these experiences are made possible by the 3 lbs. of tissue in our heads – "THE BRAIN!"
2. Show a picture of the neuron and mention its various parts.
3. Have students label the parts of the neuron and color if desired.

Activity 1 – Message Transmission: Explaining How Brain Cells (Neurons) Work

A message traveling in the nervous system of the brain can go 200 mph. These signals are transmitted from neuron to neuron across synapses. To understand this system, have students act out the neuron process.

1. Instruct students to get into groups of five. Each group should choose a group leader.
2. Direct students to stand up and form a circle. Each person is going to be a neuron. Students should be an arms length away from the next person.
3. When the group leader says "Go" have one person from the group start the signal transmission by slapping the hand of the adjacent person. The second person then slaps the hand of the next, and so on until the signal goes all the way around the circle and the transmission is complete.

Explanation: The hand that receives the slap is the "dendrite." The middle part of the student's body is the "cell body." The arm that gives the slap to the next person is the "axon" and the hand that gives the slap is the "nerve terminal." In between the hands of two people is the "synapse."

Inquiry Questions: As the activity progresses, questions will arise. What are parts of a neuron? A neuron is a tiny nerve cell, one of billions which make up the brain. A neuron has three basic parts – the *cell body*, the *dendrites* and the *axon.* Have students make a simple model by using their hand and spreading their fingers wide. The hand represents the "cell body," the fingers represent "dendrites" which bring information to the cell body, the arm represents the "axon" which takes information away from the cell body. Just as students wiggle their fingers, the dendrites are constantly moving as they seek information.

If the neuron needs to send a message to another neuron, the message is sent out through the axon. The wrist and forearm represent the axon. When a neuron sends information down its axon to communicate with another neuron, it never actually touches the other neuron. The message goes from the axon of the sending neuron to the dendrite of the receiving neuron by "swimming" through the space called the synapse. Neuroscientist define *learning* as *two neurons communicating with each other*. They say that neurons have "learned" when one neuron sends a message to another neuron (Hannaford, 1995).

Activity 2 – Connect the Dots

This exercise is to illustrate the complexity of the connections of the brain.

1. Have students draw 10 dots on one side of a sheet of typing paper and 10 dots on the other side of the paper.
2. Tell students to imagine these dots represent neurons, assume each neuron makes connections with the 10 dots on the other side.
3. Then connect each dot on side one with the dots on the other side. This is quite a simplification. Each neuron (dot) may actually make thousands of connections with other neurons.

Another part of this activity is teaching brain songs to students:

"I've Been Working On My Neurons"
(sung to the tune of "I've Been Working on the Railroad")

I've been working on my neurons, All the live long day.
I've been working on my neurons, Just to make my dendrites play.
Can't you hear the synapse snapping? Impulses bouncing to and fro,
Can't you tell that I've been learning? See how much I know!

"Because I Have a Brain"
(sung to the tune, "If I Only Had a Brain")

I can flex a muscle tightly, or tap my finger lightly,
It's because I have a brain,
I can swim in the river, though it's cold and makes me shiver,
Just because I have a brain.

I am really fascinated, to be coordinated,
It's because I have a brain.

I can see lots of faces, feel the pain of wearing braces
Just because I have a brain.

Oh, I appreciate the many things that I can do,
I can taste a chicken stew, or smell perfume, or touch the dew.

I am heavy with emotion, and often have the notion,
That life is never plain.
I have lots of personality, a sense of true reality,
Because I have a brain.

Multiple Intelligences Learning Activities

Linguistic	writing a reflection about the activity, researching how a neuron works
	keeping a study journal about how neurons work
Bodily/Kinesthetic	move like a neuron
	group drama: signal transmission
Visual/Spatial	mapping the connections of the brain (connect the dots)
Musical	singing songs about neurons
	tapping out rhythms to the song "Because I Have a Brain"
Naturalist	describing changes in your brain environment
	illustrating a dendrite connection
Interpersonal	participate in (act out) a group signal neuron transmission
	observing/recording
Intrapersonal	reflecting on being a neuron
	keeping a journal of how the brain works
Mathematical/Logical	calculating neuron connections

Evaluation: Each group will write a reflection on the activity. Journal reflections should tell what they learned about neurons and how that helps them understand how the brain works.

Brain Research and Learning

The unique aspects of the brain cells are arranged in such a way that it is malleable or plastic enough for learning to occur and stable enough for the learning to solidify into wisdom. Recently a report was issued that promises to upset what has been one of the long-held certainties about the brain: the adult brain cannot form new neurons (people are born with a fixed amount of neuron cells, they die off one by one, and they're lost forever). A shocking experiment found that thousands of new neurons a day were being formed in the brains of monkeys, migrating into areas of the brain in charge of intelligence and decision-making. If a steady stream of new brain cells is continually arriving to be integrated into new circuitry, then the brain is more malleable than anyone had realized. This contradicts the idea that the most important neurological action occurs in the first three years of human development. "Our brains remain remarkably plastic and we retain the ability to learn throughout our lives" (J. Bruer, 1999). Another study finds a small well-connected region of the brain in charge of organizing and coordinating information, acting like a global workspace for solving problems. Neuroscientists also emphasize that the brain is extremely plastic and dynamic, very responsive to experience, "its an ever-changing place." More action research of evidence of successful learning applications in the classroom is still needed.

Intellectual Tools of the Future

Since it is so difficult to figure out what knowledge will be crucial to students in the future it makes sense to pay more attention to the *intellectual tools* that will be required *in any future*. This suggests focusing on how models of critical thought can be used differently, at different times and in different situations. The idea is to put more emphasis on concepts with high generalizability – like collaborative problem-solving, reflection, perceptive thinking, self-direction, and the motivation needed for life-long learning. A more thoughtful and personalized brand of learning is the goal.

Information isn't a substitute for thinking. But information and thinking are not antithetical. At higher levels thinking requires quickly sorting through a wealth of information to be effective. There will never be enough time to teach all the information that we feel is useful. But time must be taken to be sure that student thinking can transform knowledge in a way that makes it transferable to the outside world. When there is time for inquiry and reflection, covering less can actually help students learn more deeply.

Within this context the following thinking skills can be taught directly:

- generating multiple ideas about a topic
- figuring out meaning from context
- understanding analogy
- detecting reasoning fallacies

Topical knowledge (content facts), procedural knowledge (how to study and learn), and self-knowledge are all part of critical thinking. All of these thinking skills are learned through interaction with the environment, the media, peers, and the school curriculum. Some students pick it up naturally while others learn reasoning skills with difficulty or not at all. Everyone can do it.

Providing Access to the Thoughtful Life

Children can demonstrate what their reasoning ability is in a number of ways: think-outlouds, videos, performances, photo-collage, stories for the newspaper, Web sites on the Internet, or multimedia projects that can be shared with other students and members of the community. We are already seeing glimmers of a computer-based medium that is broadly expressive and capable of capturing many aspects of human consciousness (Bruce Mao, 2004). As we move into the twenty-first century it is bound to reshape the whole spectrum of expression. Communication and information technology sometimes complements and sometimes supersedes previous media. Still the basic learning process and the essence of any curriculum will continue to involve ways of engaging students in thought that matters and sharing what they find . . . information/knowledge/wisdom. Wisdom gives you the power to change the shape of ideas.

By giving students the truth of others teachers can make it possible for them to discover their own. Feeling and meaning can be turned inside out as children learn how to construct their own knowledge and absorb new literacy experiences in ways that make sense to them. In one form or another literacy has long been seen as providing access to creative expression and a thoughtful life. This extends to anticipating and exploring (from many angles) the depths that await us under the surface of things, whatever those things may be. There is no reason to wait around for the new millennium in hopes of getting the kind of changes we want. A better approach is for every literate teacher and every literate citizen to push for changes in their domain of influence.

The ability to think critically and act creatively is an essential part of today's concept of literacy. Fostering the critical and creative imagination is one of the most important recommendations found in the new subject matter standards. In unique ways each set of standards suggest helping students move beyond literal meanings to critically interpret texts. More than recording facts, "writing" with various media is viewed as a special vehicle for analyzing, interpreting, and explaining (NCTE & IRA, 1996; NSTA, 1996; NCTM, 1989; NSEA, 1994).

Education is fluid and organic. Practice is enriched by theory. Theory is transformed in the light of practice. And research plays a clarifying role in this complimentary process. The standards are grounded in a framework that relies on all three. Understanding the relationship between theory, research, and practice is the foundation of pedagogical knowledge. The new content standards build on this cycle to give us a coherent, professionally defensible conception of how a subject can be framed for instruction. They do not put forward one best way to teach content. They leave room for interpretation.

The future is not just something that happens to us. It is something we make. And it is something that we should be prepared to revise. We have to be prepared (like any profession) for changes as new data and concerns spring to life. As we work to make connections across subjects and to everyday life it soon becomes apparent that teachers are never finished with learning how to teach. Like this last line in an Octavio Paz poem: "tomorrow we shall have to invent, once again, the reality of this world."

RESOURCES AND REFERENCES

Baron, J. (1988). *Thinking and deciding.* New York: Cambridge University Press.

Barell, J. (1995). *Teaching for thoughtfulness.* White Plains, NY: Longman.

Berman, L., Hultgam. F., Lee, D., Rivkin, M., & Roderick, J. (1991). *Toward a curriculum for being.* Albany, NY: State University of New York Press.

Boomer, G. (1992). *Negotiating the curriculum.* Busingstake, U.K.: Falmer Press.

Browne, M. N. & Keeley, S. M. (2001). *Asking the right questions: A guide to critical thinking.* (6th ed.). Upper Saddle River, NJ: Prentice Hall.

Bruce Mao Design and the Institute Without Boundaries. (2004). *Massive change.* New York: Phaidon Press Limited.

Bruer, J. T. (1999). *The myth of the first three years.* New York: Free Press.

Bruner, J. (1973). *Going beyond the information given.* New York: Norton.

Case, P. (1992). *Creativity, thinking skills, critical thinking, problem solving.* Boston, MA: University of Massachusetts.

Council of Chief State School Officers (CCSSO) (1994). *Annual Report.* Washington, D.C.: Author.

Checkley, K. (1997). The first seven . . . and the eighth a conversation with Howard Gardner. *Educational Leadership. 55* (1): 8–13.

Dissanayake, E. (1992). *Homo Aestheticus.* New York: Free Press.

Gardner, H. (1987). Developing the spectrum of human intelligences. *Harvard Educational Review. 57*: 187–193.

Gardner, H. (1993). *Creating minds.* New York, NY: Basic Books.

Gardner, H. (1983). *Frames of mind.* New York, NY: Basic Books.

Gardner, H. (1997). Multiple intelligences as a partner in school improvement. *Educational Leadership. 55*(1): 20–21.

Gladwell, M. (2005). *Blink: The power of thinking without thinking.* New York: Little, Brown and Company.

Good, T. & Brophy, J. (1994). *Looking into classrooms,* (sixth edition). New York: Harper Collins Publishers.

Goodlad, J. (1983). *A place called school: Prospects for the future.* New York: McGraw-Hill.

Hannaford, C. (1995). *Smart moves: Why learning is not all in your head.* Arlington, VA: Great Ocean Publishers.

Hunter, M. (1990-91). Seven step lesson design. *Educational Leadership* Dec. Jan. 1990–1991, pp. 79–81.

Jacobs, H. Hayes. (Ed.). (2004). *Getting results with curriculum mapping.* Alexandria, VA: Association for Supervision and Curriculum Development.

Jenson, E. (1998). *Teaching with the brain in mind.* Alexandria, VA: Association for Supervision and Curriculum Development.

Kidder, T. (1989). *Among schoolchildren.* New York, NY: Houghton Mifflin.

Martinello, M. & Cook, G.(1994). *Interdisciplinary inquiry in teaching and learning.* New York: Macmillan.

Marzano, R., Brandt, R., Hughes, C., Jones, B., Presssein, B., Rankin, S. & Suhor, C. (1988). *Dimensions of thinking: A framework for curriculum and instruction.* Alexandria, VA: Association for Supervision and Curriculum Development.

Mayfield, M. (1997). *Thinking for yourself.* Belmont, CA: Wadsworth Publishing.

National Assessment of Educational Progress. (1995). Washington, D.C.: U.S. Government Publications.

National Council of Teachers of English & International Reading Association. (1996). *Standards for the English language arts.* Urbana, IL: Author.

National Council of Teachers of Mathematics (NCTM). Commission of Standards of School Mathematics (1989). *Curriculum and evaluation standards for school mathematics.* Weston, VA: Author.

National Science Teachers Association (NSTA). (1996). National Science Education Standards. Washing, D.C.: National Academy Press.

National Science Teachers Association. (1997). *NSTA Pathways to the science standards.* Arlington, VA: NSTA.

National Standards for Education in the Arts (1994).*The Arts and Education Reform Goals 2000.* Washington, D.C.: U.S. Office of Education, p. 3.

Piaget, J. (1962). *The language and thoughts of the child.* (M. Warden, Trans.). New York: Humanities Press.

Resnick, L. B. & Klopfer, L. (1989). *Toward the thinking curriculum: Current cognitive research.* Alexandria, VA: ASCD Publishing.

Sanders, W. (1998). Guide to teachers, good and bad. *San Francisco Chronicle* Fri. July 17, p. A 23.

Sears, J. & Marshall, J. D. (1990). *Teaching and thinking about curriculum.* New York: Teachers College Press.

Segal, J. W., Chipman, S. F. & Glaser, R. (Eds). (1985). *Thinking and learning skills.* Hillside, NJ: Teachers College Press.

Sigler, R. S. (1985). *Children's thinking.* Englewood Cliffs, NJ: Prentice Hall.

Sprenger, M. (1999). *Learning and memory: The brain in action.* Alexandria, VA: Association for Curriculum Development.

Sternberg, R. & Wagner, R. (1986). *Practical intelligence: Nature and origins of competence in the everyday world.* New York: Cambridge University Press.

Whyte, D. (1994). *The heart aroused.* New York: Currency Doubleday.

Chapter 3

COLLABORATIVE LEARNING:
THE SHARED RESPONSIBILITY IN
THE COOPERATIVE CLASSROOM

Language makes us human
Literacy makes us civilized
Technology makes us powerful
The arts add resources for thoughtfulness and enlightenment
Inquiry gives us intellectual tools for making sense of the world
And being in community with others can make us free.

Cooperative learning is one of the major developments of the last twenty years that is helping shape education in the new century. Building on a solid data base, it has been recognized by educators as a successful framework for learning. The research suggests that students learn more, increase their understanding, and enjoy learning in cooperative learning groups (Burton, 1987; Lee & Jacobs, 1998). A number of studies have also pointed to the positive effect of collaboration on student achievement and attitudes towards learning (Slavin, 1989, 1995; Cohen, 1995).

Active team learning has significant advantages for enhancing social and intellectual development that includes building on teacher familiarity with small group work. Cooperative learning is making its appearance in teachers' lesson plans, teacher inservice programs, and subjects from one end of the curriculum framework to the other.

THE INFLUENCE OF ACTIVE
GROUP LEARNING

Learning takes place through interaction with the environment, family, community members, schools, and other institutions. Language is the means

35

by which meaning is translated, verified, and made conscious. By interacting with their environment, parents, siblings, and classmates, the child comes to know and make sense of the world. This early learning connects to social and cultural elements to form an experience base. Language is used to help clarify and extend these relationships and construct a more sophisticated base for additional learning.

Cooperative learning builds on the idea that much of learning is social. Working in teams provides students with opportunities to talk and participate actively in classroom life. The teacher acts as a pilot, selecting meaningful topics for discussion, mapping out opportunities for collaboration, and observing the interaction of working groups. Students then work together to make connections between new ideas discussed in class and prior knowledge. As students are encouraged to jointly interpret and negotiate meaning, learning comes alive. Constructing meaningful explanations means giving students regular opportunities to talk, read, write, and solve problems together.

It has been argued that expressive language is the foundation of student language and thinking (Jager Adams, 1990). To translate this natural process to education, students must be able to struggle with ideas informally shaping them for a public audience. Groups need time to share, clarify, suggest, and expand concepts. Starting with a student's own experiences and background knowledge, the process can move to one of a shared group idea or to a more elegant individual expression.

Unstructured interaction between peers relies heavily on shared experiences for understanding. Informal conversation with friends is often expressive, with feelings, beliefs, and opinions freely stated. The structure of such conversations can serve as a starting point for coming to terms with new ideas. Through informal conversation learners shape ideas, modify them by listening to others, question, plan, express doubt, and construct meaning. In the process they feel free to express uncertainty and experiment with new language.

Talking in mixed ability groups in school has been shown to facilitate and enhance the learning process (Johnson & Johnson, 1989). Small group discussion provides constant feedback within a supportive environment that allows individuals to become more at ease with sharing thoughts with others. This kind of expression can also help group members examine, compare and affix personal meaning to shared concepts or beliefs. A response group that places ideas into a personal and collective context can serve as a powerful motivator – with information being remembered longer because more meaning gets attached to it. Ideas take shape and become more alive. Whether using cooperative learning to build respect for other points of view, supporting group members, offering constructive criticism, or learning academic material, *there's no better way to jump-start a stalled class.*

Collaboration Builds on What Teachers Know

Elementary school teachers have always used groups. But these groups were usually based on "ability," or some kind of skill hierarchy like choosing teams. Individualized learning was different – and it had its usefulness. In this arrangement each student worked at his or her own pace and was expected to be left alone by other students. It was sometimes possible for children to self-select appropriate material and pace themselves to complete a work assignment. With this approach the individual took on the responsibility for completing the task, sometimes evaluating progress and the quality of the effort. Individualized learning forces students who are naturally social to work in isolation, struggling to piece together fragments of information. A large amount of the teacher's time is spent in correcting, testing, and record keeping. With individualized learning the goal or task objective was perceived as important, with each student expected to achieve the goal. The teacher was the major source for assistance and reinforcement. As far as it goes there is nothing wrong here. The trouble is that it filled in only part of the learning picture and missed the power of collaboration.

Another aspect of traditional learning was competition. Students monitored the progress of their competitors, and compared ability, skills and knowledge with peers. Instructional activities tended to focus on skill practice, knowledge recall, and review. The assignments were clear with rules for competing specified. The teacher was the major resource and often directed the competitive activity. A competitive atmosphere often induced anxiety, fear of failure, and ultimately withdrawal for many students. If there was an informal grading curve then someone else's success diminished your ability.

Collaborative group learning takes a different approach. It builds on what we know about how students construct knowledge, promoting active learning in a way not possible with competitive or with individualized learning. In a cooperative classroom the teacher organizes major parts of the curriculum around tasks, problems and projects that students can work through in small mixed ability groups. Lessons are designed around active learning teams so that students can combine energies as they reach toward a common goal. If someone else does well, you do well. Social skills, like interpersonal communication, group interaction and conflict resolution are developed as the collaborative learning process goes along.

Research Suggests that Cooperative Learning

- *Motivates Students.* Students talking and working together on a project or problem experience the fun and experience of sharing ideas and information.
- *Increases Academic Performance.* Studies show that classroom interaction with peers causes students – especially those from diverse cultural and linguistic

backgrounds – to make significant academic gains, compared with students in traditional settings.
- *Encourages Active Learning.* Extensive research has shown that students learn more when they're actively engaged in discovery and problem solving.
- *Increases Respect for Diversity.* Students who work together in mixed ability groups are more likely to select mixed racial and ethnic acquaintances and friendships. When students cooperate to reach a common goal they learn to appreciate and respect each other.
- *Promotes Literacy and Language Skills.* Group study offers students many chances to use language and improve speaking skills. This is particularly important for second language students.
- *Helps Prepare Students for Today's Society.* Team approaches to solving problems, combining energies with others and working to get along are valued skills in the world of work, community, and leisure.
- *Improves Teacher Effectiveness.* Through actively engaging students in the learning process teachers also make important discoveries about their students learning. As students take some of the responsibility for some of the teaching, the power of the teacher can be multiplied (Slavin, 1983, 1989; Sharon, 1980; Abraham & Campbell,1984; Levine & Trachtman, 1988).

Promoting Active Learning

Whether finding out about new concepts, solving problems, or questioning factual information, a collaborative approach has shown that it helps develop academic skills. At the same time it taps students' social nature to build self-esteem and social understanding (Moore Johnson, 1990). Collaborative skills are more important than ever in today's academic setting, workplace, and civic culture.

Years of research and practice suggest that cooperative learning can work to promote active learning (Johnson, et al., 1981). This kind of problem solving with others has been shown to spark an alertness of mind not achieved in passive listening. When students talk and reason together to complete a task or solve a problem they become more involved in thinking and communicating (Carnegie Foundation for the Advancement of Teaching, 1988). The research and the literature support cooperative learning. But the main reason it is catching on is because *teachers can tell that it works.*

Successful collaborative learning promotes interaction through face-to-face communications and links individuals to group success. Students are supported, encouraged, and given feedback as they critically analyze problems and issues. Group members are held responsible individually and collectively. Everyone has a responsibility to finish all assignments, master instructional objectives and ensure that all group colleagues do the same.

As individuals work with a small group of supportive classmates, children develop a sense of community and caring. Collaborative learning communities develop many social skills: communication, confidence in their ability, respect for others, and a sense of value ("I've got something to offer"). In a collaborative classroom students are frequently engaged in interpersonal skills such as shared decision-making, managing conflict situations, and maintaining good working relationships among group members. When a lesson is over a group typically takes time to reflect on how well they did as a group – and what could be done better. All of these skills will be crucial in the workplace of tomorrow.

Collaborative learning thrives in an atmosphere of mutual helpfulness where students know about what is happening – and why. Part of creating the right environment means having *the teacher* define objectives, talk about the benefits of cooperative learning, explain expectations, and explain behaviors such as brainstorming, peer teaching, constructive criticism, and confidence building.

For the students it is more than having something meaningful to work on. They need to learn how to be good listeners, communicate effectively, and receive constructive criticism. Learning to engage in productive conversation, how to help a group member without simply telling him the answer, how to give and take constructive criticism takes effort (Vaughn, S. and Linan-Thompson, 2004).

Professional Support Groups Work for Teachers

Teaching is a dynamic act that creates and realizes decision making power over what happens in the classroom. A professional work environment supports responsible, autonomous problem-solvers. The new wave of school reform moves organizational structures from top-down management to teacher empowerment. Professional power must go hand-in-hand with responsibility.

As a student of teaching, teachers cannot put in their class time and skip the homework. Assessing and coaching colleagues is now part of the job description. Professional development and peer coaching work best when they are based on the concept of collaborative learning. A small support group of colleagues, bound by an ethic of caring, can go over the work done by individual teachers, offer constructive criticism, and give suggestions. Professional development and support is for *everyone*. Schools are offering counseling from outstanding teachers and remedial intervention programs to teachers who are having trouble.

The actual hands-on, minds-on interaction with peers raises awareness and instills confidence in a way that reading or hearing about a new teaching strategy cannot. After some initial experiences with cooperative learning, the rough edges can be smoothed with additional reading, practice, and on-site peer mentoring. Teacher workshops and university classes can help – especially when teachers try activities, share experiences, and give and receive assistance within a collegial structure that supports collaboration. As a group becomes comfortable with sharing their concerns, teachers can discover each others personal and professional roles. As peers help with planning, implementation and feedback, teachers themselves experience the various processes of cooperative learning and come to more fully understand the power of the technique (Moore Johnson, 1990).

Individual and Group Accountability

Like any instructional strategy, implementing collaborative learning principles requires multiple objectives and approaches to reach the best a student has to offer. Cooperative group interaction can start by having students help each other in solving problems and completing academic tasks. The next step is to combine this idea with positive interdependence between group members and individual accountability. Group interdependence means that each individual plays a unique role. The team loses if they don't put out individual effort; they win or lose together. Whatever the outcome, students learn to think and act within multiple contexts.

Accountability ensures that everyone is contributing to a common goal. Individual accountability gives teachers a way of checking the role that each student is playing in the group's work. Individual accountability is accomplished through:

1. Group rewards that are based on individual performance, (for example, totaling scores on individual quizzes)
2. Having students make individual presentations on a group project or do unique tasks in their group which contribute to group presentation. (For example, one group member reports on the homes of the Navaho Indians, one reports on foods, another on rituals, and so on)
3. Providing incentives for students to work *together* to learn new material, but being *tested* individually.

Group accountability is also essential. If students are discussing last night's basketball game instead of working on mathematics, they aren't going to get much mathematical knowledge from their group discussion. Teachers must clearly define the task and closely monitor groups to ensure they are on task. When children expect positive interaction they naturally share ideas and materials, and become accountable for their own knowledge. All group members are expected to contribute to the group effort by dividing the tasks among them to capitalize on a wide range of strengths. Individuals receive support for risk taking, other group members are perceived to be the major source for assistance, support, and reinforcement.

Being willing to learn from failure, becoming more attuned to resources, and working beyond personal limits were the attitudes that teachers frequently mentioned as affecting success with cooperative learning (Slavin, et al., 1985). When teachers and students are encouraged to work collaboratively there is a positive effect on the overall school environment (Connelly & Clandinin, 1992).

Organizing An Interactive Learning Environment

Collaborative learning will not take place with students sitting in rows facing the teacher. Desks must be pushed together in small groups (two or more) or students can sit at small tables to facilitate group interaction. Groups of three or four usually work better than groups of six or seven. Resource and hands-on materials must be made readily accessible. Collaboration will not occur in a classroom which requires students to raise their hands to talk or move out of their desks. Instead of waiting with their hands up, they ask the student next to them. A basic rule of the game is that they have to ask at least two students before asking the teacher for help when they don't understand something or get stuck on a problem.

Other changes involve the noise level in the room. Sharing and working together, even in well-controlled environments, will be louder than an environment where students work silently from textbooks. Putting old carpets and other sound absorbing things in the room helps. Still, teachers need to tolerate higher noise levels and learn to evaluate whether or not it is constructive.

Evaluating cooperative learning requires a variety of procedures. In spite of new evaluative techniques on the horizon, some learning outcomes will probably continue to be measured by such instruments as standardized tests, quizzes, and written exams. Fortunately, new performance-based tests that have open-ended questions and problem-solving functions are starting to be used. The collaborative classroom also makes use of these tests and other measures like portfolios, and holistic grading. Students need to be involved in evaluating learning products, the classroom climate, and individual skill development. Self-evaluation and peer evaluation have been added to teacher assessment in cooperative learning. Otherwise the teacher can be trapped under an avalanche of minutia. One of the goals is to help teachers do a better job by *not* taking work home every night.

As they organize interactive learning environments everyone involved learns to shape questions, interpret data, and make connections between subjects. Students can learn to take responsibility for their own learning and assist others in their small group. Task oriented work groups can combine student initiative with social responsibility. This allows those with more information to stimulate the students with less – and vice versa. The same thing is true when it comes to teaching thinking processes like comprehension, decision-making, and problem solving (Trumbell, E. & Farr, B., 2005).

In a pluralistic society, we have in the United States various mixed racial, gender, ethnic, and ability group structures that can help students understand each other. They can also provide the structure for personal learning agendas and the joint application of critical thinking skills. By working together students can distinguish hypotheses from verified information and recognize reasoning based on misconceptions. In cooperative groups everyone is an active player in classroom activities. Topical projects, writing assignments, problem-solving or journal reaction papers are just a few examples of activities that require active group planning, negotiating, and the collaborative distribution of work.

As groups try to reach a consensus they can create an analysis grid or management plan whereby comparisons and contrasts can be made as well as students' speculations about outcomes. Within the tension of discussing different points of view (even heated discussion), learning takes place.

How To Structure Collaborative Groups

Johnson et al. (1984) suggest these steps for teachers interested in implementing small-group interactive learning:

1. Specify content and cooperative group objectives.
2. Determine the size of the group (typically from two to six depending on the nature of the task and the time available).
3. Divide students into groups (you may assign students or allow students to form their own group).
4. Arrange the room so that the teacher is accessible to all groups and so that group members can sit close enough to communicate effectively and not disturb another group.
5. Plan instructional materials (this can be accomplished in a variety of ways – you may wish to give only one set of materials to each group or give each group member different materials so as to force task differentiation).
6. Assign roles such as summarizer-checker, facilitator, recorder, runner, encourager, and observer.
7. Explain the task.
8. Implement strategies such as positive goal interdependence, peer encouragement, and support for learning (the group may be asked to produce a single product or put in place an assessment system where rewards are based on individual scores and on the average for the group as a whole).
9. Structure intergroup cooperation.
10. Go over the success criteria by explaining the guidelines, boundaries and roles.
11. Specify desired behaviors (taking turns, using personal names, listening carefully to each other, encouraging everyone to participate).

12. Monitor students (circulate to listen and observe groups, note problems).
13. Provide assistance when asked.
14. Intervene where groups are having problems in collaborating successfully.
15. Provide closure to the lesson.
16. Evaluate the quality of students' learning.
17. Have students assess how well the group functioned together.
18. Give and encourage feedback. Discuss how they could improve.

Shared Responsibility, Group Roles, and Respecting Differences

Collaborative group structures involve shared responsibilities. This means that a variety of tasks must be performed by group members. Each member (or pair) in the group assumes the charge of making sure that all group members work toward a group goal or objective. When students are new to cooperative learning, teachers may wish to assign certain roles to group participants. Many teachers divide the roles in the following way:

1. Facilitator
   - organizes the group's work
     makes certain students understand the group's job
   - takes the group's questions and concerns to the teacher *after* the group attempts a solution and tries alternatives.
2. Checker
   - checks with group members to make sure that everyone understands their task
   - checks to be sure that everyone agrees with the group response and can explain it.
3. Reader
   - reads the problem or directions to the group
4. Recorder
   - writes the groups response or data collection on a group response sheet or log.
5. Encourager
   - offers support and encouragement to group members.
   - Keeps others feeling good about working together (Johnson & Johnson, 1975).

If there are four students in a group you can combine facilitator and checker or reader roles. If it's a group of three: checker, reader, and recorder – the other roles are shared. Even teachers that work a lot with cooperative groups do not always assign roles. Students who are used to the process can naturally share the roles.

All students assume responsibility for promoting and maintaining positive attitudes and a positive group spirit. This doesn't mean using the "team spirit" to suppress dissent or intimidate individuals. In fact, those with an undeveloped sense of self (personal efficacy or self-esteem) have a more difficult time sharing deeply with others. Differences of opinion and conflicting views can actually result in constructive conflict and provide an important source of learning.

Organizing a group plan of action is an important part of shared responsibility and shared leadership. Learning how to search out, share and receive information to continue progress on a group task are important skills in working collaboratively. Students also need to learn how to summarize and clarify that information so as to move the group in the direction of completing their task or goal. Sometimes it may be necessary to test the consensus of a group – how many members agree that a particular direction is advisable or that a particular conclusion is accurate. Other task behaviors include:

- getting the group started
- staying on task
- getting the group back to work
- taking turns
- asking questions
- following directions
- staying in the group space
- keeping track of time
- helping without giving the answer

The idea is to play to each other's strengths and support each other's weaknesses. Teaching and learning in a cooperative environment means considering ways to encourage ourselves and others to learn. It doesn't mean that everyone has to agree about everything. Square holes make for square pegs. Collaboration doesn't equal conformity. In spite of the traditional Japanese maxim to the contrary, "the nail that sticks up" *shouldn't* be "hammered down." Rather it is important to become comfortable with the differing opinions of others whose dimensions can't be calibrated or arbitrarily controlled (Thornburg, D., 2002).

Group Support Systems

In addition to helping the group reach its goal and get the job done, a group member also has the responsibility to show support and empathy for other group members and their feelings. Agreement *isn't* required, support *is*. It is also important for everyone to have an opportunity to express ideas, to reflect on the process, and to analyze the feelings and ideas that other group members express.

There is a complex emotional geometry that connects individuals to one another in a group. When group interactions become tense, a release of that tension is needed; *humor* is a good way to ease members' frustrations. As Plato said, "the gods love a good joke." On a tough day so does everyone else. Support or maintenance behaviors that help keep things on an enjoyable keel:

1. *Compromising* – coming to an agreement by meeting half way, "giving in" to other group members when necessary.
2. *Empathizing and encouraging* – showing understanding and helping others feel a part of the group.
3. *Gate keeping* – giving everyone a chance to speak in the group, checking to see that no one is overlooked.
4. *Liberating tension* – creating harmony in the group.
5. *Expressing group feelings* – helping the group to examine how they are feeling and operating.

Teachers can help by:

- using names
- responding to ideas
- showing appreciation
- paraphrasing

- encouraging others to talk
- using eye contact
- not letting things get too heated
- criticizing an idea, not a person

As the group members learn to focus energy on the learning task, they also learn to identify with the group process. This helps members grow and develop by compromising, creating harmony, coaching, sharing, and encouraging which are learned behaviors. When group responsibility and support behaviors are in balance, group members can work collaboratively to achieve important group objectives. When the group task is over it's helpful for groups to evaluate effectiveness and make suggestions for improvement. This provides feedback and insights into the collaborative process.

Resolving Conflict and Solving Problems

The ability to solve problems and smoothly resolve conflict in the group are important tasks of cooperation and collaboration. Group members need strategies for negotiating and problem-solving to successfully defuse conflict and create harmony. Some conflict strategies include:

1. *Withdrawal* – the individual withdraws from interaction recognizing that the goal and the interaction are not important enough for excessive conflict.
2. *Forcing* – the task is more important than the relationship, members use all their energy to get the task done.
3. *Smoothing* – the relationship is more important than the task. Individuals want to be liked and accepted – and they work at it.
4. *Compromising* – the task and the relationship are both important, but there is a lack of time. Both members gain something and lose something, but meet the deadline.

5. *Confrontation* – Task and relationship are equally important, the conflict is defined as a problem-solving situation and not personalities.

Problem-solving is a useful group strategy to assist in conflict resolution. This systematic five-step process of constructively addressing conflicts involves:

1. Defining the problem and its causes.
2. Generating alternative solutions to the problem.
3. Examining advantages and disadvantages to each alternative.
4. Deciding upon and implementing the most desirable solution.
5. Evaluating whether the solutions solve the problem.

Group members must define exactly what the problem is. On occasion, this can be difficult, but it is worth the effort. Once the problem is defined, group members can then suggest alternative solutions and explore the consequences of each of those alternatives. The group members then make a decision to *try* an alternative and to review the results within a stipulated period of time.

It can also be important to teach *confrontation skills* and techniques for *successful resolution*. Some of these suggestions include teaching students to:

1. Describe behavior, do not evaluate, label, accuse or insult.
2. Define the conflict as a mutual problem. Rather than a win-lose situation, it's a win-win.
3. Use "I" statements.
4. Communicate what you think and feel.
5. Be critical of ideas, not people, affirm other's competence.
6. Give everyone a chance to be heard.
7. Follow the guidelines for rational argument.
8. Make sure there is enough time for discussion.
9. Take the other person's perspective.

Negotiating is also a learning part of problem resolution. It involves mutual discussion and arrangement of the terms of an agreement. The process of learning to "read" another's behavior for clues as to a problem solution is crucial in being able to guess what will appeal to another person and how to make a deal in which each participant's preferences or needs are considered.

Complementing the *task* and *support* behaviors are such communication skills like *active listening*. This means both attending to and responding to group and individual efforts. Active listening allows all group members to be fully in tune with each other while allowing for conversation overlaps. Acknowledging the content, feelings, or meaning of what another person is communicating lends itself to good will and deeper understanding. When everyone is given a chance to express their ideas it assures that all members of the group participate. And it makes group members secure in the knowledge that they are contributing to the group.

Constructing Cooperative Learning Environments

Once upon a time a second-grade teacher might have three groups: the bluebirds, the blackbirds, and the gorillas. And once you were in the high, medium, or low group you were likely to stay there. And cooperative learning offers the most promising ways out of the ability grouping maze.

A multidimensional collaborative classroom will make learning more accessible to more students, more valuable, and more interesting. Simply putting students in heterogeneous classes and teaching the same old curriculum isn't good enough. Other aspects of instructional practice must also be meaningfully changed – deepened, extended, and strengthened. As schools focus on the depth and quality of thoughtful work, classes will be far more useful for students and teachers. Teachers need methods, materials, and time to plan, before they can make untracked classes work up to their potential. To move toward untracking the curriculum requires patience, cooperation, thorough planning, and professional development.

In a cooperative classroom the teacher organizes major parts of the curriculum around tasks, problems and projects that students can work through in active learning teams. Students then combine energies to reach common group objectives. Whether it's finding out about new concepts, solving problems, or questioning factual information, a collaborative approach has shown that it helps develop academic skills, while promoting understanding and self-esteem (Kagan, 1986). The new wave of school reform moves organizational structures from top-down management to teacher empowerment.

Changing classroom organizational patterns and teaching strategies requires systematic staff development and the association of like-minded colleagues. It also takes time, practice, and systematic support for the vital energy inherent in new skills to become part of teachers' repertoire. Such basic changes in the organization of learning requires a school environment where it is safe to make mistakes and where it is safe to learn from those mistakes.

The approaches described here are all fairly easy to try. When students push two or three desks together they can begin helping each other learn. This kind of learning is seen as social, fun, and under their control. With the teacher acting as a resource person, learners create a climate of acceptance and a spirit of camaraderie.

Suggestions for Small Group Collaboration

It often takes several attempts with cooperative learning techniques to get groups working effectively. Like teachers, students must be gradually eased into the process through a consistent routine. The more teachers and students work in groups the easier it becomes. Some students may encounter initial problems because they are accustomed to being rewarded for easy-to-come-by answers that require little thinking. It may take some time and teacher assistance for them to become comfortable working cooperatively with more ambiguity.

Some useful strategies for helping students adjust include:

1. Adjust the group size to suit the activity. Groups of 2, 3, or 4 work well for many activities like mathematics problem-solving.
2. Groups of 5 or 6 may work better for activities that require larger group participation (creative dramatics, larger social studies projects, certain writing projects, etc.).
3. Experiment with different group patterns and size.
4. Accept a higher working noise level in the classroom.
5. Do not interrupt a group that is working well. If a group seems to be floundering, ask a student to describe what the group is discussing or what part of the problem is causing difficulty. Try not to speak loudly to a group across the room. Go to them if you want to say something.
6. Try interacting with the groups from time to time.
   Listen to their discussions.
7. Give students rules for group work. Some suggestions:
   a. Individuals must check with other members of the group before they may raise their hands to ask the teacher for help.
   b. Help can then be given to the group collectively.
   c. Try to reach a group consensus on a problem.
   d. All students should participate.
   e. Be considerate of others.
   f. Students are to help any group member who asks.

Collegial Collaboration: Peer Coaching in a Supportive Environment

Peer coaching is a model that can provide opportunities for teachers or students to assist and receive assistance from peers. Team members provide feedback, plan projects, help implement teaching suggestions, offer support, and give constructive criticism. Collegial cooperation serves as a caring support group that helps individuals over rough spots. It offers the possibility for groups to reflect, check perceptions, share frustrations and successes. As members of the group grow to respect one another, they form caring relationships. By sharing personal interpretations they collectively weave messages in ways that reaches the mind and the heart.

When a teacher is a part of a support team that encourages others to be openly exploratory and inquiring, they have opportunities to affirm their understanding and share their insights and ways of thinking with others. The give-and-take among group members of a peer coaching team is constructively critical at times. Good coaches are honest about their peer's work. Peer coaches need to work together and share their ideas with other members of the collaborative team. Team leaders learn how to promote positive learning transactions in the classroom. As active problem-solvers and analytical thinkers they strive to see all parts of a problem and the ways peers are thinking. As a team they delve deeply into inquiry and possible solutions to problems.

In peer coaching dialogue involves the interplay between feeling and thinking. Built on trust and the ethic of caring, dialogue becomes an integral tool of learning. The purpose of dialogue is to "come into contact with ideas, to understand, and work cooperatively (Nodding, 1984, p. 186). Caring teachers think of themselves as facilitators of learning not just knowledge imparters. In this role they open doors to complex interaction among each student's past experiences, personal purposes, and subject matter requirements. By connecting topics to students' lives, schools can develop a vital link to those realities.

Suggestions for Successful Group Work

1. Stress Collaboration: Some of the more successful cooperative multicultural models view collaborative intimacy as a natural condition between teachers and students (Hamm & Adams, 1992). The collaborative process works best when teachers provide students with the larger meaning (or purpose) for learning cooperative group skills. Students of mixed ability, gender, race, and ethnic groups can learn to function as a team that sinks or swims together. The basic idea is to have the group take responsibility for the learning of individual members, and within this collaborative framework individuals are held accountable.

Learning how to search out, share, and receive information to continue progress on a group task are important skills in working collaboratively. Students also need to learn how to summarize and clarify that information so as to move the group towards completion of their task or goal.

2. Assign Roles: This teamwork approach with specific roles can be useful when analyzing videos, newspaper articles, or literary works. After viewing a video clip or reading together a literary work, students can learn to construct a coherent argument or support a particular point of view through debate and compromise. Two or more groups of four and five can be assigned to argue conflicting points of view and to gather evidence to support their particular argument.

This activity works particularly well when analyzing a poem, which is often more open to interpretation than other literary works, and, because of its length, can more easily be discussed within a classroom hour. The poem "Mother to Son" by Langston Hughes, for example, can provoke a lively classroom discussion. The class can be divided into groups of three consisting of (1) a **checker**/animator, who makes sure everyone understands the directions (see below) and keeps the discussion lively, but also focused on the questions,

(2) a **reader** who reads the poem and the directions to the group, and (3) a **recorder** who explains/defends the small group's interpretation of the poem to the rest of the class.

The Unifying Effect of Collaboration

An important finding of recent research is that cooperative learning improves social relations between racially and culturally different students. After working in cooperative groups, all members became more accepting of classmates who were different (Davidson & Worsham, 1992). Sports teams have long had a similar unifying effect on teammates.

Interracial or diverse cultural learning teams can be useful for organizing classrooms in support of multicultural harmony. Studies from social psychology suggest that dividing the class into interracial learning teams reduces prejudice by undercutting the stereotyped categories while encouraging group members to pull together (Costa, 1991) Other researchers (Davidson & Worsham, 1992), have found that cooperative groups are particularly beneficial for Hispanic, African-American, and other minority students.

Since the basic plan for cooperative learning revolves around the idea of active small group learning environments, it's a natural vehicle for promoting multicultural understandings. Positive interdependence, shared responsibilities, social skills development and heterogeneity separate cooperative groups from traditional work in groups. Students at various "ability" levels, cluster together, discuss topics and learn to take charge of their own learning. They can also look for common ground, rather than emphasizing differences.

Educators have been searching for techniques to teach today's students to think clearly, creatively and cooperatively. By actively engaging students in the collaborative process teachers have been able to integrate social skills and critical thinking with academic content. With the support of teachers and a solid research base it is becoming the most widely used instructional innovation in American education (Clarke et al., 1990). Cooperative learning brings students to the edge of many possibilities – sharing visions and understandings that can enhance individual learning. It seems destined to make a real difference in American education.

RESOURCES AND REFERENCES

Abraham, S. Y. & Campbell, C. (1984). *Peer teachers as mirrors and mentors.* Detroit, MI: Wayne State University Press.

Carnegie Foundation for the Advancement of Teaching. (1986). Task forum on education and the economy, task force on teaching as a profession. *A nation prepared: Teachers for the 21st century.* New York: Carnegie Foundation.

Cohen, E. G. (1994). Restructuring the classroom: Conditions for productive small groups. *Review of Educational Research, 64,* 1–35.

Cohen, E. G., Lotan, R., and Catanzarite, L. (1990). Treating status problems in the cooperative classroom. In S. Sharan (Ed.), *Cooperative learning: Theory and research,* (pp. 203–229). New York: Praeger.

Connelly, M. F., & Clandinin, D. J. (1988). *Teachers as curriculum planners: Narratives of experience.* New York: Teachers College Press.

Costa, A. L., (Ed.). (1991). *Developing minds: A resource book for teaching thinking.* Alexandria, VA: Association for Supervision and Curriculum Development.

Darling-Hammond, L. (1999) "Teacher quality and student achievement," Palo Alto, Center for the Study of Teaching and Learning.

Davidson, N. & Worsham, T. (1992). *Enhancing thinking through cooperative learning.* New York: Teachers College Press.

Dixon-Krauss, L. (1996). *Vygotsky in the classroom: Mediated literacy instruction and assessment.* White Plains, NY: Longman.

Hamm, M. & Adams, D. (1992). *The collaborative dimensions of learning.* Norwood, NJ: Ablex.

Hughes, L. (1990). *Collected Poems of Langston Hughes.* New York: Knopf.

Jager Adams, M. (1990). Beginning to read: *Thinking and learning about print.* Cambridge, MA: MIT Press.

Johnson, D. W. & Johnson, R. (1989). *Joining together: Group theory and group skills.* (5th Ed.). Englewood Cliffs, NJ: Prentice Hall.

Johnson, D. W. & Johnson, R. (1975). *Learning together and alone.* Englewood Cliffs, NJ: Prentice Hall.

Johnson, D. W., Johnson, R., Holubuc, E. J. & Roy, P. (1984). *Circles of learning: Cooperation in the classroom.* Alexandria, VA: Association of Supervision and Curriculum Development.

Johnson, D. W., Maruyama, G., Johnson, R., Nelson, D., & Skon, L. (1981). Effects of cooperative, competitive, and individualistic goal structures on achievement: A meta analysis. *Psychological Bulletin, 89,* 47–62.

Kagan, D. (1986). Cooperative learning and sociocultural diversity: Implications for practice. In *Beyond language minority students* (pp. 98–110). Los Angeles: Evaluation, Dissemination and Assessment Center, California State University.

Lee, C., Ng, M., & Jacobs, G. M. (1998). Cooperative learning in the thinking classroom. In M. L. Quah & W. K. Ho (eds), *Thinking processes: Going beyond the surface curriculum* (pp.223–237). Singapore: Simon & Schuster.

Moore Johnson, S. (1990). *Teachers at work: Achieving success in our schools.* New York: Basic Books.

Nodding, N. (1984). *Caring: A feminine approach to ethics and moral education.* Berkeley: University of California.

Slavin, R. E. (1995). *Cooperative learning: Theory, research and practice* (2nd ed.) Boston, MA: Allyn and Bacon.

Slavin, R. E. (1990). *Cooperative learning: Theory, research, and practice.* Englewood Cliffs, NJ: Prentice Hall.

Slavin, R. (1989). *Schools and classroom organization.* Hillside, NJ: Erlbaum.

Slavin, R., Sharan, S., Kagan, S., Hertz-lazarowitz, Webb, C. & Schmuck, R. (Eds.). (1985). *Learning to cooperate, cooperating to learn.* New York: Plenum.

Slavin, R. (1983). *Cooperative learning.* New York: Longman.

Sprenger, M. (1999). *Learning and memory: The brain in action.* Alexandria, VA: Association for Supervision and Curriculum Development.

Thornburg, D. (2002). *The new basics: Education and the future of work in the telematic age.* Alexandria, VA: Association for Supervision and Curriculum Development.

Trumbull, E. & Farr, B. (2005). *Language and learning: What teachers need to know.* Norwood, MA: Christopher-Gorden Publishers.

Vaughn, S. & Linan-Thompson, S. (2004). *Research-Based methods of reading instruction.* Alexandria, VA: Association for Supervision and Curriculum Development.

Chapter 4

COMMUNICATION TECHNOLOGIES

*New technologies have been disrupting existing equilibria for
centuries, yet balanced solutions have been found before.*
— Pamela Samuelson

From chalk to the printing press, technology has always been part of the classroom literacy scene. New ways of communicating and relating to information have always required a break from habit. A thousand years ago it was the written word. For the last five hundred years or so, the printing press has been central to just about everything. The arrival of a new medium has always been exhilarating, frightening, and finally just part of life. A few decades into the twentieth century it was the telephone that began to be taken for granted. By the 1950s it was television. Now, many children see the Internet as a natural way to extend their information and communication reach. The coming together of computers, video, satellites, and the World Wide Web is both evolutionary and revolutionary.

Emerging electronic information and communications technology can conjure up new environments for critical thinking and creativity. When used intelligently, digital technologies can help you do all kinds of things better. In a school setting they can connect subjects to collaborative inquiry. As educators take an active role in the development of educational technology the process can have a liberating effect on their imagination. New technological possibilities can encourage new habits of the mind and fresh perspectives. For American teachers this means that professional development is no longer a luxury, it's a necessity.

Performed incorrectly, technology-intensive activities can be sad and lonely. Performed correctly, digital technology allows an active meaning-centered curriculum to flourish in (and beyond) the classroom. A medium like the Internet can, for example, help turn parents from spectators into active participants in their children's learning. AOL@School (www.school.aol.com) is just one of the ad free portals for connecting teachers, students, parents, and school administrators. It is arranged by grade level, encourages parent/teacher interaction, and includes links to the Smithsonian Institution and The New York Times Learning Network.

Unleashing the potential of digital media requires serious thinking, research, and experimentation on the connections between the characteristics of effective instruction and educational technology. Future directions are open to question. But it is clear that the information technology revolution and the globalization of the economy heralds the arrival of a different educational configuration (Coppola, 2004).

Powerful Tools and Unexpected Possibilities

Computers and their associates are potentially powerful tools for communications and academic work. They have the power to move literacy and learning patterns off established roads. Multimedia computing and the Internet, for example, add a new dimension to learning by communicating meaning with video, animation, and sound. With Netcams (or Webcams) the immediate visual environment of the computer user becomes part of the communication process. By motivating students through the excitement of discovery, a wide assortment of technological tools can assist the imaginative spirit of inquiry and make lessons sparkle. It can even put students right out on the edge of discovery – where truth throws off its various disguises.

As human horizons shift, a sort of flexible drive and intent is required for innovation and progress. Technology can add power to what we do and help us kick against educational boundaries. The vivid images of electronic media can stimulate students as they move quickly through mountains of information, pulling out important concepts and following topics of interest. The process changes students' relationship to information by allowing them to personally shift the relationship of knowledge elements across time and space. Learners can follow a topic between subjects, reading something here, and viewing a video segment there. All of this changes information that is structured and how it is used. It also encourages students to take more responsibility for their own learning.

> *All media as extensions of ourselves serve to provide new*
> *transforming vision and awareness.*
>   – Marshall McLuhan

Be ready for the unexpected. Things don't always go as planned. Alexander Graham Bell thought, when he invented the telephone, that it would be used to listen to distant symphony concerts. Thomas Edison thought that the phonograph record would be used to send messages. Some of the best thinkers often miss the potential of their inventions. For example: physicist Heinrich

Hertz was the first to generate and detect radio waves, yet he dismissed the notion that his findings might ever have any practical value. Human advances often come from what may go unnoticed or seem trivial at the time.

Anything that changes perspective – from travel to technology – can help generate new ideas. The motivation is also there because it's usually more fun to do things where the unexpected may turn up than sticking with the easily predictable. Playfulness and experimentation can often open up to creative possibilities, increasing the capacity to fashion ideas or products in a novel fashion. Creatively playing with various ideas, some of which may seem silly at the time, may result in getting lucky with one or two of them.

It is often difficult to detect the subtle happenstance and how we make room in our own lives for positive accidents to happen. Being exposed to different experiences and paying attention to what's going on in the world helps by opening up all kinds of serendipitous possibilities. Training the eye to notice things goes a long way towards making unpredictable advances happen. Each new finding can open up fresh questions and possibilities – breaking the habits that get in the way of creative thinking and change. Rx for thinking in the future: following curiosity, leaving doors open, using technological tools, and making room for good luck to happen.

The Technological Dimensions of Learning in a New Era

The playful gleam in the eye is often an engine of progress. There are multiple tools and modes of expression that schools need to build on to promote the multitude of strengths and imaginations found in all students. Many schools are mired in unproductive routines that prevent teachers from making creative breakthroughs. However, before we get too critical, we should recognize that it's difficult to redesign the plane when you're the pilot and flying at 30,000 feet. Seldom is enough time taken to go back to the drawing board and use good data and experience to get it right. Educators need time, space, support, and time for collegial professional development to make all the changes required.

Powerful forms of face-to-face learning within schools must not be neglected as we sort out the new media possibilities. Intelligent use of electronic forms of learning have proven to be helpful in improving student learning. But when it comes to the professional development of teachers their value is not as clear. Electronic learning can, however, make a contribution. And it is a useful supplement to the professional development toolkit.

It is difficult to unravel issues of creativity or analyzing without taking into account influential media, like computers and television. They have a tremendous impact on children. We shape them and they shape us. Some are often written about as Lady Caroline wrote about Lord Byron *"mad, bad and dangerous to know."* Others see technology, such as computers and the Internet, as a particularly dangerous enemy, creating a culture of electronic peeping Toms without a moral foundation.

To be valuable, educational technology must contribute to the improvement of education. Digital devices and their accessories should be designed to help open doors to reality and provide a setting for reflection. By making important points that might otherwise go unnoticed these technological tools can help students refine and use knowledge more effectively. For example, computers can use mathematical rules to simulate and synthesize life-like behavior of cells growing and dividing. It's a very convincing way to bring the schooling process to life.

The yeast of knowledge, openness, and enterprise raises the need for a multiplicity of learning media and technological tools. Schools can teach students to recognize how technology can undermine social values, human goals and national intention. They can also help students learn to harness these powerful tools so that they might strengthen and support the best in human endeavors. It is our belief that when the pedagogical piece is in place technology can support and strengthen the best in student learning. This cannot only change what teachers teach but how they go about doing it.

As new technologies and related products start to fulfill their promise, students will become active participants in knowledge construction across a variety of disciplines. We have had only a glimpse of the technological gateways to learning that will open in the twenty-first century. As state-of-the-art pedagogy is connected with state-of-the-art technological tools, the way knowledge is constructed, stored, and learned will be fundamentally altered (Moersch, 2002).

The Future of Narrative in Cyberspace

The idea of print as an immutable cannon may or may not be an historical illusion. One thing for sure, the way print is being mixed electronically with other media changes things. Although the American book industry is rushing into the emerging electronic literary market, book pages made of paper will not go away. And print is here to stay. Even the doomsayers usually use books to put forward their argument that the medium is a doomed and outdated technology. In the future will books be confined to dusty museum libraries? No, they remain an elegant user-friendly medium. With books you don't need batteries and don't have to worry about the technological platform becoming obsolete and unusable.

There are at least two fairly new digital approaches to books that are finding a niche in the literacy universe. One is much like an electronic version of printed books. E-books by Microsoft, Time Warner and others are print-based. The other approach to electronic books is interactive and visually-intensive. It takes the narrative and places it in randomly accessible blocks of text, graphics, and moving video. The "reading" skills that will come to be associated with such "books" have implications that cut across the curriculum. The major goal of any form of reading instruction will continue to incur students to comprehend what they read. High or low tech, once children get the hang of it many of the purposes remain the same. For example, with stories, students must learn to go beyond merely following the action of the plot in order to learn about characters, explore different ideas, and enter other minds.

An interactive story places students in charge of how things develop and how they turn out. Participants are able to change the sequence or make up a new beginning to a multidimensional story. They can take the opportunity to find out additional information and they can change the ending. Navigating interactive stories with no fixed center, beginning or end, can be very disconcerting to the uninitiated. It requires different "reading" skills. To make sense of the anarchy and chaos a reader has to become a creator. This means following links around so that they can discover different themes, concepts and outcomes. "Interactive Storytime" is an early example. It tells stories with narration, print, music, sound effects and graphics. Children can click on any object and connect spelling to the pronunciation.

Literature has traditionally had a linear progression worked out in advance by the author. The reader brought background knowledge and a unique interpretation to what the author had written. But it was the author who provided the basic sequential structure that pushed all readers in the same direction. Computer-based multidimensional literature is quite different. The reader shapes the story line by choosing the next expository sequence from a number of possibilities.

With early versions of interactive computer-based literature, readers are connected to a vast web of printed text, sound, graphics, and life-like video. When key words or images are highlighted on a computer screen the reader clicks what they want next with a mouse (or finger on a touch screen) and the reader hops into a new place in the story, causing different outcomes. With a virtual reality format the "reader" uses their whole body to interact with the story. Whatever the configuration, interactive literature causes the user to break down some of the walls that usually separates the reader from what is being read.

The forking paths in this electronic literature poses new problems for readers — like how do you know when you have finished reading when you can just keep going all over the place. Judy Malloy's *It's Name was Penelope,* for example, shuffles 400 pages of a fictional woman's memories so that they come together very differently every time you read it. The ambiguity of these programs isn't as bothersome as it used to be. Today, children are used to television and computer programs that deal with quick movement between short segments of information. In addition, many video games and computer simulations require students to wander in a maze of ideas. As a result, children are usually not as disoriented by the various forms of interactive literature as adults.

Odd varieties of e-stories can be found, free of charge, on the Internet. Some are free, some are comparable to a traditional book in price, and others require a multimedia or virtual reality platform. Many of these efforts at constructing interactive stories were more like interactive comic books than literature. Programs are becoming more sophisticated and are giving us some advance warning of a new literary genre. One thing is for sure. Something important to the future of literacy is happening and schools will have to tie some of the results into their curriculum.

Conveying Meaning With Powerful Visual Models

One way to enhance the power and permanency of what we learn is to use visually-based mental models in conjunction with the printed word. Inferences drawn from visually-intensive media can lead to more profound thinking. In fact, children often rely on their perceptual (visual) learning even if their conceptual knowledge contradicts it. In other words, even when what's being presented runs contrary to verbal explanations, potent visual experiences can push viewers to accept what is presented. Children can become adept at extracting meaning from the conventions of video, film, or animation – zooms, pans, tilts, fade-outs and flashbacks. But distinguishing fact from fiction is more difficult.

The ability to understand what's being presented visually is becoming ever more central to learning and to our society. Most of the time children construct meaning for television, film, computer, or Internet content without even thinking about it. They may not be critical consumers, but they attend to stimuli and extract meaning from subtle messages. The underlying message children often get from the mass media is that viewers should consume as much as possible while changing as little as possible. How well content is understood varies according to similarities between the viewers and the content, in which viewers' needs, interests, and age are important factors. Sorting through the themes of mental conservatism and material addition requires carefully developed thinking skills.

Meaning in any medium is constructed by each participant at several levels. For better or for worse, broadcast television used to provide us with a common culture. When viewers shared a common visual culture they also shared a similar set of tools and processes for interpreting these signals (construction of meaning, information processing, interpretation, and evaluation). The greater the experiential background in the culture being represented, the greater the understanding. The ability to make subtle judgments about what is going on in any medium is a developmental outcome that proceeds from stage to stage with an accumulation of experience.

Relying upon a host of cognitive inputs, individuals select and interpret the raw data of experience to produce a personal understanding of reality. What is understood while viewing depends on the interplay of images and social conditions. Physical stimuli, human psychology, and information processing schemes taught by this culture helps each person make sense of the world. In this respect reacting to the content of an electronic medium is no different from any other experience in life. It is just as possible to internalize ideas from electronic visual imagery as it is from conversation, print, or personal experience. Its just that comprehension occurs differently.

Reflective thought and imaginative active play are an important part of the growth process of a child. Even with a "lean back" passive medium like television, children must do active work as they watch, make sense of its contents, and utilize its messages. With a "lean forward" medium like the Internet this work is fairly evident. Evaluative activities include judging and assigning worth, assessing what is admired, and deciding what positive and negative impressions should be assigned to the content. In this sense children are active participants in determining meaning in any medium (Brooks-Young, S., 2002).

Adults Influence How Children Learn To Assess Media Messages

Children learn best if they take an active role in their own learning although parents, teachers and other adults are major influences. They can significantly affect what information children gather from television, film, or the Internet. Whatever the age, critical users of media should being able to:

1. understand the grammar and syntax of a medium as expressed in different program forms.
2. analyze the pervasive appeals of advertising.
3. compare similar presentations – those with similar presentations or those with similar purposes in different media.
4. identify values in language, characterization, conflict resolution, and sound/visual images.
5. utilize strategies for management in regard to duration of viewing and program choices.
6. identify elements in dramatic presentations associated with the concepts of plot, story line, theme, characterizations, motivation, program formats, and production values.

Parents and teachers can affect children's interest in media messages and help them learn how to process information. Good modeling behavior, explaining content, and showing how the content relates to student interests are just a few examples of how adults can provide positive viewing motivation. Adults can also exhibit an informed response by pointing out misleading messages – without building curiosity for undesirable programs.

The viewing, computer, and Internet using habits of families play a large role in determining how children approach a medium. The length of time

parents spend watching television, the kinds of programs viewed, and the reactions of parents and siblings toward programming messages all have a large
influence on the child. If adults read and there are books, magazines, and
newspapers around the house, children will pay more attention to print.
Influencing what children view on television or the Internet may be done with
rules about what may or may not be watched, interactions with children
during viewing, and the modeling of certain content choices. A tip for parents: it is usually a good idea to keep the computer or WebTV in the family
room.

Whether co-viewing or not, the viewing choices of adults in a child's life
(parents, teachers, etc.) set an example for children. If, for example, parents
are heavy watchers of public television or news programming then children
are more likely to respond favorably to this content. If parents make informed
intelligent use of the Internet then children are likely to build on that model.
Influencing the settings in which children watch TV or use the computer is
also a factor. Turning the TV set off during meals, for example, sets a family
priority. Families can also seek a more open and equal approach to choosing
television shows – interacting before, during and after the program. When it
comes to the Internet, keep the computer in the family room rather than in a
private isolated space. Time limits must be placed on today's electronic gad-
gets. Parents can organize formal or informal group activities outside the house
that provide alternatives to Internet use or TV viewing.

It is increasingly clear that the education of children is a shared responsibility. Parents obviously play a central role and they need connections with
what is going on in the schools. Working together, parents and teachers can
use the television, computers, and the Internet to encourage students to
become more intelligent media consumers. But when it comes to schooling it
is the teachers who will be called upon to make the educational connections
entwining varieties of print and visual media with language arts, reading,
mathematics, science, and art.

Communications Technology and Public Conversations

A democratic community is defined by the quality of its educational institutions and its public conversations. Democracy often becomes what it pays attention to. American national values, supported by our constitution, require an
educated citizenry that can think, respond to leaders, and are willing to actively go beyond the obvious. Patriotism isn't just the flag and stern rhetoric,
it's a thinking, decent, and literate society. Exercising citizenship in a world of
accelerated change requires the preservation of our human values.

Ignoring the societal implications of technology means ignoring looming
changes. Whether it is technologically-induced passivity or the seductive
charms of believing in simplistic technological solutions, it is only through the

educational process that people can gain a heightened awareness of bright human and technological possibilities. The question that we need to answer is: how may the technology be used to spark a renaissance in human learning and communication?

The long-term implications of recent changes in information and communications technology are important, if not frightening. The convergence of technologies is causing a major change in societal behaviors, lifestyles and thinking patterns. With few people monitoring digital technology or theorizing its health, the human race is being forced to swim in an electronic sea of information and ideas. In the early part of the twenty-first century there is little question that reality is being shaped by electronic information and electronic illusions.

Activities for Making Sense of Visual Media

1. *Help students critically view what they see.* Decoding visual stimuli and learning from visual images requires practice. Seeing an image does not automatically ensure learning from it. Students must be guided in decoding and looking critically at what they view. One technique is to have students "read" the image on various levels. Students identify individual elements and classify them into various categories, then relate the whole to their own experiences, drawing inferences and creating new conceptualizations from what they have learned. Encourage students to look at the plot and story line. Identify the message of the program. What symbols (camera techniques, motion sequences, setting, lighting, etc.) does the program use to make its message? What does the director do to arouse packaging, color and images) that influence consumers and often distort reality. Analyze and discuss commercials in different media. How many minutes of ads appear in an hour? How many ads do you have to sort through before you can watch a program or use a search engine to pull up some Web sites? What should be done about the ad glut?

2. *Create a scrapbook of media clippings.* Have students keep a scrapbook of newspaper and magazine clippings on computers, television, the Internet or other digital devices. The *New York Times* "Science" and "Circuits" section are both good for older students. Paraphrase, draw a picture, or map out a personal interpretation of the articles. Share these with other students.

3. *Create new images from the old.* Have students take rather mundane photographs and multiply the image, or combine it with others, in a way that makes them interesting. Through the act of observing it is possible to build a common body of experiences, humor, feeling and originality. And through collaborative efforts students can expand on ideas and make the group process come alive.

4. *Use debate for critical thought.* Debating is a communications model that can serve as a lively facilitator for concept building. Taking a current and relevant topic, and formally debating it, can serve as an important speech/language extension. For example, the class can discuss how mass media can support political tyranny, commercialism, public conformity or the technological enslavement of society. The discussion can serve as a blend of social studies, science, and humanities study.

The following activity can be used to test students knowledge of media use. [Leave the answers blank and ask small groups of students or teachers to estimate the percentage.]

Media Use and Literacy

1. Only ___% of teens say they don't watch TV during the week.
2. ___% of teens know Regis Philbin vs. ___% the Speaker of the House of Representatives.
3. The number of words in the vocabulary of a 14-year-old in 1950: was ___ vs. ___ words in 1999.
4. The average 18 year old has spent ___ hours watching television by age 18.
5. In a 1999 AOL online survey, what percentage of children used computers by age two ___% by age 6 ___%
6. What % of children get information on the Internet from peers? ___% What % from teachers? ___%

Answers

1. Only *2%* of teens say they don't watch TV during the week.
2. *66%* of teens know Regis Philbin vs. *6%* the Speaker of the House of Representatives.
3. The number of words in the vocabulary of a 14-year-old in 1950: *25,000* vs. *10,000* words in 1999.
4. The average 18-year-old has spent *22,000* hours watching television by age 18.
5. In a 1999 AOL online survey the percentage of children who used computers by age two was *25%*, by age 6, *90%*.
6. What % of children get information on the Internet from peers? *54%*. What % from teachers? *6%*.

[The first four points are from a *Newsweek* poll published May 10, 1999. The last two are from an AOL survey of customers. Presented by Steve Case at the ASCD annual conference, March, 2000. You might have students or teachers guess in a group of two or three – then you could see how close different groups came.]

Media often goes through stages of acceptance and use. There are many ways to set this up and our Internet example is just one way to conceptualize what has been going on with that medium. For a few years after the Internet got off the ground in 1995 it was centered on providing data for people to read and measuring how many visitors a Web site received. The second stage featured a rush to get business transactions onto the Web — with or without turning a profit. The third stage might be viewed as a focus on activities that pay more attention to transactions that contribute to profitability and making better use of knowledge workers. As things now stand, information can be personalized to meet the needs of these workers. Communications may now come in many ways, forms, from many sites, and on a variety of digital devices.

Different Media Symbol Systems

Print and visually-intensive media take different approaches to communicating meaning. Print relies upon the reader's ability to interpret abstract symbols. A video or computer screen is more direct. Whatever the medium, thinking and learning are based on internal symbolic representations and the mental interpretation of those symbols. When they are used in combination one medium can amplify another.

We live in a complex society dependent on rapid communication and information access. Life-like visual symbol systems are comprised in part, of story structure, pace, sound track, color, and conceptual difficulty. Computers, the Internet, television, and digital devices are rapidly becoming our dominant cultural tools for selecting, gathering, storing and conveying knowledge in representational forms.

Various electronic symbol systems play a central role in modern communications. It is important that students begin to develop the skills necessary for interpreting and processing the full range of media messages. Symbolically different presentations of media vary as to the mental skills of processing they require. Each individual learns to use a media's symbolic forms for purposes of internal representation. To even begin to read for example, a child needs to understand thought-symbol relationships. To move beneath the surface of electronic imagery requires some of the same understandings. It takes skill to break free from a passive wash of images and electronically induced visual quicksand. These skills don't just develop naturally, training is required to develop critical media consumers who are literate in interpreting and processing print or visual images.

Unlike direct experience, print or visual representation is always coded within a symbol system. Learning to understand that system cultivates the mental skills necessary for gathering and assimilating internal representations. Each communications and information medium makes use of its own distinctive technology for gathering, encoding, sorting and conveying its contents associated with different situations. The technological mode of a medium affects the interaction with its users – just as the method for transmitting content affects the knowledge acquired.

The closer the match between the way information is presented and the way it can be mentally represented, the easier it is to learn. Better communication means easier processing and more transfer. At its best, a medium gets out of your way and lets you get directly at the issues. New educational choices are being laid open by electronic technologies. Understanding and employing these technological forces requires interpreting new media possibilities from a unique and critical perspective.

Understanding and Creating Electronic Messages

Understanding media conventions helps cultivate mental tools of thought. In any medium this allows the viewer new ways of handling and exploring the world. The ability to interpret the action and messages requires going beyond the surface to understanding the deep structure of the medium. Understanding the practical and philosophical nuances of a medium moves its consumers in the direction of mastery.

Simply seeing an image does not have much to do with learning from it. The levels of knowledge and skill that children bring with them to the viewing situation determine the areas of knowledge and skill development acquired. Just as with reading print, decoding visually-intensive stimuli and learning from visual images requires practice. Students can be guided in decoding and looking critically at what they view. One technique is to have students "read" the image on various levels. Students identify individual elements, classify them into various categories, and then relate the whole to their own experiences. They can then draw inferences and create new conceptualizations from what they have learned.

Planning, visualizing and developing a production allows students to critically sort out and use media techniques to relay meaning. Young producers should be encouraged to open their eyes to the world and visually experience what's out there. By realizing their ideas through media production students learn to redefine space and time as they use media attributes such as structure, sound, color, pacing and imaging.

Since the field of educational technology is in a period of introspection, self doubt, and great expectations, theoretical guidelines are needed as much as specific instructional methods. It is dangerous to function in a theoretical or research deprived vacuum because rituals can spring up that are worse than those drained away. As schools are faced with aggressive marketing for electronic devices we must sure that a pedagogical plan that incorporates technology is in place. For technological tools to reach their promise requires close connection between educational research, theory, and classroom practice.

Reaching students requires opening students' eyes to things they might not have thought of on their own. This means using technological tools as capable collaborators for tapping into real experience, fantasies, and personal visions. This way previously obscure concepts can become comprehendible, with greater depth, at an earlier age. Technology and metacognitive strategies can come together as students search for data, solve problems, and graphically simulate their way through multiple levels of abstraction. The combination of thoughtful strategies and the enabling features of media tools can achieve more lasting cognitive change and improved performance (National Educational Standards for Students, 2002).

Social Equity and a Modern Philosophy of Teaching

When it comes to solving our educational problems technology isn't the only thing. But it is an important thing. As we put together the technological components that provide access to a truly individualized set of learning experiences it is important to develop a modern philosophy of teaching, learning, and social equity. While new information and communications technologies have the potential to make society more equal, it sometimes has the opposite effect. As we enter a world of computers, camcorders, interactive TV, satellite technology, and the Internet, everyone must have access.

Many American school districts lack the money to train teachers to use computers effectively. So in some schools children are still taught to use the computer primarily for typing, drill, and workbook-like practice. In contrast, affluent schools often encourage students to use computers for creative exploration – like designing multimedia presentations and collaborating with classmates in problem-solving experimentation. Everyone deserves access to a provocative and challenging curriculum. To become an equal instrument of educational reform technology, we must do more than reinforce a two-tier system of education; otherwise, many children will face a discouraging picture of technological inequality.

There are serious social consequences surrounding the inequalities of access to telecommunications and advanced information technology. Future connections to faculty, other students, databases, and library resources will change the way that information is created, accessed, and transmitted. Those denied access may have their academic ambitions stifled, causing them to fall further and further behind. The challenge is to make sure that this information is available for all in a twenty-first century version of the public library.

Digital technology gives us the ability to change the tone and priorities of gathering information and learning in a democratic society. Taking the right path requires learning to use what's available today and building a social and educational infrastructure that can travel the knowledge highways of the future. Electronically connecting the human mind to global information resources is shifting human consciousness in ways similar to what occurred in moving from an oral to a written culture. The ultimate consequences are unclear. But the development of basic skills, habits of the mind, wisdom, and traits of character will be increasingly affected by the technology.

The curriculum materials that are most effective and most popular are those that provide for social interaction and problem-solving. Information can be embedded in visual narratives to create contexts that give meaning to dry facts. Computer-controlled interactive activities can challenge students on many levels and even serve as a training ground for responsibility, persistence, and collaborative inquiry. It's relatively easy to buy the hardware and and get children interested. The difficult thing is connecting to deep learning in a manner that advances curriculum goals.

Schools of the future need more adults than ever: teachers aides, parents, older students, and more. Technological tools can be a unique and useful supplement that allows teachers to enhance what they are already doing – and do some new things.

> *True teachers use themselves as bridges over which they invite their*
> *students to cross; then, having facilitated their crossing joyfully*
> *collapse, encouraging them to create their own.*
>
> — Nikos Kazantzakis

Learning to Evaluate Software

Curriculum is a cooperative and interactive venture between students and teachers. On both an individual and social level those directly involved with the process must be taken seriously. Working together they can decide what benefits are gained from particular software programs. After all, the software user is in the best position to decide if the program is taking people out of the process – or whether learners are in control of the computers. Good software programs let students learn together at their own pace – visualizing, talking together, and explaining abstract concepts so that they can relate them to real-life situations.

There are time-consuming evaluation issues surrounding the multitude of software programs to be dealt with. Multimedia, simulation, microworlds, word processing, interactive literature, spreadsheets, database managers, expert (AI) systems or getting the computer in contact with the outside world all increase the potential for influencing impressionable minds. That is too large a universe for the teacher to figure out alone. Teachers can help each other. Another thing that helps the task become more approachable is getting the students to take on some of the responsibility.

Children can learn to critique both computer software and Internet Web sites much as they learned to critique the dominant media of yesteryear – books. One of the first tenants of book review criticism is to critique what is usually taken for granted. Another is that a critic must have at least a little affection for the media being critiqued. Why not have students do "book reports" on computer software and the quality of sites on the World Wide Web. Students can do this by sifting through some of the software reviews in newspapers, magazines and journals. The Web is a good source for information.

Students can quickly check to see if the flow of a program makes sense. Next they can try out the software as they think a successful or unsuccessful student might. What happens when mistakes are made? How are the graphics? Do you think you can learn anything from this? Is it exciting?

Without question, teachers and students are the ones who experience the consequences of making good or bad choices in software selection. And they are the ones who most quickly learn the consequences of poor choices.

Criteria For Software Evaluation

The teacher can apply the same assessment techniques used on other instructional materials when they evaluate courseware. The following list is an example:

1. Does the program meet the age and attention demands of your students?
2. Does the program hold the student's interest?
3. Does the program develop, supplement, or enhance curricular skills?
4. Does the program require adult supervision or instruction?
5. Children need to actively control what the program does. To what extent does the program allow this?
6. Can the courseware be modified to meet individual learning requirements?
7. Can it be adjusted to the learning styles of the user?
8. Does the program have animated graphics which enliven the lesson?
9. Does it meet instructional objectives and is it educationally sound?
10. Does the program involve higher level thinking and problem solving?

Student Evaluation Checklist

Name of student evaluator(s)_____

Name of software program_____

Publisher_____Subject_____

1. How long did the program take?_____minutes
2. Did you need to ask for help when using this program?_____
3. What skills do you think this program tried to teach?_____

Please circle the word that best answers the question.

4. Was the program fun to use?   yes   no   somewhat not very
5. Were the directions clear?   yes   no   somewhat not very
6. Was the program easy to use?   yes   no   somewhat not very

7. Were the graphics (pictures) good?　　yes　　no　　somewhat not very
8. Did the program get you really　　yes　　no　　somewhat not very
   involved?
9. Were you able to make choices in the program?　yes　　no
10. What mistakes did you make?_____
11. What happed when you made a mistake?_____
12. What was the most interesting part of the program?_____

_____
13. What did you like least? _____
14. What's a good tip to give a friend who's getting started with this program?

_____

Extended Activities

- Make up a quiz about the program and give the questions to other students in the class who have used the program.
- Create your own soundtrack for part of the program.
- Make up a student guide for the program. Use your own directions and illustrations.
- Write or dramatize a TV interview with one of the characters in the program.
- Interview other students who have used the program and write their responses.
- Write a review of the program for a magazine.

Remember, there are many *top ten* or *best of* lists out there for consideration.

Serving Pedagogy

The curriculum should drive the technology rather than the other way around. The most effective use of such tools occurs when desired learning outcomes are figured out first. Once standards have been set you can decide what technological applications will help you reach your goals. Technology can help when it serves clear educational goals. But there is much work to be done. Put an "e" and a dash in front of education. However, by working together teachers can learn from each other, push on to other innovations, and build a medium worthy of our students (Willard, N., 2002).

Converging communication technologies can serve as a great public resource. Commercial profit alone should not determine how these new technologies will be exploited. The airwaves and the information highways are owned by the public. Emerging public utilities must show a concern for learning and responsible social action. Any new media system is a public trust that should enable students to become intelligent and informed citizens.

In today's world children grow up interacting with electronic media as much as they do interacting with print or with people. Unfortunately, much of the programming is not only violent, repetitious, and mindless but also distracts students from more important literacy and physical exercise activities. New technologies, software, and interactive media amplifies everything. To deal with these new digital realities requires a new approach to curriculum and instruction. It also requires a heightened sense of social responsibility on the part of those in control of programming.

Not only has the media changed but we now live in a society that is ruled by profits. It is the time to go back to considering the public interest and devise rules to insure that the mass media takes responsibility for the fact that they influence the foundation on which formal learning takes place.

> *The main purpose of education is to prepare citizens to be productive in a democratic society.*
> – Thomas Jefferson

Tips on Using Technology

- Technology is an important thing, but not the only thing.
- Put the learning piece in place first.
- Don't panic or be intimidated by technology.
- Make mistakes and learn from your failures.
- Don't be afraid to learn from your students.
- Bring everybody along; leave no-one behind.
- Teach your teachers; invest in teacher training.
- Two-way is the only way. Foster active conversation.
- Have fun. Be sure that there is some joy in it.

(This list is built around ten points that Steve Case emphasized at the ASCD annual conference. March, 2000.)

The human imagination can be enhanced by technology-based instruction in a way that makes actual experiences more meaningful. With computer control you can speed it up, slow it down, go into an atom, or go back into the past. On occasion, the experience can even transcend print or actual experience as an analytical tool.

Looking Forward to Tomorrow

Amid all the commercial maneuvering, new technologies have potential for empowering students to take more control of their learning. It can also extend our reach for new knowledge and assist in the search for new ways of learning.

Digital technology not only can make information more visually intriguing, but also can provide two-way communication with live or artificially intelligent experts. Tutoring, for example, will be done by live, recorded, or computer-composed experts. (See the AOL Internet resource at the end of the chapter.)

Digital interactive storytelling techniques will allow plot lines to evolve in almost infinite directions. Characters can even be programmed to surprise us in ways that have never been programmed or written. Lessons can play to our cognitive strengths. There are at least three ways to think of spelling a word, for example. One is to picture it. This may be thought of as an experiential kinesthetic approach. Another way is to sound a word out, an audio approach. A third approach is visual. You see the word in your mind and spell it. This same formula may work for other tasks.

By putting on glove controllers and a helmet-like device, players can put themselves inside a simulation and use a wide range of media to participate. Instead of manipulating images on a flat screen, players can move their bodies around, pivot up, and duck down as they capture or escape villains. Head-mounted displays have separate liquid crystal display screens for each eye to create three-dimensional effects and stereo earphones for high quality sound. When certain gloves are used, wearers can even feel their hands grip objects. The next step is becoming immersed in the stories and vicarious experiences without the bulky equipment.

Computer-generated technology can give the user a sense of being in another reality. Tank commanders and pilots used virtual reality simulators for years. Astronauts use VR programs to train for future missions in which they use manned maneuvering units (jet packs) to move around in space. As the technology improves and the cost drops virtual reality is moving from an expensive military/space program to arcade attraction and home entertainment possibility.

From theme park attractions to simulated surgery in virtual operating rooms, the technology is moving through its infancy and into early childhood. Within the multisensory world of virtual reality, people can see, hear, and touch objects. Some of the applications being developed involves what has been called "telepresence," which gives the operator the sensation of putting his/her hands and eyes in a remote location. One could, for example, send a robot to "Mars" or the bottom of the ocean, control the action, see what it sees and feel what it feels. Can we predict where all of this wiz-bang technology will take us? The best advice is pursue multiple paths and not be afraid to change direction. In this way we can push back the horizon of predictability. The more unsettled things become the more important it is to have a range of possibilities. Even luck is the residue of design. If you think through the implications of multiple versions of the future you will be better prepared for whatever happens.

Opportunities Today and Challenges Ahead

When considered collectively, digital technology is the most powerful representational medium ever invented. It should be put to the highest tasks of society. As far as the schools are concerned, this means using technology to motivate students to explore school subjects with passionate curiosity.

Digital devices will continue to evolve in ways that extend human capabilities and compensate for the limits of the human mind. Clearly, dealing with emerging digital technologies is one of the many challenges that teachers will face in the twenty-first century. We often lament the fact that new teachers have not been provided the training to use new technologies available to them. Some teachers are still coming through teacher education programs that did not prepare them adequately to integrate digital technology with instructional tasks. In addition, some states pay little attention to the inservice needs of their teachers. This is not a question of remediation. Rather it is the fact that any profession requires its members to keep up-to-date with new findings and cutting edge technology. One way or another, technology is bound to generate new ways of thinking and working that will heat up the curriculum and instruction debate.

More and more Americans have access to computers and the Internet. Schools are coming along. But they are particularly slow to use the technology for active engagement and collaborative inquiry. Where do creative solutions come from and what small episode will spark the chain of creation?

Exploring a Future That Is Invaded by the Present

Computers, digital devices, the Internet, and the World Wide Web are redefining literacy and reshaping the architecture of learning. These technological tools help students learn in different ways and permit them to explore a much broader world of knowledge and learning. Learning to separate noise from knowledge is increasingly important in this age of information glut. Making better use of these "knowledge machines" means going well beyond "factoids" and electronic workbooks to collaboratively explore problems and tinker with disparate ideas. Will artificial intelligence be used to enhance the real thing? This will take a while since we are a long way from an understanding of human or computer consciousness.

The human mind can create beyond either what it intends or what it can foresee. Combinations of electronic media will be with us no matter how far the electronic environment expands. The problem is being sure that it works to human advantage. The informing power of technological tools can help change the schools. It can also make learning come alive and breathe wisdom into instructional activities.

Harmonizing the present and the future requires more than reinventing the schools. It means attending to support mechanisms and global trends. On one level globalization and the Internet have an American face. On another level the more the world integrates the more it disintegrates into ever smaller ethnic groups. To successfully sail through the crosscurrents of a transitional age requires

Americans to develop stronger habits of the intellect and a willingness to learn about the rest of the world. If we simply combine superpower omnipotence with public ignorance we are mixing a dangerous cocktail.

Technological application go a long way towards explaining the shape of the today's industrialized world. The futures that shape people's lives are often the imaginary ones that can stir them to action. We have grown used to having technology between us and reality. The future that this sets up may be bumpy, but it doesn't have to be gloomy. We can learn to be proactive in a rapidly expanding electronic world. What's needed is a controlling vision that can help explain technological innovation and pedagogical principles. In the meantime, we can educate the whole person to be productive in a changing democratic society. Teachers can be sure that when they educate students for a changing world they can help them become one of the individuals who is changing it.

> *The future is not a result of choices*
> *among alternative paths offered by*
> *the present, but a place that is created*
> *– created first in the mind and will,*
> *created next in activity.*
> *The future is not some place we are going to,*
> *but one we are creating.*
>   – John Schaar

RESOURCES AND REFERENCES

AOL @ SCHOOL is a series of six learning portals: K–2, 3–5, middle school, high school, teachers, and administrators. AOL partnered with the Family Education Network to create these Web sites for schools across America. Educators were involved in the design process and every effort was made to make it easy-to-use. A panel assembled by the American Association of School Administrators worked with AOL to set up links to useful and age-appropriate online content sites. Teachers can decide if and when they want students to use communication features like e-mail, chat, and instant massaging. AOL @ SCHOOL first became available during the 2000/2001 school year. The price is right, it's free. For more information call 1–888–468–3768.

Armstrong, A. (2001). *The child and the machine*. Beltsville, MD: Robins Lane An imprint of Gython House.

Bauer, D. (2000). *Technology funding schools*. San Francisco, CA: Jossey-Bass.

Boler, M. (1999). *Feeling power: Emotions and education*. New York: Routledge.

Bransford, J. D, Brown. A. L. & Cocking, R. R. (Eds.). (1999). *How people learn: Brain, mind, experience, and school*. Washington, DC: National Academy Press.

Brooks-Young, S. (2002). *Making technology work for you*. Eugene, OR: International Society for Technology in Education.

Brown, J. & Duduid, P. (2000). *The social life of information.* Boston, MA: Harvard Business School Press.

Coppola, E. M. (2004). *Powering up: Learning to teach well with technology.* New York: Teachers College Press.

DePalma, A. (2001). *Here: A biography of the New American Continent.* Public Affairs.

Gardner. H. (1999). *The disciplined mind.* New York: Simon & Schuster.

Gruber, S. (Ed.). (2000). *Weaving a virtual web: Practical approaches to new information technologies.* Urbana, IL: National Council of Teachers of English.

Healy, J. (1998). *How computers affect our children's minds.* New York: Simon & Schuster.

Higgins, C. (2001). *ICT in the primary school.* New York, NY: Falmer Press.

Hird, A. (2000). *Learning from cyber-savvy students.* Herdon, VA: Stylus Publishing.

Leask, M. (2000). *Teaching and learning with ICT.* New York: Routledge.

Moersch, C. (2002). *Beyond hardware: Using existing technology to promote higher-level thinking.* Eugene, OR: International Society for Technology in Education.

Murray, J. (1997). *The future of narrative in Cyberspace.* New York: The Free Press.

National Educational Technology Standards for Students. (2000). *Connecting curriculum and technology.* Eugene, OR: International Society for Technology in Education.

National Standards for Students. (2002). *Connecting curriculum and technology.* Eugene, OR: International Society for Technology in Education.

Samuelson, P. (1995.) Copyright and Digital Literacies. *Communications of the ACM,* April 1995, 38:3, pp. 15–21, 110.

Willard, N. (2002). *Computer ethics, etiquette, and safety for the 21st-century student.* Eugene, OR: International Society for Technology in Education.

Chapter 5

ASSESSMENT

INTEGRATED PERFORMANCE ASSESSMENTS IN THE ELEMENTARY AND MIDDLE SCHOOL CLASSROOM

Since teachers have to perform many types of assessment, they are in the best position to put the data to good use. Official assessment, instructional assessment, and social (sizing-up) assessment are the most common. *Official (administrative) assessment* includes formal grading, interpreting standardized test results, and testing for special needs placement. *Instructional assessment* is used to plan how and when instruction will be delivered. What materials will you use? How is the lesson progressing? What changes have to be made in the planned activities? *Social (sizing-up) assessment* involves figuring out how to set up groups and enhancing communication within the classroom community.

There is general agreement that the methods for assessing educational growth have not kept up with the new subject matter standards and the way the curriculum has changed. Multiple choice testing just doesn't do a very good job of capturing the reality of today's students. Such tests convey the idea to students that bits and pieces of information count more than deep knowledge. On the other hand, assessing performance conveys the notion that reasoning, in-depth understanding, taking responsibility, and the ability to apply knowledge in new situations is what counts. Here we concentrate on how performance portfolios can help you energize small-group instruction in the 3 Rs.

Howard Gardner (1997) argues for assessment practices that "look directly at the performance that we value, whether it's a linguistic, logical, aesthetic, or social performance." We suggest including diagnostic assessment for prior knowledge, teacher observations, interviews, response to prompts, self-assessment, peer reviews, products, projects, and even the occasional quiz. This chapter focuses on how certain elements of performance assessment, like portfolios, can be helpful in teaching the basics. We view performance portfolios as a good way to link assessment directly to instruction. Within this context, the teacher and the students jointly develop some important criteria for assessment; they go on to use this criteria to determine the quality of the product or performance.

Portfolios are different things to different people. How you define the term has a lot to do with how you are planning to use them. In our view, the portfolio is a purposeful collection of student work that can be used to describe their effort, progress, and performance in a subject. There is no harm in using portfolios to showcase the best of what a student has achieved. But most elementary school teachers get more useful information when portfolios reflect student growth over a period of time. Before you get started, it is best to figure out whose intersects are going to be served and what processes do you want the portfolios to measure.

Assessment can be used to motivate students in several ways. To begin with, children can be assigned to cooperative teams for interdisciplinary inquiry and peer assessment. As students are brought into designing assessment procedures as responsible partners, the whole process is enhanced. Students can then use portfolios to keep their own records and reflect on how well they are doing. By viewing the evidence of their increasing proficiency they become reflectors of their own progress. Finally, learning to communicate with peers, teachers, and parents about their achievement means taking more responsibility for academic success (Popham, W. James, 2003).

Using Growth Portfolios

Many teachers share a vision of what they think should be happening in their classes. It goes something like this: Students work in small groups doing investigations or accomplishing tasks using tools such as manipulative materials, blocks, beakers, clay, rulers, chemicals, musical instruments, calculators, assorted textbooks, computers, the Internet, and other references. They consult with each other and with the teacher – keeping journals and other written reports of their work. Occasionally the entire class gathers for a discussion or for a presentation. They want students to be motivated and responsible. Traditional testing methods do not support this vision.

As students and teachers use product criteria (the performance or work samples) and progress criteria (effort or class participation) they conduct experiments, collaborate in interdisciplinary projects, and construct portfolios. Portfolios represent a more authentic and meaningful assessment process. They are a major performance assessment tool for having students to select, collect, reflect and communicate what they are doing. Having children think about the evidence that they have collected – and deciding what it means – is clearly a good way to increase student engagement.

Portfolios have long been associated with artists and photographers as a means of displaying collected samples of representative work. They have also been used for over ten years by various reading and writing projects (Graves, 1994). In the 1990s the National Assessment of Educational Progress has suggested using portfolios to assess students' writing and reading abilities. In addition, portfolios have been helping some teachers monitor student performance in the language arts for the better part of a decade. They usually begin by specifying the essential concepts to be covered, figuring out how to link what is taught to the assessment process, and finding ways to display an understanding of the results. What is new is the interest in using these performance assessment techniques that now stretches across the curriculum.

Teachers have found that collecting, organizing, and reflecting on work samples ties in nicely with active interdisciplinary inquiry. Portfolios not only capture a more authentic portrait of a child's thinking but can serve as an excellent conferencing tool for meetings with children, parents, and supervisors. In addition to portfolios, teachers often create other performance assessment tasks: projects, exhibitions, performances, and experiments. By creating opportunities for students to reveal their growth we help them understand *what* they are doing and why they are doing it.

Drawing Meaning from What is Observed or Measured

Assessment and evaluation are so intertwined it's hard to separate them. Assessment is collecting data to gain an understanding or make a judgment. Evaluation is judging something's value based on the available data. You can have assessment without evaluation, but you cannot have evaluation without assessment. Assessment is a broader task than evaluative testing because it involves collecting a wider range of information that must be put together to draw meaning from what was observed or measured. Of course, the first use of assessment is within the classroom, to provide information to the teacher for making instructional decisions. Teachers have always depended on their own observations and examination of student work to help in curriculum design and decision-making. Teachers need ongoing support in their efforts to set high goals for student achievement.

Lately, we have been hearing a lot about "authentic assessment." The term implies evaluating by asking for evidence of the behaviors you want to produce. For assessment to be authentic the form and the criteria for success must be public knowledge. Students need to know what is expected and on what criteria their product will be evaluated. Success should be evaluated in ways that make sense to them. It allows students to show off what they do well. Authentic assessment should search out students' strengths and encourage integration of knowledge and skills learned from many different sources. It encourages pride and may include self and peer evaluation.

Equally important is the use of assessment in the world outside of school where people are valued for the tasks they do, their ability to work with others, and their responses to difficult problems or situations. To prepare students for future success both curriculum and assessment must encourage this kind of performance assessment (Stenmark, 1989). Assessment of products that students produce may include portfolios, writing, group investigations, projects, interactive web sites, class presentations, or verbal responses to open-ended questions. Whether it's small-group class presentations, journal writing, story-tellings, simple observation, or portfolios, alternative assessment procedures pick up many things that children fail to show on pencil-and-paper tests.

Purposeful Assessment

Learning demands communication with self, peers, and knowledgeable authorities. It also asks for effort and meaningful assessment. A lesson from twentieth century physics is that *the world cannot ultimately be objectified.* The same is true of people. Still, whether in science or education, we need to know where we're going, how we're going to get there and how far we have progressed. Although goals and accompanying testing may be limiting, moving on school reform requires identifying and measuring some of the desired results at various levels of schooling. Comparisons sometimes prod schools to improve. Like movie reviews, school rankings can make or break the reputation of a school. Public shaming may be embarrassing and painful. But it often leads to improvement. National tests, goals, and subject matter standards help us know where we are going. The next step is to be sure that highly competent teachers are given the chance to get us there.

Standardized multiple choice tests have not shown themselves to be all that helpful for teachers facing complex and multifaced socioeducational problems. Portfolio assessment is more dynamic and does a better job of demonstrating proficiency or progress towards a preset purpose. It can be used to meet the needs of evolving definitions of literacy – allowing students and teachers to create, reflect, evaluate, and act upon material that is highly thought of by those most directly involved. This helps us all go beyond simply recognizing that a mistake was made to imagining *why*, getting feedback from others, and finding practical ways to do something about it (Reeves, 2004).

The Portfolio as a Tool for Understanding

A portfolio is best described as a container of evidence of someone's skills and dispositions. Its a portfolio, not an archive, so avoid being trapped under an avalanche of information. More than a folder of a student's work, portfolios represent a deliberate, specific collection of an individuals important experiences and accomplishments. The items are carefully selected by the student and the teacher to represent a cross section of a student's creative efforts. It isn't just the best stuff, its what is most important to all concerned. Portfolios can be used as a tool in the classroom to bring students together, to discuss ideas, and provide evidence of understanding. The information accumulated also assists the teacher in diagnosing learners' strengths and weaknesses. It is clearly a powerful tool for gaining a more powerful understanding of student achievement, knowledge and attitudes.

The portfolio assessment process helps children become aware of their learning history and the development of their reasoning ability. Prospective teachers can find out a lot about themselves by sketching the most important events and efforts in their school days. As students become directly involved in assessing progress towards learning goals, the barrier between the learner and the assessment of the learner is lowered. Through critical analysis of their own work – and the work of peers – students gain insight into many ways of thinking about and resolving problems.

Portfolios are being used by teachers to document students' development and focus on their growth over time. The emphasis is on performance and application, rather than on knowledge for knowledge's sake. Portfolios can assist teachers in diagnosing and understanding student learning difficulties. This includes growth in attitudes, thinking, expression, and the ability to collaborate with others. There is clearly more to learning than multiple choice. Assessing the student over time (with portfolios) brings academic progress into sharp focus and promotes reflection on the larger issues of teaching and learning.

The Design and Purpose of a Portfolio

Portfolios are a means of bringing together representative material over time. Building such a picture of students' understanding is not a one-time collection of examples. This material should reflect students' knowledge and performance. The purpose is to gain an accurate understanding of students' work, development, and growth. The intent is to recapture the past to more effectively shape the future.

Careful attention should be given to:

- what is being evaluated
- the purpose of the portfolio
- the appropriateness of the contents to what is being assessed
- the audience for which it is intended

The purpose behind the portfolio should determine its design. The portfolio's range and the depth can be determined by the teacher, the student, or the nature of the portfolio's contents. Students may choose the contents based on specific categories. For example, teachers could ask students to select examples of their work that fit into categories such as:

- a sample that reflects a problem that was difficult for you
- work that shows where you started to figure it out
- a sample that shows you reached a solution
- a sample that shows you learned something new
- a sample of your work where you need to keep searching for ideas
- two items you are proud of
- one example of a comical disaster

Involving students in the selection process gets them directly participating in their own learning and their own evaluation. Learners, teachers and parents can gain a better understanding of the "student" in and out of school because portfolio contents can reveal a surprising depth of thinking and provide insights into personal issues. *Collecting, selecting,* and *reflecting* on their school experience (and that of their peers) allows students to communicate who they are and how they view themselves in relation to others. What to put in portfolios:

- group assignments and ideas
- teacher assessments and comments
- student writings and experimental designs
- student reflections, journal entries, reactions and feelings
- research, collected data entries, and logs
- problems, investigations
- individual and group projects
- creative expressions (art, photographs, audio, and videotapes)
- rough drafts and finished products.

Items selected should be dated and described. A cover letter by the author, a table of contents, and a description of the assignment or task are other ways of assisting the reader. As the portfolio develops, the contents can be added to, deleted, improved, revised, edited, or discarded.

Portfolio Tips

- Portfolio assessment is not just for younger students. Portfolios can be used with students from kindergarten through graduate school.
- Assessment should be integrative and oriented toward critical thinking and solving problems, not simply recall based. These may include observational notes by the teacher and student self-assessment.
- evidence of creative and critical thinking
- quality of activities and investigations
- variety of approaches and investigations
- demonstrate understanding and skill in situations that parallel prior classroom experience.

Suggestions for Getting Started

- Primary teachers often use large boxes to contain student portfolios. Children can place their written work in folders by subject area and the folder is put in a decorated box with the student's name. Boxes are stacked for easy access and neatness.
- For older students a three-ring binder is most frequently used for items such as: oral history interviews, copies of historical documents, photos of community service activities, worksheets, and class notes. Handouts can be 3-hole punched and added, along with journal entries, written comments, quizzes, and other documents.
- An artist's folder is useful for gathering things like video cassettes and three-dimensional kinds of projects. Photographs can be taken of large projects and videotapes made of others.

Using Portfolios for Professional Development

Student input adds to the process of professional knowledge building and assures the internal commitment of those involved. We ask our students to contribute to our development as teachers by writing down two things they like about some aspect of the class and one thing that we could do better. Only one complaint is allowed! Being curious about how students *think* and learn has always been part of a teachers job description. What's new is including ourselves and systematically attacking the issue, sharing the information, and looking for more professional development opportunities.

Information and observations garnered from your own classroom ("action research") is part of performance assessment and can be used to improve practice. This approach can help the best teacher in the country make better informed choices about learning activities and teaching methods. As far as student research is concerned, all projects require the formulation of a good problem (one that can be stated in question form). They also require focusing on the relationship between variables, and some way of objectively testing the hypothesis. The factors (variables), like time or group, should be kept constant. Some teachers find it best to work with another teacher to collect the data, organize and figure out a way to share with others. This might mean graphing results, mapping out a teaching strategy, video sharing of classroom events, informal readings of class essays, or simply a few overheads to share at a faculty meeting.

The construction of teaching portfolios has to be a teacher-designed process to get a real conversation about teaching going. We need to be constantly reminded that reimaging teaching is a continuing process that looms larger than the success or failure of any single lesson or project. It connects to teachers taking charge of their professional growth and development. Risk taking is essential for change and must be considered an asset – even when everyone agrees there has been a miscue. A few of the entries in a teaching portfolio might well be lessons that went astray yet still revealed important insights into future possibilities. Far from using this to criticize a teacher, administrators are professionally required – like doctors, lawyers or clergy – *not to use this information in a harmful way*. If used to criticize, you can be sure that the next year's teaching portfolio will be designed to cover up weaknesses rather than an instrument for positive self-initiated change.

> *If the highest aim of a captain was to preserve his ship*
> *then he would stay in port.*
> – Thomas Aquinas

The level of courage needed for the level of self-revelation for a good teaching portfolio requires a supportive caring environment where successes are celebrated and failures are seen as possibilities for growth. The objective of a teaching portfolio must be clear to everybody and it's simply not ethical to put something together for development and then have it misused for formal evaluation. If the goal is to assist professional development and help the teacher in self-motivated growth then this must be adhered to.

Portfolio Assessment Exam

Portfolios can help provide an ongoing conversation about processes relating to teaching and learning. They can also help us attend to subjects that don't lend themselves to traditional testing methods (Michell, 1989). Portfolios also assist in exploring what is going on *in* and *between* subjects. These samples, drawn from different times and contexts, can serve as an ongoing means of getting people talking and learning across disciplines.

A PORTFOLIO EXAM FOR PROSPECTIVE TEACHERS

Consider *your work as a whole* and select significant pieces from your notebook, readings, class experiences, and activities assignments. Each item should encourage you to reflect on your performance and illustrate each of the categories below. Discuss why you included each sample, how your ideas have changed over the course of the semester, and how your understanding of the subjects covered have grown over time.

Category 1. How has your knowledge of teaching grown or changed? Include an example that reflects a growth in personal understanding and samples of activities that were meaningful to you (or enlarged your understanding).

Category 2. How have your attitudes, beliefs, and personal confidence about educational concepts changed? Samples might include questions you raised or beliefs that you held at the beginning of the semester and a comparison with later ideas. This category may include some reflection on your views and how these attitudes will translate into your classroom practice.

Category 3. How have your experiences – in and out of the classroom – helped you understand yourself and the learning process? What have you found out about your personal learning style, strengths, weaknesses, self-esteem, and group communication skills? What does this mean for your students in the future?

Category 4. What relationships/connections do you see in your work (all subjects) this semester? Look over *all* of your notes, handouts, activities, readings, assignments, etc., and select pieces that make meaningful connections for you – or form relationships between concepts that you have not explored before.

Category 5. How can what you have learned be applied to elementary school students with special needs? Include personal insights and samples from children.

Linking Assessment with Instruction

Portfolios are proving useful in linking assessment with instruction at every level because they allow students and teachers to reflect on their movement through the curricular process (Mumme, 1990). They also provide a chance to look at what and how students are learning while paying attention to students' ideas and thinking processes. We do not suggest that the "pure" objectivity of more traditional testing has no place in the classroom. Rather we must respect its limits and search for more connected measures of intellectual growth. But there is no question that when coupled with other performance measures, like projects, portfolios can make an an important contribution to new literacies.

Rules for Assessing and Evaluating

1. Conduct all assessment and evaluation in the context of *learning teams.* You must assess each student's achievement, but it's far more effective when it takes place in a cooperative setting.
2. Continual Feedback and Assessment
   Learning groups need continual feedback on the level of learning of each member. This can be done through quizzes, written assignments, or oral presentations.

3. Develop a list of expected behaviors:
   Prior to the lesson _____
   During the lesson _____
   Following the lesson _____
4. Directly involve students in assessing each others learning.
   Group members can provide immediate help to maximize all group members learning.
5. Avoid all comparisons between students that is based solely on their academic ability. Such comparisons will decrease student motivation and learning.
6. Use a wide variety of assessment tools.

Cooperative Learning Activity and Assessment Grid

RISKY BUSINESS

A recent survey in Dun's Review lists the most perilous products or activities in the United States (based on yearly death statistics). Your group task is to rank each item in order of dangerousness according to the number of deaths caused each year. Place number 1 next to the most dangerous, number 2 next to the next most dangerous, and so forth.

mountain climbing ____	surgery _____	
swimming _____	smoking _____	
railroads _____	motor vehicles _____	
police work _____	pesticides _____	
home appliances_____	handguns _____	
alcohol_____	bicycles _____	
nuclear power_____	fire fighting _____	

Answers: 1. smoking   2. alcohol   3. motor vehicles   4. handguns   5. swimming   6. surgery   7. railroads   8. bicycles   9. home appliances   10. fire fighting   11. police work   12. nuclear power   13. mountain climbing   14. vaccinations   15. pesticides

Assign students to mixed-ability teams. Be sure that the team takes charge of the quality of the work of its members.
Team members must
– learn how to define and organize work processes.
– assess the quality of the processes by recording the indicators of progress.
– place the measures on a quality chart for evaluating effectiveness.

An important **assessment part of the activity** is an observational record that is kept by one member of the group or by the teacher. It can be arranged on a grid and may be marked during the activity. [Keep it simple so that the rater can participate.]

OBSERVATION FORM

Group	Explaining Concepts	Encouraging Participation	Checking Understanding	Organizing the Work
1				
_____/_____/_____/_____/_____				
2				

etc.

Involving Students in Performance Assessment

With performance-based assessment, students demonstrate what they can do by performing a procedure or documenting a skill. Performance assessment also involves students in the evaluation of their own work. Educators no longer view assessment as residing only with the teacher or as an end point to learning. As teachers and students work together to design assessments, everybody develops an understanding of what needs to be learned. Performance assessment is not new or difficult. Basically it's something that good teachers have always done: questioning and observing students to evaluate their progress and then modifying instruction based on these observations (Hales, L., 2004).

Through performance assessment teachers are encouraged to:

- incorporate assessment into the teaching and learning process;
- use their own judgment when evaluating learning;
- establish criteria to assure reliability;
- describe the skills, attributes, and qualities to be developed;
- focus on important concepts and problem-solving skills, rather than memorization of facts;
- design tasks to provide opportunities for students to perform, create or produce a satisfying product;
- involve students in the evaluation of their work;
- build commitment to change.

The object of performance assessment is to look at how students are working as well as at the completed task or product. An observer or interviewer may stay with the group or make periodic visits. Activities may be videotaped, tape recorded or recorded in writing by an outside adult, the teacher, or the students. Looking at student performance gives teachers information about students' abilities to reason and raise questions. This type of group assessment focuses on finding out what students know and building experiences around that information. This involves student groups working together gathering information and supporting their data. Often teachers construct a chart at the beginning of a unit showing:

- what students already know.
- what they want to find out.
- how data was collected as evidence.

At the beginning of each unit of study, teachers measure students' understanding and establishes learning objectives by also writing them on the chart "What our class wants to find out." Next, the teacher introduces hands-on activities. Through first-hand experience students discuss and develop their own meanings. Throughout the unit teachers and students refer to the chart to find out how thinking and questions have changed, and what new questions have arisen. At the end of the unit students complete the chart stating what they have learned as supported by the gathered data. This knowledge is then incorporated into group writings entitled "What our group learned." Student groups meet as a class to discuss their findings, compare and review concepts learned and check to see if they met all the objectives. This gives the teacher insights into how well students are concentrating, how they communicate, how well they work together, organizing and presenting information.

Teachers of kindergarten and primary age children have always relied on performance and product assessments. In the lower grades children often have limited communication skills and are in the process of being socialized into the school culture. Observing the child's performance is about the only way you can assess behaviors like self control, getting along with others, and working independently. In addition, observation and the products of the child's work are key ingredients in assessing basic literacy development. In spite of calls for accountability, its hard for a five-year-old to take a standardized test.

By the time students get into the upper elementary grades assessment often morphs into standardized tests and more formal measurement. At the classroom level this includes quizzes and graded writing tasks. Still, there is plenty of room for using performance assessment to help everyone understand daily work, observations, conferences, and interviews. In mathematics, for example, this might include involving students in a mathematical task, project, or investigation. Its a good way to document the degree to which a child thinks of himself or herself as an observant investigator. The next step is to observe, interview, and look at student products so that you can actually see what they can *do*. Many of the same performance assessment techniques work for reading and writing. With these subjects teachers are even more likely to use anecdotal records, checklists, group evaluations, and individual portfolios to document the students' language learning process while documenting the degree to which a child thinks of himself or herself as an observant investigator (Tierney, 2003).

No matter how you go about it, its hard to measure intellectual curiosity or the creative imagination. But portfolios and other performance assessment techniques certainly go a long way towards giving us the information we need.

Changing Schools Means Changing Assessment

Generating the energy to change school culture and act on new practices and new assessment possibilities is an art. It has a lot to do with understanding human nature, establishing a readiness for change, and developing an intellectual understanding of new practices. The most effective innovations are usually research-based and classroom friendly. Change is a personal process but things work out best when it is supported by a team approach. School reform without teachers is a contradiction in terms. To move educational reform from talk to action requires the involvement of informed teachers who can make use of new concepts. If their voice is left out then we will miss a real opportunity.

When teachers arrange for their students to spend significant amounts of time in small cooperative groups, their assessment techniques change dramatically. Within this context, more emphasis is placed on student understanding and less on content recall assessed through multiple choice tests. Assessment is bound to become more authentic and dynamic as it changes to reflect the changing nature of instruction in the classroom.

The social context of the students' performance is an important issue in teaching the three Rs. Teachers need this information so that they can organize mixed ability groups in a way that reflects the amount and type of help students need to perform tasks. By designing grouping arrangements and adjusting instruction you will be able to include students from diverse backgrounds in challenging activities. The amount of help that children need can be adjusted by observing and analyzing the interaction that occurs during the learning task. As students gain social and subject matter competence, the teacher can provide less assistance and shift more responsibility to the student groups.

Performance assessment requires students to demonstrate the desired procedure or skill in a "real life" context. It must also be informed by the goals of instructional practice. When it comes to portfolios and evaluating performance, teaching, learning, and assessment are intimately connected. Such techniques allow students and teachers to display growing strengths, rather than simply exposing weaknesses.

Portfolios are associated with the performance assessment approach and receive a great deal of attention here. They promote ownership of learning by encouraging students and teachers to use, shape, and reflect on the social interaction and the knowledge that is important to them. A collaborative approach works as well for the teacher's professional development as it does for students.

When favorable new approaches like portfolios are shared with others everyone gains. For teachers sharing might involve collecting and organizing data, graphing the results, presenting a teaching strategy, and an informal discussion of authentic assessment with a colleague. Remember, when you set out to improve something, it is important to have a goal in mind and room for serendipity. When it comes to possibilities for practice we have to be ready for chance finds. Who, for example, would have predicted today's Internet based on the 80s original?

Professionals don't blossom when they spend their careers enfolded in the logic of others. Teachers themselves are in the best position to identify the key issues, question, probe, try to attain clarity, and *do* something in an ambiguous world. Informal belief systems are just as important as methodology. When teachers become students of their own learning, they discover the inconsistencies between what they believe about gaining knowledge and how they practice teaching. Discoveries they make themselves are more convincing and make them more willing to change what they do. The thoughtful reflection about practice that comes with performance assessment can play a major role in helping teachers become autonomous professionals.

> *I believe that we should get away altogether from tests*
> *and correlations among tests and look instead*
> *at more naturalistic sources of information*
> *about how peoples around the world develop*
> *skills important to their way of life.*
> – Howard Gardner

RESOURCES AND REFERENCES

Airasian, P. W. (2000). *Classroom assessment: Concepts and applications.* New York, NY: McGraw-Hill.

Bailey, K. M. (1999). *Learning about language assessment: Dilemmas, decisions, and directions.* Stamford, CT: Wadsworth Publishing Company.

Barrentine, S. J. (editor) (1999). *Reading assessment: Principles and practices for elementary Teachers: A collection of articles from the Reading Teacher.* Newark, DE: International Reading Association.

Betz, N. E. (2000). *Tests and assessment.* Upper Saddle River, NJ: Prentice Hall.

Fiderer, A. (1999). *40 rubrics and checklists to assess reading and writing: Time-saving reproducible forms and great strategies for meaningful assessment.* New York, NY: Scholastic, Inc.

Gardner, H. (1997, September). Multiple intelligences as a partner in school improvement. *Educational Leadership, 55*(1), 20–21.

Glasgow, N. A. (2000). *New curriculum for new times: A guide to student-centered problem-based learning.* Thousand Oaks, CA: Corwin Press.

Graves, D. (1994). A fresh look at writing. Portsmouth, NH: Heinemann.

Guskey, T.R. and Bailey, J.M. (2000). *Developing grading and reporting systems for student learning: Experts in assessment.* Thousand Oaks, CA: Corwin Press.

Hales, L. (2004). *Developing effective assessments to improve teaching and learning.* Norwood, MA: Christopher-Gordon Publishers.

Homan Shearer, S. P. (2001). *Linking reading assessment to instruction: An application worktext for elementary classroom teachers.* Mahwah, NJ: Lawrence Erlbaum Associates, Inc.

Linn, R. L. L. & Gronlund, N. E. (1999). *Measurement and assessment in teaching.* Upper Saddle River, NJ: Prentice Hall.

Marzano, R. (2000). *Transforming classroom grading.* Baltimore, MD: Association for Supervision and Curriculum Development.

McMillan, J. H. H. (2000). *Classroom assessment: Principles and practice for effective teaching.* Boston, MA: Allyn & Bacon, Inc.

Michell, R. (1989). Portfolio newsletter of *Arts PROPEL.* Cambridge, MA: Harvard University Press.

Montgomery, K. (2000). *Authentic assessment: A guide for elementary teachers.* Boston, MA: Addison Wesley.

Mumme, J. (1990). *Portfolio assessment in mathematics.* Santa Barbara, CA: California Mathematics Project, University of California, Santa Barbara.

Nitko, A. J. (2000). *Educational assessment of students.* Upper Saddle River, NJ: Prentice Hall.

Popham, W. James. (2003). *Test better, teach better: The instructional role of assessment.* Baltimore, MD: Association for Supervision and Curriculum Development.

Puckett, M. B. & Black, J. K. (1999). *Authentic assessment of the young child: Celebrating development and learning.* Upper Saddle River, NJ: Prentice Hall.

Reeves, D. (2004). *Accountability for learning: How teachers and school leaders can take charge.* Baltimore, MD: Association for Supervision and Curriculum Development.

Salvia, J. (2001). *Assessment.* Boston, MA: Houghton Mifflin.

Stenmark, J. K. (1989). *Assessment alternatives in mathematics: An overview of assessment techniques that promote learning* (Prepared by the EQUALS staff and the Assessment Committee of the California Mathematics Council Campaign for Mathematics). For information contact EQUALS, Lawrence Hall of Science, University of California, Berkeley, CA 94720.

Stiggins, R. J. (2000). *Student-involved classroom assessment.* Upper Saddle River, NJ: Prentice Hall.

Swearingen, R. & Allen, D. D. (1999). *Classroom assessment of reading processes.* Boston, MA: Houghton Mifflin Company.

Tierney, R. (2003). I*nteractive assessments: Teachers, parents and students as partners with CD-ROM.* Norwood, MA: Christopher-Gordon Publishers.

Trice, A. D. (1999). *A handbook of classroom assessment.* Boston, MA: Addison-Wesley Educational Publishers, Inc.

Walker, B. J. J. (1999). *Diagnostic teaching of reading: Techniques for instruction and assessment.* Upper Saddle River, NJ: Prentice Hall.

Chapter 6

LANGUAGE ARTS IN A NEW ERA

SOCIAL INTERACTION, DIGITAL TECHNOLOGY, AND LANGUAGE LEARNING

Language learners must invent and try out the rules of
language for themselves through social interaction as
they move toward control of language-for-meaning.
— Glennellen Pace

Using all the available tools to accomplish shared literacy goals is widely recognized as one of the keys to effective language arts instruction. Certain simple truths about learning are sometimes lost in the smoky quarrelsomeness of the American education debate. One of these simple truths is that language learning is social and that instruction is most effective when it is holistic and in context. Another is that integrating the language arts is a powerful way to connect students to the full range of real communication possibilities.

As the concept of literacy expands to include electronic media, it is important to realize that each communication medium relates directly or indirectly to every other. The development of language and literacy is much more than learning subskills. It involves becoming active, critical, and creative users of print, spoken language, and the visual language of film, television, digital media, and more. Information and communication technology are not only part of the fabric of contemporary life but an increasingly important part of language arts instruction. Technological resources can do many things — including linking the classroom to the outside world in ways that extend the boundaries of learning.

Wiz-bang technology, collaborative learning, and a standards-based curriculum all help. But the key to high quality instruction is a cooperative language-rich classroom where the teacher knows the characteristics of effective instruction. Meaningful group activities and settings can help students learn how to use language to communicate, solve problems, and meet the diverse literacy demands that they will encounter throughout their lives. As teachers look for new ways to make the language arts more active, dynamic, purposeful, and fun, it is important to recognize the importance of personal adaptability and creativity. No single instructional method will meet the needs of all students in all situations. Rigid scripts designed by others have always been a poor substitute for well-educated teachers who can combine professional flexibility with a thorough knowledge of effective instruction.

Making Connections In Groups

Whether old or new media, the whole range of language skills can be helped by communicating with peers who provide immediate feedback during the reading, writing, and revision process. The most competent readers tend to be the most competent talkers, listeners, writers, viewers, and thinkers (Barr, Kamil, Mosenthal, & Pearson, 1993).

Let's look at how younger children can share big books:

Steps in Sharing a Big Book

- The teacher introduces the book and has children to predict what it is about.
- The teacher reads the book to the students – holds so children can see words.
- The teacher sometimes pauses so students can think what will happen next.
- The teacher rereads the book – students can read along (outloud) with the teacher.
- Students may pair up for a rereading – taking turns reading small parts.

A beginning reader may have to be repeatedly exposed to a book by hearing the story read well several times before they develop oral fluency themselves. The old fashioned round robin style doesn't work well. Just about anything else will get the job done. If you want to do a lot of oral reading simply do paired reading in groups of two. Get close, point the chairs in opposite directions, and take turns reading. Don't assume that a student – or even an adult – can make a book sound exciting when reading outloud. Many new teachers have to practice and get suggestions from their peers to do the job well. So you know that young readers will have to go over the text several times with a friend or two.

Just about any activity that you can think of can be employed. For example: children can work in small groups to act out a story or practice reading the lines in a readers theatre activity. They can also work in small groups to discuss the theme, plot, characterization, or difficulty to be overcome in the story. Felt pens and large paper can be used for semantic maps or webs of their answers. These can be put up and shared with the whole class. The most important thing is to get children thinking, discussing, and interacting with literature.

> *Reading is thinking with the mind of a stranger*
> – Jorge Luis Borges

Social Processing and Thinking About Written Expression

The development of a writing community is a very powerful way for students to collaborate in developing their writing voice (Heilbrun, 1989). Whether writing is self, peer, or teacher evaluated, it is important not to lose sight of the connection between what is valued and what is valuable. Jointly developed folders (portfolios) have a major role to play in student writing assessment. By selection samples these folders can provide a running record of students' interests and what they can and cannot do.

To work toward less control teachers need to help students take more responsibility for their own learning. The ability to evaluate does not come easily at first, and peer writing groups will need teacher-developed strategies to help them process what they have learned. The ability to reflect on being a member of a peer writing team is a form of metacognition – learning to think about thinking. The skills of productive group work may have to be made explicit. This requires processing in a circular or U-shaped group where all students can see each other. Questions for evaluative social processing might include:

1. How did group leadership evolve?
2. Was it easy to get started?
3. How did you feel if one of your ideas was left out?
4. What did you do if most members of your group thought that you should write something differently?
5. How did you rewrite?
6. Did your paper say what you wanted it to?
7. What kind of a setting do you like for writing?
8. How can you arrange yourself in the classroom to make the writing process better?
9. What writing tools did you use?
10. How do you feel when you write?
11. Explain the reasoning behind what you did?

Remember, its just as important for students to write down their reasoning as it is to explain their feelings and preferences.

The recognition of developmental stages in social skills must be taken into account as teachers incorporate literature-based writing concerns into their classroom routines. For the younger students, the writing process can take the form of jointly produced language experience stories. These can be placed on large charts with the teacher or an upper-grade student doing the writing. As soon as they can write on their own the children can keep a private journal where they label drawings, experiences and writing samples.

As students learn to expand their perspectives they can begin to carry a story from one page (or day) to the next. Time may be set aside each day for a personal journal entry. Although it's important that the language be in a student's own words the teacher can make comments without formal grading.

There are times when teachers have to intervene to assess students' writing or do some final editing before something is widely shared. Remember to stamp "draft" or "creative writing – work in progress" on anything that might go home before it reaches its final form. A "work in progress" stamp would save you from a little embarrassment when a misspelled word or some bad grammar reaches parents.

Structured and Unstructured Poetry Experiences

A twentieth century American may disagree with Wordsworth, a nineteenth century Englishman who explained poetry as "emotion recollected in tranquility." People reach for poetry today because in its own peculiar way poetry tells truths that other communication techniques often miss. Teachers must have some basic knowledge of the vocabulary of poetry in order to help children enjoy and mature in their understanding and appreciation of it. One thing they can do is to share some of their efforts at poetry with their students – as well as reading published poetry to their class. Reading or writing poetry involves awareness of certain elements that make it unique. Some poetry characteristics that students should know about:

1. Poetry uses condensed language so *every* word becomes important.
2. Poetry uses figurative language (e.g., metaphor, simile, personification, irony)
3. The language of poetry is often rhythmical (regular, irregular, metered).
4. Some words may be rhymed (internal, end of line, run-over) or non-rhyming.
5. Poetry uses the language of sounds (alliteration, assonance, repetition).
6. The units of organization are line arrangements in stanzas or idea arrangements in story, balance, contrast, build-up, or surprise.
7. Poetry uses the language of imagery (sense perceptions reproduced in the mind).

Different Kinds of Poetry

1. *Fixed Forms*
   a. Narrative or storytelling
   b. Literary forms with prescribed structures (e.g., limerick, ballad, sonnet, haiku, others)
   c. Lyric

2. *Free Verse*
   a. Tone: humorous, serious, nonsensical, sentimental, dramatic, didactic
   b. Content: humor, nonsense, everyday things, animals, seasons, family, fantasy, people, feelings, adventure, moods
   c. Time of Writing: contemporary, traditional (Nell, 1989)

3. *An Example of Collaborative Poetry*
   Students work in small collaborative groups. Each team or partnership is given a short time (one or two minutes) to compose the first line of a poem. On a signal from the teacher, each team passes their paper to the next group and receives one from another. The group reads the line that the preceding team has written and adds a second line. The signal is given and the papers rotate again – each time the group reads and adds another line. Teams are encouraged to write what comes to mind, even if it's only their name. They must write something in the time allotted. After 8 or 10 lines the papers are returned to their original team. Groups can add a line if they choose, revise, and edit the poem they started. The poems can then be read orally with team members alternating reading the lines. Later, some of them can be turned into an optic poem (creating a picture with computer graphics using the words of the poem) or acted out using ribbons or penlights (while someone else reads the poem).

Writing Poetry in Small Collaborative Groups

The collaborative writing of poetry intertwines process with content and students with learning. The cooperative linking of poetry concepts will often turn mundane work into poems rich in detail, sentiment, and humor. The importance of an audience for poetry will help at every stage of the writing.

Working in cooperative groups helps students become more responsible in communicating their understanding to other group members and an audience. The sharing of ideas helps each child develop a better understanding of the writing process and stimulates student conversations around literary pursuits.

When poetry is fused with collaborative dreams, emotions, and comedy it can foster personal and intellectual growth. If poetry is viewed as a solitary and dour undertaking than little space is left for the role of humor in explaining life's goofy splendors.

A group's interaction encourages building and changing ideas to foster the development of collaborative poetry. The interaction between peers can amplify the process. It's good to stir things up, but sometimes a few rules will help the group to be more productive:

1. One person should not do all the talking.
2. Accept everyone's ideas.
3. Stick to the topic.
4. Remind each other of the rules or appoint a group leader to help.

Poetry is more than just printed words on a page. Poetry comes alive when the reader and the words connect in a way that provides meaning and build upon the reader's experiences. External stimuli, like some of the methods presented here, can build on sights, sounds, thoughts and tensions to create poems. Unsaid inner meanings can be revealed in the "music" or rhythm of a poem. Poetry often happens between sensibility, control of language and rhythm.

A good place to begin is with a subject that offers a sense of metaphysical possibility. How do real writers write? Beethoven, for example, would write fragments in notebooks that he kept beside him; later he would develop these themes. He got ideas from every conceivable direction – including other composers, folk music, and myths. Like other writers he needed a thorough knowledge of the language (music) and a broad range of experience to build upon. Children can do the same thing by keeping a notebook of ideas about experiences, books, and how their thinking changes in regard to different subjects.

Beyond having some mastery of language, being able to think in images is certainly useful. So is the ability to concentrate. Poetry, like any kind of writing requires many revisions along the way. It's important to get something – almost anything – down and go from there. Sketching out an idea and developing it into a clear vision can foster language growth and help illuminate the reading and writing process.

Since what you read influences how you write, there is a natural connection between a student's written poetry and the richness of the literature program they are exposed to. By leading students to appreciate literature and poetry across time and cultures, teachers can enhance a child's ability to write. Thus, a variety of children's literature and poetry can become a source of vocabulary, metaphor and conceptual material. Experiencing the language and rhythm of good poetry gives students the building blocks for creating their own poetic patterns. By exposing students to various kinds of poetry patterns teachers enable them to do a better job of creating poetry on their own.

Experiences with Poetry

1. Poetry with Movement and Music. Poems can be put to music and movement. One student can read the poem and the rest of the group can use streamers, penlights in a darkened room to move down to the pen. Students can also illustrate picture books to go with poems that they can later share with younger children.

2. *Daily Oral Reading of Poetry.* Students sign up and read aloud at the of each day. Other students "point," commenting on parts of the poem that catch their attention. A classroom anthology of poetry can be illustrated and laminated.

3. *Responding During Free Writing Period.* Thirty minutes to an hour and one-half is set aside each day for students to write on any topic, in whatever form they choose. A share time follows so that other students may respond to each other's writing by pointing and asking questions.

4. *Literature Share Time.* Students gather in small groups once a week to share books they have been reading. The groups are structured so that each student

1. reads the author and title of each book,
2. tells about the book,
3. reads one or two pages aloud,
4. receives responses from members of the group, specifically pointing out parts they liked and asking questions.

5. *Wish Poems.* Each student writes a wish on a strip of paper. The wishes are read together as a whole for the group. Students then write individual wish poems which are shared.

6. *Group Metaphor Comparisons.* Poems containing metaphors are read aloud. Group comparison poems are written on the board. Students write individual comparison poems and share them with the class.

7. *Sample Poetry Lesson.* A lesson developed from *Dinosaurs*, a poetry anthology for children edited by Lee Bennett Hopkins.

1. Teacher reads poems aloud.
2. Students brainstorm reasons why the dinosaurs died, and words that relate to how the dinosaurs moved.
3. Models of dinosaurs and pictures are displayed and talked about.
4. Students write poems and share them.

8. *The Fame to the Name.* This activity can be adapted to suit class and curriculum needs, integrating whole language, cooperative learning and poetry. It is a simple lesson with lots of flexibility that integrates social studies, history, and mathematics. The form of the poem is in the name. The name chosen is written vertically on a chart pad or on the board.

Beginning with each letter in the name the class brainstorms a sentence or phrase that tells something about the name. Here is an example using the state of Alaska:

A lot of fresh air
L and of the froze
Athabaskans, Eskimos, Aleuts
Seals, bears, moose and more
Kaleidoscope in the night sky
A state to be proud of.

Model the first poem with the class. This will give the children an idea of how it is to be done. Using alliteration can add excitement.

Another idea is to make a list of nouns or adjectives that pertain to the theme. Incorporate cooperative learning by breaking the students into small groups. One method is to have each group work on one letter of the thematic poem or invent their own topic. Be sure to allow time for group presentations. As a parental involvement activity have each student with his or her family, write a poem using their last name. Families with several names can be encouraged to use both, or individuals can write a poem using their own name.

This fun activity can be used throughout the whole year. Life experiences can broaden the world knowledge base of these poems. To incorporate writing across the curriculum, pull names or subjects from the children's life experiences, science, social studies or history and math. Encourage the students to write about animals, their habitats, the weather, or other scientific facts about the state or city. Suggested social studies topics might include the people, their culture, and the history of the place.

Children may also wish to include personal school or family history in their poem. Math could be incorporated by using population, or area size of a state. Another idea is to have students figure out how many students in each grade within a school and how many students there are total.

9. *Creating Poems from Words in the Environment.* This activity is designed to increase students' observation of words in their environment and create poetry from printed words they observe around them. This can be in the classroom, at school, on field trips, at the bus stop, or walking down the street.

Pair children up or have them grouped in threes. Set the physical boundaries, limiting them to the classroom, hallway, playground, etc. Set expectations based on the needs of the class. Each group armed with writing/sketching supplies is instructed to gather.

Newspapers and World Knowledge are Important

Newspapers can be an excellent supplement to literature, original documents and oral histories. With upper grades, middle school, and high school students, newspaper articles can spark ideas for group discussion and provide writing models for analysis. Students can see how a composition is organized as they read, rather than watch television. They can also compare the evening news, which is often based on items in national newspapers with written stories. *The New York Times, The Washington Post, The Los Angeles Times,* or the local newspaper can be more stimulating than textbooks. With younger children simple pieces (with pictures) and publications like the *Weekly Reader* can replace more difficult newspapers.

The daily newspaper, particularly if it's in a second language, can be an intimidating document for students to tackle. It is imposing in format and vocabulary for early readers who are accustomed to materials geared toward their competency levels. By preparing imaginative exercises using a newspaper and a taped news broadcast, a teacher can provide an introduction and demystify those pages filled with newsprint and connect to a second language video segment.

It is important that the newspaper and video segment cover some of the same ground. The TV news items or conversations should be shown first so that what the students have listened to (and seen) is then applied to print. This means using print and video material from the same day.

The following example called *The Newspaper Scavenger Hunt* is an exercise that can be applied to a variety of reading levels. A list is drawn up with columns of words and phrases extracted from a sample paper. This list of cartoons, pictures, words, concepts, and short phrases (to be found in the newspaper) is handed out to pairs of students along with the paper. They are then asked to begin the hunt: Students put the page number which the item is located on the answer sheet and then circle the item in the newspaper. A time limit is set for the search to take place. When time is up, the students can compare their "success" rates. This exercise can be modified for a range of ability levels.

The teacher can go over the newspaper with them as the class collaboratively searches for connections with nightly news program the students are asked to watch as homework. Small groups can also make up a creative story composed almost entirely of headlines, subheadings, and a few connections of their own. Political cartoons, with their words removed, can also be presented, groups can come up with their own caption.

Integrating the Language Arts with Readers Theatre

Readers theatre is the oral presentation of prose or poetry by two or more readers. Complete scripts can be provided or students can write them after reading a story or a poem. The actual story or chapter may be ten or twenty pages long – the finished readers theatre script may only be two or three pages. We recommend trying some prepared scripts first (so that children get the basic idea) and then have the students work as a small group to transform a story or poem into a script.

The typical readers theatre lesson involves script writing, rehearsal, performance, and follow-up commentary for revision. Before the class presentation children need a chance to practice and refine their interpretation. Everybody eventually gets their own copy so that they can read their role from a hand-held script. (A few mistakes in reading are good for a laugh.)

When reading they stand up (from a chair) or face the audience; when their turn is over they sit down or turn their back to the audience. If there are four roles and five children than two read the same thing at the same time; if there are four students and six roles than two members of the group read two roles. Lines, gesture, intonation, and movement are worked out in advance. Individual interpretations are negotiated between group members. The performance in front of an audience can intensify the experience and connect the reader to the audience.

Readers theatre can be a good informal cooperative learning activity where students not only respond to each each other as character to character but in spontaneous responses that ties the group together with the situation of the text. The idea is to use a highly motivating technique to engage children in a whole range of language activities and literate behaviors.

Combining Poetry and Readers Theatre

Poetry is an art form that allows us to think deeply about ourselves and others. It doesn't have to be solitary, in the schools, and off the streets. Wordsworth may have been wrong when he explained poetry as "emotion recollected in tranquility." Teachers can always be looking for ways to make poetry interactive and stretch the possibilities. Readers theatre is one way to make poetry inclusive and fun.

Students can divide up a poem in several ways, read each version out loud in their small group, and discuss which division lent dramatic effect to the piece. Other questions: Which script has the best logical breaks or shifts? What are the dramatic or thematic advantages to the different arrangements? How would different interpretations of what the poem is saying effect the division? If there are four students and three roles, two students can read in unison.

Script #1

Reader 1: *Abandoned Farmhouse* by Ted Kooser
     He was a big man,
          says the size of his shoes on a pile of broken dishes by the house;

a tall man too, says the length of the bed in an upstairs room;
and a good, God-fearing man, says the Bible with a broken back —
    on the floor below the window, dusty with sun;
but not a man for farming
    say the fields cluttered with boulders and the leaky barn.

Reader 2: A woman lived with him,
    says the bedroom wall papered with lilacs and the kitchen shelves
    covered with oilcloth,

Reader 3: and they had a child says the sandbox made from a tractor
    tire

Reader 2: Money was scarce,
    say the jars of plum preserves and canned tomatoes
    sealed in the cellar-hole,
    and the winters cold, say the rags in the window frames
    It was lonely here, says the narrow gravel road.

Reader 1: Something went wrong, says the empty house
    in the weed-choked yard.
    Stones in the fields say he was not a farmer;

Reader 2: the still-sealed jars in the cellar say she left in a nervous haste

Reader 3: And the child?
    Its toys strewn in the yard like branches after a storm
    — a rubber cow, a rusty tractor with a broken plow,
    a doll in overalls. Something went wrong, they say.

"After Reading" Questions

Why do you think the characters left? Does this readers theatre version of the poem help you get to know more about the characters? Does each reader have an equal share? What are the dramatic or thematic advantages to this division?

Script #2

Reader 1: *Abandoned Farmhouse* by Ted Kooser
Reader 2: He was a big man,
Reader 4: (echoes) a big man
Reader 1: says the size of his shoes on a pile of broken dishes by the house;
Reader 2: a tall man too,
Reader 4: (echoes) a tall man
Reader 1: says the length of the bed in an upstairs room;

Reader 2: and a good, god-fearing man,
Reader 3: (echoes) good and God-fearing
Reader 1: says the bible with a broken back
        on the floor below the window, dusty with sun;
Reader 2: but not a man for farming,
Reader 1: say the fields cluttered with boulders and the leaky barn.
Reader 3: a woman lived with him,
Reader 1: says the bedroom wall papered with lilacs
        and the kitchen shelves covered with oilcloth,
Reader 4: and they had a child
Reader 1: says the sandbox made from a tractor tire,
Reader 3: Money was scarce,
Reader 1: say the jars of plum preserves
        and canned tomatoes sealed in the cellar-hole,
Reader 2: and the winters cold,
Readers 3 and 4: "oh, so cold"
Reader 1: say the rags in the window frames,
Reader 3: It was lonely here,
Readers 3 and 4: "so lonely"
Reader 1: says the narrow gravel road.
Everyone: Something went wrong,
Reader 1: says the empty house in the weed-choked yard.
Reader 2: Stones in the fields say he was not a farmer;
Reader 3: the still-sealed jars in the cellar say she left in a nervous haste,
Reader 4: And the child? Its toys are strewn in the yard
        like branches after a storm – a rubber cow,
        a rusty tractor with a broken plow, a doll in overalls.
Everyone: Something went wrong, they say,
Reader 4: (echoes) Something went wrong.

Questions: Are there any dramatic or thematic advantages to this division? Explain the thinking behind your preferences. How would your conception of what happened to the characters influence how you would divide the poem up?

Creative Drama in the Language Arts Classroom

Creative drama can serve as a tool for integrating language learning experiences. It also offers teachers a medium that can make important contributions to children's literacy development (Johnson, et al., 1987). Engaging in literacy-related creative drama should be part of every language arts program. These activities can be done with small groups with few props, no memorization of lines, and no chance for failure.

Dramatic play can be used to bridge the gap between written and visual forms of communication. For example, students can work in small groups to script, act, and even videotape a one-minute commercial. They pick a topic, develop a skit, practice, and perform it for the class. They can then critically examine the reasoning behind each group's presentation to the class. The original commercials developed by the students can also be compared to those done on television.

Creative drama can help students reconstruct their own meanings as they respond to literature, writing and ideas. The way students are asked to go about this process influences their development as readers, writers, and thinkers.

Creative Drama

- Doesn't emphasize performance.
- Adapts to many types of books, lessons, and subjects.
- Encourages the clarification of ideas and values.
- Evokes contributions and responses from students who rarely participate in "standard" discussions.
- Can be used to assess how well students understand what they are reading – characterization, setting, plot, conflicts, etc.
- Provides a stimulating pre-writing exercise.

Teaching Story Dramatization and Teamwork

1. Select a good story – and then tell it to the group.
2. With the class, break the plot down into sequences, or scenes, that can be acted out.
3. Have groups select a scene they wish to dramatize.
4. Instruct the groups to break the scene or scenes into further sequence, and discuss the setting, motivation, characterizations, roles, props, etc. Encourage students to get involved in the developmental images of the characters – what they did, how they did it, why they did it. Have groups make notes on their discussions.
5. Meet with groups to review and discuss their perceptions. Let them go into conference and plan in more detail for their dramatization.
6. Have the whole class meet back together and watch the productions of each group. Instruct students to write down five things they liked and five things that could be improved in the next playing.
7. Let the players return to their groups at the end of all group performances and evaluate the dramas using the criteria in number 6.
8. Allow groups to bring back their group evaluations to the whole class. Discuss findings, suggestions, and positive group efforts.

Creative Drama with Active Learning Teams

1. *Personification:* (This can also be used as a pre-writing activity.) Each student draws the name of an inanimate object (pencil sharpener, doorknob, waste basket, alarm clock, etc.) Students pick a partner and develop an improvisation.
2. *Using Drama To Extend a Story.* Creative drama can extend a story. Try "blocking" a play as you read it aloud in class. Giving such a visual perspective increases concentration.
3. *Increasing Research and Journalism Skills.* Using techniques of role playing and creative drama, have student groups show *how* to interview (give good and bad examples). Short excerpts from TV news or radio information programs provide good models for discussion and creative drama activities.

Creative drama has long been used to help students learn speaking, listening, thinking, and social skills. After they reflect the theme and action of drama children can compare character development in plays and written literature. By drawing on prior knowledge and tapping so many modes of expression creative dramatics ties in nicely with Howard Gardner's ideas about multiple pathways to learning. Creative dramatics can be a motivating foundation linking all of the language arts by engaging students in the full range of language expression. Reading, writing, and the other language arts occurs in a social context. As students experience puppetry, pantomime, improvisation, and other dramatic activities they develop teamwork skills that can be applied to a wide range of comprehension strategies.

Connecting Language, Thinking Skills, and Literature

Literature is a key to literacy. However to reach its full power it must be integrated with the other language arts. Students use oral language to talk about what they are reading, they also listen to others, write in their response journals, and dramatize stories. Connecting the story to creative drama and writing are good ways for students to share imaginative ideas with their peers. This can create an atmosphere where unconscious thought can flow freely. Students can also be asked to record how they think and make inferences about what they read.

Exploring the lives of elders in the community can be more than informative, it can make use of the full range of communication skills to connect generations. We like to ask five or six elders in for an oral history project. (You could, for example, focus on an era by inviting World War II veterans in.) Each elder gets assigned to a small group and is interviewed by students who take notes and later write up the "history." The students need to do a little homework on the time period in question and prepare some questions. The local newspaper may even be willing to come in and cover the event. In a small town the local newspaper might even carry the final version of what the students write about each visitor.

The integrated language arts approach encourages long periods of self-selected reading, teachers reading out loud to students, the use of technology, and the sharing of books and response projects. Response projects emphasize reflection and interpretation, not summarizing the plot of a story. These methods for analyzing literature can also help the teacher find special student interests in an author, illustrator, or theme. Students and teacher can even plan a unit together – choosing books around a topic or person of interest and planning reading and response activities. Students can also keep response journals and focus on a few favorite books through writing, art, drama, or a particular line of research.

Some teachers like to use what they call a "think-aloud." They choose one or two strategies to teach, such as prediction, visualization, confirming, elaborating, or summarizing. Next, they talk about how they use these strategies to activate prior knowledge as they read. The next step is to have the students practice the meaning-construction strategy – working with a partner as they read, think out loud, and jot down a few notes. This helps students develop their own critical reading and writing skills as they experience a variety of viewpoints.

Literacy at Home Supports Literacy at School

When children learn language and literacy skills in active ways they can construct their own meaning with the full range of communication tools. This means interacting with peers, electronic media, and literature to accomplish genuine goals. All of the adults in a child's life can help create a rich learning environment while providing information that students need to know when they need to know it. Parents, as much as teachers, need to create a literate environment, mediate the learning, and be good literacy models.

Whatever adults want to make important to children, they must make important to themselves as well. For example, its hard for a teacher to teach reading if they don't read newspapers and books. Likewise, its hard for a parent to instill a love of literature if there are no reading materials (books, magazines, and newspapers) around the house. If parents read and have a highly developed vocabulary children follow suit. Reading in the home environment precedes reading in the world.

Parents need to know what's going on so that they can help out at home. In the twenty-first century many parents are employed. A few can't read well in any language, others can't read English. Parents with the most highly developed language skills are most likely to be working outside the home. Caught between 50-hour work weeks and functional illiteracy teachers have more trouble than ever with home-school connections to language and literacy.

When teachers change their methods and classroom organizational structures they need the understanding of parents and administrators. When other colleagues help, things usually work out for the better. Some teachers meet with parents before school starts to set cooperative goals and ask parents about the child's strong and weak points – what works for them and what doesn't. We need to leave no stone unturned when it comes to helping parents realize how they can make a big contribution to their child's success in school by helping children use reading, writing, listening, speaking, and communication technology for real purposes.

E-Books: Here Today, More Tomorrow

Only a few years ago you could find only a small number of electronic books stored at universities. A few were available over the Internet, most you couldn't get no matter what. Until 2000 they were hard to access and it was even harder to read the scrolling text. Today we have tens of thousands of titles that are available in different formats on several devices. They have become easy to get and much easier to read. Major publishers have jumped on the bandwagon and are now selling a range of titles designed to be read on hand-held computers called *Readers*.

Microsoft Reader, Softbook, Rocket eBook, NuvoMedia, and their associates are complicating the publishing business to say nothing of reading and the language arts instruction. Hardware companies like Compaq, Casio, and Hewlett-Packard are rolling out palm to book-sized reading devices. Colorful, cuddly, and cute. . . . They come loaded with *ClearType* from Microsoft or *Cool Type* from Adobe. This software smoothes the jagged edges of electronic type in a way that makes the words on the screen about three times as easy to read.

Electronic book devices cost several hundred dollars and can hold the equivalent of five to ten books at a time. Titles can be delivered via the Internet in a few minutes. Some of the *Readers* or *Bookpads* like Softbook, can simply be plugged into a telephone line for downloading. Wireless downloading is next. Whatever the platform, nonfiction works can be constantly upgraded and books can be customized so that you only read the parts that you want. Special features also allow you to adjust the size of the print, the sound, or the background lighting. Unlike paper books, e-books can be read in the dark.

E-book Readers are able to search for strings of ideas or words within the text and quickly find information, interesting passages, and references. A menu lets readers jump quickly to a particular chapter or a favorite scene. E-book software can even read out loud to you in ways that reinforce the speaking and listening dimensions of language and literacy. As you might imagine, children are very attracted to these digital reading tools. A common question when they see one: "When can I read my books on one of these?"

Microsoft and some of their associates believe that a sea change from paper to electronic books is on the horizon. Don't count on it. Paper books will *not* "go the way of the quill pen." E-books are, however, finding a comfortable niche in the publishing world – along with Web appliances, broadband Web access, Palm Pilots and other wireless communication technologies. Digital technologies will increasingly reshape the way education is practiced. Although much of language arts instruction will continue along traditional paths, the schools cannot avoid the most powerful information and communication technologies of our time.

In spite of inevitable changes, the wood-pulp business has little to fear. Paper documents have proved more resistant than expected. In fact, print on paper is doing much more than hanging on. So many new avenues for paper documents continue to develop that we are using more paper than ever. Books in the traditional mode will be with us throughout the twenty-first century. They are, after all, an elegant user-friendly medium that will not become unreadable when the technology changes.

There are some concerns surrounding electronic books. They are published more quickly and with less editorial oversight so there is a greater chance for error. Publishers need to ensure that the positive qualities of the paper book system – quality controls, selectivity, etc. – be maintained in the new environment. Publishing companies certainly have made sure that late twentieth century copyright law is applied in the twenty first century e-book context. The notion of a public library where we can all check out books is viewed as an unprofitable relic. Don't even think what might happen if you share an e-book with a friend.

All of this is so new and futuristic that citizens have not even begun to consider the social issues that surround the use of such new technology. Lobbyists for the publishing industry, with little public attention, managed to get Congress to pass the Digital Millennium Copyright Act. Now people who use specially designated software to read an e-book are identified every time they read something. It is a publisher's dream: if you aren't authorized to read an e-book you are committing a crime. Fortunately, we still have the freedom to read and share paper books.

Since e-books are part of our future we had better consider them in a social and educational context. There are some advantages to carrying fifty pounds of books on a Reader that weighs a couple of pounds. Although they are not superior to printed books, the e-book opens a range of possibilities for helping readers master words, passages, and concepts in a new way. Stumble over a word that you can't pronounce or a concept that you don't understand. The e-book will give you the correct pronunciation and an explanation.

It is unlikely that any electronic media will become the main container of content. E-books are simply one of the new waves from the literary future.

They will become part of the many ways we will use digital tools to read, watch, and investigate. An array of digital products will continue to evolve as they spread across the landscape. An exotic collection of literary hybrids will change how we read, write, and communicate. Already some books have become part of distant databases, allowing readers to extract and combine what they want from pools of digital information.

Electronic Readers make it easier for a book to be customized as it is downloaded from the Internet. When publishers allow books to be reduced to digital pieces readers only have to pay for the pages or chapters that they use. The online world is well suited for those who want to buy only specific chapters of a book. It is also possible to chop different books up into interchangeable parts and allow customers to buy a highly targeted text. This customization is made possible by online services like IDG and iUniverse. Publishers have farmed out some of their titles to these and other companies with online digital systems that allow readers to assemble and pay for the specific pieces they want.

Within five years the bookpad will reproduce text with greater clarity than ink-on-paper and the equivalent of 500 books can be stored on a chip. They will have the thickness and the flexibility of a magazine. It will look and feel like paper and when you are ready to go on it will be like changing the TV channel. Technology is an important thing. But it isn't the only thing. Caring and capable teachers are required to change the schools for the better. Once the pedagogical piece is in place we can figure out how technological tools like electronic books can help us achieve our instructional goals.

In and out of school, avoiding the most powerful information and communication technologies of our time is not an option. There are plenty of entrepreneurs out there who would like to set things up for you. If you let them, they will be happy to impose their version of the future. A better arrangement is for the American public, educators, and policymakers to exert some control over the vested interests and the rough edges that surround new technologies. As far as the schools are concerned, this means being proactive about how the instructional environment is being constructed. The future is, after all, not just some place that we are going to but one that all of us should be involved in creating.

In the hands of a skilled teacher, technology can provide powerful tools for opening pathways to learning. If the teacher doesn't know how to make good use of it, technology can be just another annoying distraction.

> *The more powerful technology becomes,*
> *the more indispensable good teachers are.*
> – Michael Fullan

On or Off-Line, Learning Can be a Shared Experience

Language learning is, at its best, a shared experience. At home this means stories at bedtime, a discussion of the news, adults who read, museum excursions, and library visits. At school it means encouraging a cooperative environment so that students can actively construct knowledge together and perform alone when they need to. Teamwork skills can help students maintain a healthy balance between believing that they have the ability to learn and knowing that effort will help them maximize their ability (Bempechat, Graham, and Jimenez, 1999). A common element in successful classes and successful schools is a socially integrating sense of purpose and a shared sense of community.

> *What children can do together today,*
> *they can do alone tomorrow.*
> – Vygotsky

Active team learning provides students with opportunities to jointly interpret and negotiate meaning as they work together to make connections between prior knowledge and new ideas. Starting with the child's own experiences and background knowledge the collaborative process can lead to both a shared group idea and a more elegant individual expression. Small cooperative groups need time to share, clarify, suggest, and expand concepts. By giving students regular opportunities to talk, read, write, go online, and solve problems together, language learning can really come alive.

Programs with connected language and literature components provide a solid foundation for approaching language instruction in a natural and holistic manner. A major goal of language arts instruction is to enable students to apply a wide range of strategies to comprehend, evaluate, and appreciate spoken, written, and visual language. Powerful approaches to literacy development requires intrinsically motivating activities that help students draw on their cultural and personal resources as they develop productive habits of the mind. Engaging youngsters in an active group exploration of ideas is an exciting and powerful way for children to take an active part role in both their learning community.

Providing an engaging language-rich environment for all children requires the opening of social pathways to literacy. A caring learning community is built on students feeling connected to their peers as well as significant adults. The social side of learning has a profound effect on language and literacy. The interpersonal nature of literacy development gives students new tools for reflecting on a whole range of communication possibilities. By sharing knowledge among peers the seeds of literacy can grow – allowing students to adjust the language medium that they are using so that they can communicate effectively with a variety of audiences.

The specific methods that a teacher chooses to teach the language arts will probably reflect a unique combination of professional knowledge, policy requirements, personal choice, and passion for the subject being taught. Good teachers may take surprisingly different paths, but informed enthusiasm is one trait that successful teachers have in common (Applebee, 1996). Like many things in the classroom, the degree of success for integrated language arts instruction depends upon the enthusiasm and energy of the teacher. When teachers are truly energized their students are more likely to communicate with others and make sense of the world around them (Bempechat, 2000). To paraphrase William Blake, *energy is an external delight.*

RESOURCES AND REFERENCES

Applebee, Arthur. (1996). *Curriculum as conversation: Transforming traditions of teaching and learning.* Chicago: University of Chicago Press.

Bempechat, J., Graham, S., & Jimenez, N. (1999). The socialization of achievement in poor and minority Students: A comparative study. *Journal of Cross-Cultural Psychology 30,* no. 2 (March 1999):139–158.

Bempechat, J. (2000). *Getting our kids back on track: Educating children for the future.* San Francisco: Jossey-Bass.

Bromley, H., & Apple, M. (1999). *Education/technology/power: Educational computing as a social practice.* Albany: SUNY Press.

Brown, J. S. & Duguid, P. (2000). *The social life of information.* Cambridge, MA: Harvard Business School Press.

Burns M. S., Griffin P., & Snow E. (Eds.), (1999). *Starting out right: A guide to promoting children's reading success.* Washington, DC: National Research Council. National Academy Press.

Coles, G. (2000). *Misreading reading.* Portsmouth, NH: Heinemann.

Fink, D. (2000). *Good schools/real schools: Why school reform doesn't work.* New York: Teachers College Press.

Fleischer, C. (2000). *Teachers organizing for change: Making literacy everybody's business.* Urbana. IL: NCTE.

Gordon, D. (Ed.), (2000). *The digital classroom: How technology is changing the way we teach and learn.* Cambridge, MA: Harvard Education Letter.

Graves, M. & Graves, M. (2003). *Scaffolding reading experiences: Designs for student success.* (2nd ed.) Norwood, MA: Christopher-Gordon Publishers.

Heilbrun, C. (1989). *Writing a woman's life.* New York: W. W. Norton.

Johnson, K. (1987). *Doing words: Using the creative power of children's personal images to teach reading and writing.* Boston, MA: Houghton Mifflin.

Mitchell, K. (Ed.), (2000). *Adventuring with books.* Urbana, IL: NCTE.

Morrell, E. (2004). *Linking literacy and popular culture: Finding connections for lifelong learning.* Norwood, MA: Christopher-Gordon Publishers Inc.

Murray, J. (1997). *Hamlet on the holodeck: The future of narrative in cyberspace.* New York: The Free Press.

National Council of Teachers of English & International Reading Association (1996). *Standards for the English Language Arts.* Urbana, IL and Newark, DE.

Nell, V. (1989). *Lost in a book.* New Haven, CT: Yale University Press.

Oczkus, L. (2004). *Super six comprehension strategies: 35 lessons and more for reading success with CD-ROM.* Norwood, MA: Christopher-Gordon Publishers Inc.

Rasinski, T. V., & Padak, N. (2000). *Effective reading strategies: Teaching children who find reading difficult.* Englewood Cliffs, NJ: Prentice Hall.

Smith, F. (1998). *The book of learning and forgetting.* New York: Teachers College Press.

Stoll, L., & Fink D. (1996). *Changing our schools.* London: Open University Press.

Strickland, D. (2004). *Improving reading achievement through professional development.* Norwood, MA: Christopher-Gordon Publishers Inc.

Vygotsky, L. S. (1978). *Mind in society: The development of higher educational processes.* Cambridge, MA: Harvard University Press.

Chapter 7

A VISION FOR MATHEMATICS IN THE TWENTY-FIRST CENTURY

Imagine a classroom, a school, or a school district where
all students have access to high-quality,
engaging mathematics instruction.
– National Council of Teachers of Mathematics

The new millennium has ushered in extraordinary changes. In mathematics new knowledge, new ways of learning, doing and communicating continue to evolve. Today, inexpensive calculators are pervasive. Powerful media outlets widely disseminate information as mathematics continues to filters into our lives.

The need to understand and use mathematics in everyday life has never been greater. Mathematics for life should be part of school culture. Personal satisfaction and confidence come with making wise quantitative decisions, whether it's buying a house, solving problems on the job, choosing health insurance or voting intelligently. As part of our cultural heritage, mathematics is one of the greatest achievements. Our careers, our workplace, our community all require a foundation of mathematical knowledge. Mathematical proficiency opens doors to future achievements. With this in mind everyone needs to understand mathematics. All students should have the opportunity to learn important mathematics with meaningful understanding and depth (Burris, 2005).

We want all students to be involved in high-quality engaging mathematics instruction. High expectations should be set for all, with accommodations for those who need them. Students will confidently engage in mathematics tasks, explore evidence, and provide reasoning and proof to support their work. As active resourceful problem solvers, students will be flexible as they work in groups with access to technology. Students value mathematics when they work productively and reflectively as they communicate their ideas orally and in writing (NCTM, 2000).

This is not a highly ambitious dream, but part of the vision set forth in the National Council of Teachers of Mathematics Standards 2000 document. In this chapter we will try to help teachers clarify the new mathematics standards, as well as offer suggestions for effective mathematics teaching.

The National Council of Teachers of Mathematics Standards

The Curriculum and Evaluation Standards for School Mathematics was first published in 1989. Since their inception, the math standards have changed our thinking about the content and how we teach mathematics (NCTM, 1989). The NCTM has recently updated and refined the standards creating the new *Principles and Standards for School Mathematics.*

Principles and Standards for School Mathematics proposes that all students see value in learning mathematics and increase their awareness of mathematics in their lives. The principles address issues of high-quality mathematics education. A vision of equity, good teaching and learning, effective assessment, and innovative technology are expressed throughout (NCTM, 2000).

Principles for School Mathematics

The six principles discussed below describe important issues of the mathematics program. Used together the principles will come alive as teachers develop excellent school math programs:

1. **Equity.** High-quality mathematics requires raising expectations for students' learning, all students must have opportunities to study and learn mathematics. This does not mean that every student should receive identical instruction, instead it demands that appropriate accommodations be made for all students. Resources and classroom support are also a large part of equity. This includes professional development of teachers.

2. **Curriculum.** A curriculum must be coherent, focused on mathematics, and articulated across grade levels. Interconnected strands effectively organize and integrate mathematical ideas so that students can understand how one idea builds on and connects with other ideas. Building deeper understandings provides a map for guiding teachers through the different levels of learning.

3. **Teaching.** Effective teachers understand mathematics, understand what students know and need to learn and challenge and support them through learning experiences. Teachers need several kinds of knowledge; knowledge of the subject, pedagogical knowledge – understanding how children learn, different techniques and instructional materials all affect how well their students learn mathematics (National Council of Teachers of Mathematics, 2004).

4. **Learning.** Mathematics must be learned with understanding. Students actively build new knowledge from prior experience. Students should have the ability to use knowledge in a flexible manner, applying what is learned, melding factual knowledge with conceptual understandings and making learning easier.

5. **Assessment.** Assessment should support the learning of mathematics and provide useful information to students and teachers. This enhances students' learning while being a valuable aide for making instructional teaching decisions.

6. **Technology.** Technology today is an essential part of learning and understanding mathematics. Effective mathematics teaching is dramatically increased with technological tools. Tools such as calculators and computers provide visual images of mathematical ideas, they facilitate learning by organizing and analyzing data and they compute accurately. Technology resources from the Internet, the World Wide Web, to computer programs like Logo provide useful tools for mathematics learning.

Standards for School Mathematics

The standards are descriptors of the mathematical content and processes that students should learn. They call for a broader scope of mathematics studies, pointing out what should be valued in mathematics instruction. The ten standards describe a comprehensive foundation of what students should know and be able to do. They state the understandings, knowledge, and skills required of elementary students.

All students should be provided with the opportunity to learn significant mathematics. *The Principles and Standards for School Mathematics* strengthen teachers' abilities to do that by including information about the way students develop mathematical knowledge. The standards include content (addressing what students should learn) and process (addressing aspects of doing mathematics). The content standards number and operations, algebra, geometry, measurement, data analysis and probability describe the foundations of what students should know. The process standards problem solving, reasoning and proof, communicating, making connections and representing data express ways of using and applying content knowledge.

The Principles and Standards for School Mathematics are paraphrased as follows:

Number and Number Operations Standard

• Students will understand the number system by recognizing numerals, counting, grouping, place value concepts, and fractional numbers.

- Students will comprehend the meanings of operations and how they relate to one another by constructing meaning through real-world experiences.
- Students will understand the concepts behind addition, subtraction, multiplication and division, compute fluently and make reasonable estimates.

Algebra Standard

- Students will understand patterns, represent and talk or write about mathematical relationships.
- Students will understand the concepts of algebra, analyze mathematical situations and use algebra symbols.
- Students will use mathematical models to represent quantities in mathematics.
- Students will analyze change in everyday situations to solve a variety of problems.

Geometry Standard

- Students will observe and describe a variety of shapes, focus on their properties, and develop mathematical reasoning skills about their relationships.
- Students will learn concepts of relative positions and develop spatial relationships.
- Students will use symmetry and apply their knowledge of transformation (moving shapes around) to analyze mathematical situations.
- Students will use visualization, spatial reasoning and geometric models to solve problems.

Measurement Standard

- Students will understand attributes of length, weight, area, volume, time, temperature and angle.
- Students will develop the process of measuring, make and use measurements in problems and everyday situations.
- Students will learn to calculate simple perimeters, areas, and volumes.
- Students will perform measurement in both metric and customary systems.

Data Analysis and Probability Standard

- Students will pose questions, that can be answered with data and collect, organize, and display relevant data when answering them.
- Students will select and use statistical methods to analyze data.
- Students will understand and apply concepts of chance and probability.

- Students will know how to construct, develop and evaluate inferences, and predictions based on data.

Problem-Solving Standard

- Students will use problem solving to explore and understand mathematical content.
- Students will build new math knowledge through solving problems.
- Students will develop and apply strategies to solve a wide variety of problems in mathematics and other areas.
- Students will confirm and interpret problem results.
- Students will develop and apply a variety of appropriate strategies to solve problems (Polya, 1957).

Reasoning and Proof Standard

- Students will recognize reasoning and proof as basic to mathematics learning.
- Students will make and use models, to make independent investigations, understand basic facts, and use properties and relationships to explain their thinking.
- Students will justify their answers and solutions, and use arguments and proofs to analyze mathematical situations.
- Students will select and apply different types of reasoning and methods of proof.

Communication Standard

- Students will organize and refine their mathematical thinking through communication.
- Students will reflect on and clarify their thinking about mathematical ideas and situations.
- Students will communicate their mathematical thinking clearly to peers, teachers and others.
- Students will use the skills of discussing, reading, viewing, writing, and listening to interpret and evaluate mathematical ideas.
- Students will discuss, analyze, and evaluate the mathematical ideas of others, make predictions, and produce convincing arguments.
- Students will use mathematics language to express ideas precisely and clearly.

Connections Standard

- Students will connect mathematical ideas and recognize how these connections can help when solving problems.

- Students will understand how mathematical ideas are interconnected and how they build on each other to form an integrated whole.
- Students will learn to use and apply mathematics in their daily lives as well as link mathematics to other subject areas like science and social science.

Representation Standard

- Students will create and use many representations to build new understandings and express mathematical ideas.
- Students will represent their thoughts about mathematical ideas through oral and written language when solving problems.
- Students will use mathematical models to interpret physical, social and real-world problems.

Principles and Standards for School Mathematics, NCTM, 2000.

The NCTM's mission is to provide vision and leadership for improving mathematics education. They also set for themselves the goal of ensuring that every teacher of mathematics is given the opportunity to grow professionally. They clearly recognize the fact that giving all children the opportunity to receive an equitable standards-based mathematics education means creating collaborative professional development situations in which the best sources of higher education expertise are merged with the experiences and needs of teachers.

The goals articulated by the standards can be responsive to accelerated changes in our society, our schools, and our classrooms. Individual teachers can make alterations within their classrooms, but the school itself must have a coherent program of mathematics study for students (Adams, 2000). No curriculum should be carved in stone at any level; rather it must be responsive to the lessons of the past, the concerns of the present, and the human and technological possibilities of the future.

Implementing the Curriculum Standards

The next section of this chapter connects the standards to classroom practice by presenting few sample activities for each standard. The intent is not to prescribe an activity for a unique grade level, but to present activities that can be used in many grades (Hattfield, Edwards, Bitter and Morrow, 2005).

Number and Number Operations Standard

Concepts and skills related to number are a basic emphasis for young children. Teachers should help children strengthen their sense of number, moving from initial basic counting techniques to a more sophisticated understanding of numbers, if they are to make sense of the ways numbers are used in their everyday world. Our number system has been developing for hundreds of years. The modern system we use today had many contributions by numerous countries and cultures (Reys et al., 2003).

There are four important features of the number system:

1. *Place value.* The position of a numeral represents its value, for example, the numeral 2 in the numbers 21, 132, 213 represents different ways of thinking about the value of the number 2. In the first case, 2 represents 2 tens or 20, the second 2 represents 2 ones or 2, and in the third case 2 represents 2 hundreds or 200.
2. *Base of ten.* Base in the number system means a collection. In our number system, ten is the value that determines a new collection. Our number system has ten numerals: 0, 1, 2, 3, 4, 5, 6, 7, 8, 9. This collection is called a *base ten system.*
3. *Use of zero:* Unlike other number systems, our system has a symbol for zero. Encourage students to think about the Roman numeral system. The reason it is so cumbersome to use today is that it has no zero.
4. *Additive property:* Our number system has a specific way of naming numbers. For example the number 321 names the number 300 + 20 + 1.

Grouping by tens or trading. Young children need experiences in counting many objects, trading for groups of tens, hundreds, and thousands; and talking together about their findings. In early grades, children need many models. Bean sticks and base-ten blocks are two models widely used by teachers. But students also need piles of materials (rice, beans, straws, counters, and unifix cubes) to practice counting, grouping, and trading.

Ask students to group by tens as they work. This makes the task of counting easier for children; counting by tens also helps students check errors in their counting. But most importantly, sorting by tens shows students how large amounts of objects can be organized.

Trading rules. The base-ten system works by trading ten ones for one ten, or the reverse, trading one ten for ten ones, ten tens for one hundred, ten hundreds for one thousand, and so on. Base-ten blocks are a great ready-made model in teaching this principle. Encourage students to make their own model. Building models with Popsickle® sticks and lima beans works equally well. Or if teachers wish to have students use construction paper and scissors, students can make their base-ten models by cutting out small squares of paper and pasting them on a ten strip to form a ten. Then after completing ten tens, paste the ten strips together to make a hundred and then paste the hundreds together to form a thousand. It is time-consuming work, but well worth the effort.

Proportional models such as base-ten blocks, bean sticks, and ten strips provide physical representation. In all the examples just mentioned, the material for ten is ten times the size of the unit; the hundred is ten times the size of the ten; the thousand is ten times the size of the hundred; and so on. Metric measurement provides another proportional model. Meter stick, decimeter rods, and centimeter cubes can be used to model any three-digit number. Nonproportional models such as money do not exhibit a size relationship, but present a practical real-life model. Because both types of models are important and should be used, we recommend starting children with proportional models, as they're more concrete and help children to understand the relationships more clearly.

Teaching place value. It is important that children think of numbers in many ways. A good place to start is to pass out a base-ten mat with the words "one," "tens," and "hundreds." Also pass out base-ten blocks to each of the students (units, longs, flats). The units represent ones, longs represent tens, and flats represent hundreds. Now have the students build the number they hear. If, for example, the teacher says the number 42, the students take four long rods (tens) and place them on the tens column of their mat, and two units, placing them in the ones column. Encourage students to test their skill in a small group by thinking of a number, verbalizing it, and then checking other students' mats.

Fractions

Fraction concepts are among the most complicated and important mathematical ideas that students encounter. Perhaps because of their complexity, fractions are also among the least understood by students. Some of the difficulties may arise from the different ways of representing fractions: spoken symbols, written symbols, manipulative materials, pictures, and real-world situations. It is difficult for children to make sense of these five ways of representing fractions and connecting them in meaningful ways. Children need many chances to work with concrete materials, observe and talk about fractional parts, and relate their experiences to science and mathematical notation. One helpful activity is to have students make a fraction kit.

Make a Fraction Kit

This introductory activity introduces fractions to students. Fractions are presented as parts of a whole.

Materials: Each student needs seven different 3" × 18" strips of colored construction paper, a pair of scissors, and an envelope to put their set of fraction pieces labeled as follows: 1, 1/2, 1/3, 1/4, 1/8, 1/12, 1/16.

Directions: Direct students to cut and label the strips:

1. Have students select a colored strip. Emphasize that this strip represents one whole, and have students label the strip 1/1 or 1.
2. Ask students to choose another color, fold it in half, cut it, and then label each piece 1/2. Talk about what 1/2 means (1/2 means 1 piece out of 2 total pieces).
3. Have students select another color, and have them fold and cut it into four pieces, labeling each piece 1/4. Again discuss what 1/4 means (1 piece out of 4 total pieces, compare the 4 pieces with the whole).
4. Have students fold, cut, and label a fourth colored strip into eighths, a fifth strip into 12ths, and a sixth strip into sixteenths.

Now each student has a fraction kit. Encourage students to compare the sizes of the pieces and talk together about what they discover. For example, students can easily observe that the fractional piece 1/16 is smaller than the piece marked 1/4. This is a good time to introduce equivalent fractions. "How many 1/16 pieces would it take to equal 1/4? What other fractional pieces would equal 1/4?" Explaining equivalence with a fraction kit makes fractions more meaningful (Burns, 2001).

Algebra Standard: Patterns and Functions

Patterns are everywhere in everyday life. People organize their home and work activities around patterns. The inclusion of patterns and functions in elementary school opens many possibilities for math instruction. Teachers can connect many ideas in mathematics to children's background knowledge by encouraging them to describe patterns and functions in their own language to help them represent those ideas with mathematical symbols. For example, if a child has described a pattern such as "each object is 3 more than the last one, they can symbolically represent the their idea as n (the object) and describe the *nth* object as $n + 2$. So patterns and functions naturally lead to an understanding of functions in algebra. In the activities that follow, we will explore only a few types of patterns and functions and ways to describe them. The more opportunities children have to describe patterns and functions with pictures, words, tables, and variables the more power with mathematics they will have (Kennedy & Tripps, 2000).

Multiplication Activity: Using Algebra To Build Rectangles

Discuss rectangles and demonstrate or review how to name them, for example, 2 × 3 (2 rows of 3 units), 4 × 5 (4 rows of 5 units). Provide students with a sheet of graph paper.

Directions: Plan a design, creature or scene that you could make using only rectangles. Cut the graph paper into rectangles. Use the whole page. Paste the rectangles onto construction paper to make your design. Write a number sentence that tells how many 1 cm. × 1 cm. rectangles are included in your design. Since all students started with the same size graph paper, they should all get the same answer although their equations will be different. If the class uses 10 cm. × 10 cm. graph paper grid, students can write statements that show what percentage of the whole picture is represented by each part. Have students write stories about their pictures. The stories should include mathematical statements using algebraic notation (Moses & Cobb, 2001).

Multiplication Factor Puzzles Activity

Place a large sheet of butcher paper on the board. Divide the paper, labeling each part with a multiplication product (18, 20, 21, 36, 40, etc.). Divide the class into teams. Ask each team to find and cut out of graph paper all the rectangles that can be made with a given number (20, for example). Have each team label and paste their rectangles on the butcher paper under that number (Newstrom, 1997). As a whole class, review the findings and determine if all the possible rectangles have been found for each number without duplicates (flips, rotations). List the factors for each number.

Geometry Standard

In the elementary grades, geometry should provide the experiences for children to develop the concepts of shape, size, symmetry, congruence and similarity in two and three-dimensional space. Children should begin with familiar objects and use a wide variety of concrete materials to develop appropriate vocabulary and build understanding.

Construct a Chinese Tangram Puzzle

Materials: 6 inch squares of construction paper, scissors
The Tangram is a Chinese puzzle made from seven geometric shapes.
The seven shapes can be put together in hundreds of ways. Tangrams are fun for students to work with in developing spatial concepts. The Tangram puzzle is cut from a square. Having students each cut their own is a good lesson in following directions.

Directions for making a tangram kit (place cut shapes in an envelope)

1. Fold the square in half. Have students cut it apart to make two triangles.
2. Have students take one triangle and fold it in half and cut.
3. Take the other triangle, and make two folds, first in half, then fold the top corner down. Cut along the folds (students should have one trapezoid and one triangle).
4. Cut the trapezoid in half.

5. Fold one trapezoid to make a square and a triangle. Cut.
6. Fold the last trapezoid to make a parallelogram and a triangle. Cut.

Tangram Shape Exploration

1. Use the three smallest triangles to make a square. Use the same pieces to make a triangle, a rectangle, a trapezoid, and a parallelogram.
2. Use the five smaller pieces (all but the two large triangles) to make the same shapes.
3. Repeat with all seven pieces.

Evaluation: When students have made a Tangram kit of their own have them put the square together. Encourage them to share their puzzle with family and friends.

Extensions:

1. Have students explore using the pieces to make a shape of their own. Have them draw an outline around the shape on drawing paper, name it, sign it and put it in a class Tangram box so that others can solve their puzzles.
2. Area and Perimeter: Encourage students to compare the areas of the square, the parallelogram, and the large triangle. Then, compare their perimeters. Have students record their findings.

Measurement Standard

Concepts and skills in the measurement standard deal with making comparisons between what is being measured and a standard unit of measurement. Children acquire measuring skills through first-hand experiences. It is important to remind students that measurement is never exact, even the most careful measurements are approximations. Students need to learn to make estimates when measuring.

Measurement tools and skills have many uses in everyday life. Being able to measure connects mathematics to the real-world environment. Being able to use the tools of measurement: rulers, measuring cups, scales, thermometers, meter sticks, and so on — and to estimate with these tools, are essential skills for students to develop.

Instruction in measurement should progress through these attributes of measurement: length, weight/mass, volume/capacity, time, temperature and area. Within each of these areas young students need to begin making comparisons with standard and nonstandard units. In older grades more emphasis can be placed on using measurement tools to measure.

Sample Measurement Activity: Body Ratios

Children need direct concrete experiences when interacting with mathematical ideas. The following activities are designed to clarify many commonly held incorrect ideas:

- **Finding the Ratio of Your Height to Your Head**
  How many times do you think a piece of string equal to your height would wrap around your head? Many children have a mental picture of their body, and they make a guess relying on that perception. Have students make an estimate, then have them verify it for themselves. Few make an accurate guess based on their perceptions.
- **Comparing Height With Circumference**
  Have students imagine a soft drink can. Then have them think about taking a string and wrapping it around the can to measure its circumference. Have students guess if they think the circumference is longer, shorter, or about the same height as the can. Encourage students to estimate how high the circumference measure will reach. Then have the students try it. Like the previous activity, many students guess incorrectly. The common misperception is that the string will be about the same length as the height of the can. There is a feeling of surprise or mental confusion when they discover that the circumference is about three times the height of the can. Repeat the experiment with other cylindrical containers. Have students record their predictions and come up with a conclusion (Burns, 2001).

Group Activity: Estimate, Measure & Compare Your Shoes

Materials: unifix cubes, shoes
Procedures:

Estimate how many unifix cubes would fit in your shoe. Write your estimate. Choose a volunteer from your group to take off their shoe. Then students are instructed to estimate how many unifix cubes would fit in the shoe. When finished with the estimate, have students actually measure the shoe using unifix cubes. Students record the measurement. Pass the shoe to the next group; they estimate and record the actual measurement. Continue passing the shoes around the class until students have recorded estimates and actual measurements of the shoes from each of the groups.

Evaluation: Instruct students to compare the shoes. Have students explain what attribute of measurement they used. Encourage students to think of another way to measure the shoes. Explain how it might be more accurate (Battista, 2002).

Metric Perimeter Using Cuisinaire Rods

Materials: Cuisinaire rods, centimeter paper
Procedure: Have students use one red rod (2 cm), two light green rods (3 cm), and one purple rod (4 cm). Arrange the rods into a shape on centimeter squared paper in such a way that when students trace around it, they draw only on the grid paper lines. Students should cut out the shape and have it remain in one piece. Make several different shapes this way. Trace each and record its perimeter. Try to get the longest and the shortest perimeter.

Data Analysis and Probability Standard

It is difficult to listen to the news on television or pick up a newspaper without noticing the extensive use of charts, graphs, probability, and statistics. Following are a few suggestions for teaching some elementary concepts for teaching probability and graphing.

The study of data analysis, statistics and probability invites students to collect, organize, and describe information. Students communicate data through tables, graphs, and other representations. Probability and statistics are mathematical tools for analyzing and drawing conclusions about data.

Classifying and Predicting

Give students a list of statements and ask them to sort them into three piles labeled "certain," "uncertain," and "impossible." Use statements such as the following:

- Tomorrow it will rain.
- I will get 100 percent on my next spelling test.
- Tomorrow we will all visit Mars.
- If I flip a coin, it will either land heads or tails.

As the children classify the statements, discuss with them the reasons for the classifications. When they have finished, ask them to further classify the uncertain statements as either likely or unlikely. In doing this students are predicting the outcome. Encourage students to give examples of activities and experiments to clarify their thinking. As a follow-up activity, have students come up with their own list of statements to classify into categories and offer their predictions.

Predicting Coins and Colors

Ask students to predict whether a coin will land on heads or tails. Flip the coin and show the result. Ask students to predict the outcome of several flips of the coin. Discuss if one flip seems to have an influence on the next flip. Events are called independent if one event has no effect on another. Give each child a penny and ask them to make a tally of the heads and tails out of ten flips. Talk about such terms as "equally likely," "random," and "unbiased."

Show the children a spinner with three colors (red, yellow, blue). Spin the spinner a few times to show that it is a fair spinner. Ask students to predict the number of times they could expect to get yellow if they spin the spinner thirty times. Can you find a formula for predicting the number of times a color will come up? If the probability of landing on each color is equally likely, they can write the probability of landing on any one color as

$$\frac{the\ number\ of\ favorable\ outcomes}{the\ total\ number\ of\ outcomes}$$

In the example of the spinner, the total number of outcomes is three because there are three colored sections altogether. Therefore, the probability of getting yellow is one out of three or 1/3. Ask the children to predict the number of times they could expect to get yellow if they were to spin the spinner thirty times.

Try the experiment using different colors and different numbers of spins. Can you find a formula for predicting the number of times a color will come up?

Exploring Sports Statistics

The following are the salaries of five professional basketball players: $80,000, $80,000, $100,000, $120,000 and $620,000, The players are complaining about their salaries. They say that the mode of the salaries is $80,000 and that they deserve more money for all the games they play. The owners claim the mean salary is $200,000 and that this is plenty for any team. Which side is correct? Is anyone lying? How can you explain the difference in the reports?

Ask students to look in newspapers and magazines for reported averages. Are there any discrepancies in the reports? Bring in reports for discussion in class. Encourage students to read any reported statistics carefully (Whitin & Whitin, 2000).

Data Investigation Exercises that Empower Learners

In the future we will all be called upon to approach and solve problems not even envisioned today. A good preparation in mathematics provides the language, the tools, and the computational techniques needed to get the job done. Understanding the conceptual bases of mathematics, having the ability to communicate mathematical ideas to others, and demonstrating mathematical competence will be more important than ever.

A mathematics investigation is more demanding than a problem or an exercise. Sometimes they are used to introduce and learn mathematical concepts. More often investigations are project-like culminating activities that help students integrate what they are learning into a comprehensible whole. Like the problem, the investigation lets students use several different approaches. It requires students to generate and structure the problem – creating a context that invites sustained work. The following activity is an example of an investigation that connects to the data analysis and probability standard:

Math Raisin Investigation

Description:
Students use science and mathematical data they have collected about raisins to decide the mean, median, mode and range of each group's raisins. Statistics are use in the research to arrive at their judgment of which group has the greatest amount (Johnson & Johnson, 1990). Students then use this information to write a brief report describing their research. This investigation involves the mathematics concepts and skills of: problem solving, communication, reasoning, making connections, number sense, computation and estimation, and statistics.

Materials: calculators, graph paper, notebook, class recording sheet

Background Information:
Students will need to be familiar with the following statistics terms:

> mean – the average of a set of data.
> median – the middle number or the average of the middle 2 numbers when the set of numbers are arranged in order.
> mode – the number occurring most often in a set of data.
> range – the difference between the largest and smallest number in a set of data.
> sample – a segment of a population selected for study to predict characteristics of the whole.
> tally – a way of recording information.

Objectives:
1. Student groups of four or five will be assigned a chart to record their group's statistics and collect the statistics from every other group.
2. Groups will collect data from the class.
3. Groups will systematically collect, organize, and describe their data on a class data sheet.

Class Raisin Data Sheet

Name of group:_____

1. Estimate the number of raisins in your individual box: _____
2. Find the group estimate: _____
   Mean _____
   Median _____
   Mode_____
   Range _____
3. When all groups have entered their data then the class is faced with the following statistical challenges:
   – Find the average number of raisins in the sample.
   – Determine the mode, range, median and mean for the class.
4. Student groups are to explain their strategies and reasoning.
5. Students will work as a team in a powerful, organized and purposeful manner.

Evaluation:

As a group write a report about the investigation your class just finished. Include at least one graph. The report should describe how their group collected and compiled the data, explaining the information the group included in their graph or graphs. Be sure the students back their recommendation with facts from their research.

Problem Solving Standard

Problem solving has been central to elementary mathematics for nearly two decades. Problem solving refers to engaging in a task where the solution is not known. George Polya, a well-known mathematician, devised a four-step scheme for solving problems: Understand the problem, create a plan or strategy, follow through with the approach selected, check back. Does it make sense?

Problems are teaching tools that can be used for different purposes. The solutions are never routine and there is usually no right answer because of the multitude of possibilities. Strategies include guessing and checking, making a chart or table, drawing a picture, acting out the problem, working backward, creating a simpler problem, looking for patterns, using an equation, using logic, asking someone for help, making an organized list, using a computer simulation, or come up with your own idea; take a risk.

Teachers should model the problem-solving strategies needed for thinking about mathematics content or responding to particular math problems. Modeling might include the thinking that goes into selecting what strategy to use, deciding what options are possible, and checking on their progress as they go along. Following are a few problemsolving activities:

Present Interesting Problems

Present a problem to the class. Have students draw pictures of what the problem is about, or act out the problem, or have one student read the problem leaving out the numbers. Once students begin to visualize what the problem is about, they have much less difficulty solving it. Students should work in small groups when arriving at strategies and when solving the problems. Students should write how they solved it and discuss and check their answers with other groups. The following is a sample problem to present to the class.

Solve This Problem:

One day Farmer Bill was counting his pigs and chickens.
He noticed they had 60 legs and there were 22 animals in all.
How many of each kind of animal did he have?

Record your strategy below:
Solve the problem another way:

Communication Standard

Outside the classroom, real world problems are rarely solved by people working alone. People work in groups and pool their knowledge. Cooperative group learning is a way to help students develop communication skills. Through listening and talking students learn to express ideas and compare them to others. Children listen to explanations and solutions of their peers and obtain information from books and electronic sources. Throughout the elementary years students develop mathematical language using precise terms to describe math concepts and procedures. The following communication activity looks at mathematics and science measurement skills:

Math/Science Nature Scavenger Hunt

Description: Mathematics and science applications are all around us. Mathematical patterns in nature abound. Architecture, art, and everyday objects rely heavily on mathematical principles, patterns, and symmetrical geometric form. Students need to see and apply real-world connections to concepts in science and mathematics. This activity is designed to get students involved and more aware of the mathematical/scientific relationships all around them, and to use technology to help report their findings.

Objectives:

1. Students will participate in observing, communicating, and collecting samples.
2. Students will exhibit their understanding by recording their observations in their notebooks.
3. Students will show their ability to work in groups in a responsible, interactive, and productive manner.
4. Students will reflect their thinking orally and in writing.

Procedures: Divide the class into four groups. Each group is directed to find and bring back as many objects as they can that meet the requirements on their list. Some objects may need to be sketched out on paper if they are too difficult to bring back to the classroom, but encourage students to try to bring back as many as possible.

Group One: Measurement Hunt

Mathematics skills: measuring, comparing, inferring, ordering by distance, formulating conclusions
Procedure: Find and bring back objects that are:

as wide as your hand	a foot long
farther away than you can throw	waist high
half the size of a baseball	as long as your arm
smaller than your little finger	wider than four people
thinner than a shoelace	as wide as your nose

Group Two: Shape Hunt

Math skills: comparing shapes, recognizing patterns, recording data
Procedure: Find and bring back as many objects as you can that have the following shapes: Record them in your notebook (triangle, circle, square, diamond, oval, rectangle, hexagon and other geometric shapes).

Group Three: Number Pattern Hunt

Math skills: Comparing number, shape, and patterns, and recording data
Procedure: Find objects that show number patterns. For example, a three-leaf clover matches the number pattern three.

Group Four: Texture Hunt

Math skills: classifying, recording data, comparing, labeling
Procedures: Find as many objects as you can that have the following characteristics: smooth, rough, soft, grooved/ridged, hard, bumpy, furry, sharp, wet, grainy.
Evaluation: When students return, have them arrange their objects in some type of order or classification. Using a graphing program on the computer or colored paper, scissors and markers, have them visually represent their results in some way (bar graph, for example).

Connections Standard

The connections standard emphasizes the many relationships between mathematics topics and everyday life. Important connections for young children is between the hands-on, intuitive, mathematics that students have learned through their own experiences and the mathematics they are learning in school. Students' abilities to experience meaningful mathematics is based on strong connections in applying math content to out of school situations.

Making Connections (Addition and Subtraction)

When children are learning about the operations of addition and subtraction, it is helpful for them to make connections between these processes and the world around them. Story problems help them see the actions of joining and separating. Using manipulative and sample word problems gives them experiences in joining sets, and figuring the differences between them. By pretending and using concrete materials, learning becomes more meaningful. Tell stories in which the children pretend to be animals or things.

Building Connections Across Disciplines

In elementary grades, students should be developing the processes of scientific inquiry and mathematical problem solving. This includes inferring, communicating, measuring, classifying and predicting. The kinds of investigations that connect the two disciplines are problems like these:

1. How many ways can you sort your bag of buttons?
2. Make a Venn Diagram using your buttons.
3. Classify the buttons (Notes: light to dark color, small to large, number of ridges, number of patterns, number of holes) (Andrews & Trafton, 2002).

Representation Standard

Representing ideas and connecting them to mathematics is the basis for understanding. Representations make mathematics more concrete. A typical elementary classroom has several sets of manipulative materials to improve computational skills and make learning more enjoyable.

Base-ten blocks will be used in these activities to represent the sequence of moving from concrete manipulations to the abstract algorithms. Students need many chances to become familiar with the blocks, discovering the vocabulary (1's = units, 10's = longs, 100's = flats) and the relationships among the pieces. The following activities will explore trading relationships in addition, subtraction, multiplication and division.

The Banker's Game (Simple Addition)

In this activity small groups of students will be involved in representing tens. The game works best dividing the class into small groups (four or five players and one banker). Each player begins with a playing board divided into units, longs, and flats. Before beginning the teacher should explain the use of the board. Any blocks the student receives should be placed on the board in the column that has the same shape at the top. A student begins the game by rolling a die and asking the banker for the number rolled in *units*. They are then placed in the units column on the child's board. Each child is in charge of checking their board to decide if a trade is possible. The trading rule states that no player may have more than nine objects in any column at the end of their turn. If they have more than nine, the player must gather them together and go to the banker and make a trade, (for example ten units for one long). Play does not proceed to the next player until all the trades have been made. The winner is the first player to earn five tens. This game can be modified by using two dice and increasing the winning amount.

The Take Away Game (Subtraction)

This game is simply the reverse of the Bankers Game. The emphasis here is on representing the regrouping of tens. Players must give back in units to the bank whatever is rolled on the die. To begin, all players place the same number of blocks on their boards. Exchanges must be made with the banker. Rules quickly are made by the students (for example, when rolling a six, a player may hand the banker a long and ask for four units back). It is helpful for students to explain their reasoning to one another. The winner is the first to have an empty playing board. Children should decide in their group beforehand whether an exact roll is necessary to go out or not.

Teaching Division with Understanding

Base-ten blocks bring understanding to an often complex algorithmic process. The following activity is a good place to start when introducing and representing division.

1. Using base-ten blocks have students show 393 with flats, rods, and units.
2. Have the students divide the blocks into three equal piles.
3. Slowly ask students to explain what they did. How many flats in each pile, how many rods, how many units?
4. Give students several more problems. Some examples: Start with 435 and divide into three piles. Encourage students to explain how many flats, rods, and units they found at the end of all their exchanges. In this problem one flat will have to be exchanged for 10 rods (tens), and then the rods divided into three groups. One rod remains. Next, students will have to exchange the one rod for ten units, and then divide the units into three groups. No units are left in this problem. Continue doing more verbal problems, pausing and letting students explain how they solved them. What exchanges were made? It is helpful to have students work

together trying to explain their reasoning, correcting each other, asking questions (Burns, 1988).

5. After many problems, perhaps the next class session, explain to the students that they're now ready to record their work on paper still using the blocks.

   a. The teacher then shows two ways to write the problem.

      $435 \div 3 =$ and 3) 435.

   b. Then the teacher asks the students three questions and waits until all students have finished with each question.

    Question 1: – How many 100's in each group? (Students go to their record sheet above the division symbol of the problem. They answer one flat, so they record 1 on their sheet).

    Question 2: – How many in all? Students check how many cubes are represented, they answer 300, so they record 300 on their sheet.

    Question 3: – How many are left? Students return to the problem and subtract $435 - 300 = 135$.

    Now the problem continues with the tens, then the ones. Again they start over asking the three questions each time (Burns, videotapes).

6. For advanced students this seems like an elaborate way of doing division. By using manipulative and teaching with understanding, beginning division makes sense to elementary students. Teachers can introduce shortcuts later to make more advanced division easier and faster.

Students learn best when they are actively engaged in meaningful mathematics tasks using hands-on materials. Such a mathematics classroom encourages students' thinking, risk-taking, and communicating with peers and adults about everyday experiences.

Reviewing the Mathematics Standards for the Twenty-First Century

We want our students to think and reason mathematically drawing on a solid base of mathematical knowledge and skills. Students must be fluent in computation, they must have efficient and accurate methods, and they must understand them. Mathematics in the twenty-first century continues the emphasis on exploring, reasoning, conjecturing, communicating, and connecting to other subjects. The days of treating mathematics as a set of isolated concepts and procedures are long past. Current mathematical applications frequently support science, in that they utilize the power of technology to solve real-world problems. To survive in the next century students need different skills. We view mathematics instruction as a developmental process of understanding of what math is, what it is not, what it can do, and how mathematical comprehension contributes to culture. The challenge for today's teachers is to awaken mathematical curiosity and motivate students for lifelong learning.

Answering questions correctly and memorizing facts won't help much. Today, we want students to relate and apply math to social problems, to use creative innovation, and to their personal lives (Reys, Lindquist, Lamdin, Smith & Suydam, 2004).

When mathematics learning is seen as a purposeful activity with real applications it can then be used as an intellectual tool to positively affect people's lives. Mathematics teaching can emphasize inquiry, promote curiosity, value original ideas, and connect to other subjects so that students can communicate their thoughts to others. It is the teacher who pulls all this together. Effective teachers create mathematical adventures for children because they understand how the components of mathematics education work together. Our goal is to help teachers develop their own understanding of mathematics and enhance their awareness of children's learning by providing some activities designed to stimulate creativity.

Suggestions for Active Thinking and Learning

Mathematics education helps students learn to think, but it must also help students take responsibility for their own thoughts. The challenge for the teacher is to engage children in mathematical curiosity so that they can create a clear inner logic. Interesting classroom math experiences stimulate students to explore and express their own ideas and connect to past understandings. This means that students have opportunities to interpret mathematics ideas/rules/principles and construct mathematical understandings for themselves. To do this students need to be involved in problem-solving investigations and projects that engage thinking and reasoning (Sharp and Hoiberg, 2005).

Some of the more recent methods for teaching mathematics are active small group participatory situations that include activities like keeping daily logs or journals, writing about paths to the solution of problems, and expressing concepts through creative endeavors from poetry to geometry to art. Projects and presentations can combine experiential knowledge with theoretical understandings. The focus should be on exciting examples, investigations, and everyday applications. Everyone needs mathematical information to make choices that arise every day. To reinforce this point the school mathematics program can extend beyond the classroom to include resources from the community. As students get better at reasoning mathematically, they become more able to apply mathematical thinking to a whole range of situations.

When teachers and students feel that they are participants in and explorers of mathematical knowledge they are more open to new uses of mathematics and new discoveries within the discipline (Chapin & Johnson, 2000). With the emphasis on thinking, communicating, and making connections between topics, students are more in control of their learning. Students in this environment have many experiences with manipulatives, calculators, computers, and working on interesting problems in cooperative groups. Computational skills and the ability to express basic mathematical understandings, to estimate confidently, and to check the reasonableness of estimates are part of what it means to be literate, numerate, and employable.

The mathematics curriculum is continuing to change to reflect the needs of today's students, society's demands, and the mathematical needs of the future. Surviving in the twenty-first century will require a deeper understanding of central mathematical ideas as well as an understanding of how these ideas relate to our day-to-day world.

In the future both students and teachers will be expected to implement new ways of interacting and thinking. It is a new world, crying out for new definitions and people who can redefine themselves in this rapidly changing environment. We need teachers and students who can learn to ask insightful questions together, self-monitor, reflect on their own thinking, and be able to deal with the empirically verifiable surprises awaiting us. It would be a shame to miss the opportunities of the new millennium.

Resources

The NCTM Standards

Principles

The school mathematics principles address the following themes:

- Equity
- Curriculum
- Teaching
- Learning
- Assessment
- Technology

Standards for School Mathematics

- Number and Operations
- Algebra
- Geometry
- Measurement
- Data Analysis and Probability
- Problem Solving
- Reasoning and Proof
- Communication
- Connections
- Representation

RESOURCES AND REFERENCES

Andrews, A. G., Trafton, P. R. (2002). *Little kids powerful problem solvers: Math stories from a kindergarten classroom.* Westport, CT: Heinemann.

Adams, T. (2000). Helping children learn mathematics through multiple intelligences and standards for school mathematics. *Childhood Education. 77,* 86–92.

Battista, M. T. (2002). Learning in an inquiry-based classroom. In J. Sowder & B. Schappelle (Eds.), *Lessons learned from research* (pp. 75–84). Reston, VA: NCTM.

Biech, E. (Ed.) (2001). *The Pfeiffer book of successful team-building tools.* San Francisco, CA: Jossey -Bass/Pfeiffer A. Wiley Co.

Burns, M. (2001). *About teaching mathematics: A K–8 Resource.* White Plains, NY: Math Solutions Publication.

Burns, M. (1988). *Mathematics with manipulatives.* Cuisinaire Company of America, six videotapes. White Plains, NY: Cuisinaire Company of America.

Burris, A. (2005). *Understanding the math you teach: Content and methods for prekindergarten through grade 4.* Upper Saddle River, New Jersey: Pearson Education, Inc.

Chapin, S. & Johnson, A. (2000). *Math matters: Understanding the math you teach.* Sausalito, CA: Math Solutions Publications.

Hattfield, M., Edwards, N., Bitter, G. & Morrow, J. (2005). *Mathematics methods for elementary and middle school teachers.* (5th Ed.). Hoboken, NJ: John Wiley & Sons.

Johnson, D. & R. Johnson. (1990). Using cooperative learning in math. In N. Davidson (ed). *Cooperative learning and mathematics,* (p. 122). Menlo Park, CA: Addison-Wesley.

Kamii, C. (2000). *Young children reinvent arithmetic: Implications of Piaget's theory.* New York: Teacher's College Press.

Kennedy, L. & Tripps, S. (2000). *Guiding children's learning of mathematics.* (9th Ed.) Belmont, CA: Wadsworth/Thomas Learning.

Moses, R. & Copp, C. (2001). *Multiple perspectives on mathematics teaching and learning.* Norwood, NJ: Ablex Publishing.

National Council for Teachers of Mathematics (NCTM). Commission of Standards of School Mathematics (2004). *Curriculum and evaluation standards for school mathematics.* Reston, VA: National Council of Teachers of Mathematics.

National Council of Teachers of Mathematics (NCTM). (2000) *Principles and standards for school mathematics.* Reston, VA: National Council of Teachers of Mathematics.

National Council for Teachers of Mathematics (NCTM). Commission of Standards of School Mathematics (1989). *Curriculum and evaluation standards for school mathematics.* Reston, VA: National Council of Teachers of Mathematics.

National Research Council (NRC). (1995). *National science education standards.* Washington, DC: National Academy Press.

Newstrom, J., Scannel, E. (1997). *The big book of team building games.* San Francisco, CA: Jossey-Bass.

Polya, G. (1957). *How to solve it.* (2nd ed.). Princeton, NJ: Princeton University Press.

Reys, R., Lindquist, M., Lamdin, D., Smith, N. & Suydam, M. (2003). *Helping children learn mathematics.* (6th Ed.) John Wiley & Sons.

Rohrich, K., Ansberry, K. & Morgan, E. (2004). *Perfect science lessons: Using children's books to guide inquiry.* Arlington, VA: National Science Teachers Association Press.

Sharp, J. & Hoiberg, K. (2005). *Learning and teaching K–8 mathematics.* Boston, MA: Pearson Education Inc.

Whitin, P. & Whitin, D. (2000). *Math is language too.* Urbana, IL: National Council of Teachers of English and Reston, VA: National Council of Teachers of Mathematics.

Chapter 8

SCIENTIFIC LITERACY: ACTIVE INQUIRY IN THE CLASSROOM

*Effective teachers design many activities for group learning,
not simply as an exercise but as collaboration essential to inquiry . . .
technology provides students and teachers with exciting tools
– such as computers – to conduct inquiry and understand science.*
– The National Science Education Standards

In a world filled with the products of scientific inquiry, scientific literacy has implications that reach beyond subject matter and the schools. Citizens need to be informed about science-related choices that arise every day. Science and its technological associates influence human interaction, communication, values, and just about everything else. Scientific concepts have been used as metaphors in everything from popular culture to newspaper accounts of foreign affairs. Even literature has not gone unscathed as science has flowered as narrative material.

As far as the schools are concerned, teachers can help their students move in the direction of scientific literacy by making connections between science, other disciplines, and real-world concerns. Thinking like a scientist, responsible citizenship, and self-understanding are all part of science education today. There is general agreement that science teaching should stress methods and processes for active inquiry into scientific concepts. Scientific inquiry involves identifying questions that can be answered through scientific investigations. This implies having the ability to conduct a scientific investigation, using technological tools, developing explanations, and thinking critically about the relationships between evidence and explanations (Ethredge & Rudnitsky, 2003).

Teaching for Scientific Literacy

To be scientifically literate today requires an awareness of what the scientific endeavor is and how it relates to our culture and our lives. The National

135

Council on Science and Technology Education identifies a scientifically literate person as one who recognizes the diversity and unity of the natural world, understands the important concepts and principles of science, and is aware of the ways that science, mathematics, and technology depend on each other (National Education Goals Panel, 1999). To be literate in science is to recognize that science is a human endeavor with strengths, weaknesses, and a host of possibilities. It is also a way of thinking and asking questions.

One of the important new goals of American education is to prepare scientifically literate citizens. This means preparing students who can make use of scientific knowledge and connect the implications of science to their personal lives and to society. Scientific literacy also involves having a broad familiarity with today's scientific issues and the key concepts that underlie them. As far as the schools are concerned this means organizing scientific inquiry around real-life problems – the kind that can elicit critical thinking and shared decision-making. Inquiry today involves curiosity, observation, posing questions and actively seeking answers. Scientific literacy implies that a person can identify scientific issues underlying national and local decisions and express positions that scientifically and technologically inform the National Science Education Standards.

The recognized importance of a scientifically literate citizenry has resulted in national efforts to reform science education. Instructional strategies include concrete, physical experiences and opportunities for students to explore science in their lives. Today's science has an emphasis on ideas and thinking skills. This involves sequencing instruction from the concrete to the abstract. Students are actively involved in the learning process, developing effective oral and written communication skills. Frequent group activity sessions are provided where students are given many opportunities to question data, to design and conduct real experiments, and carry their thinking beyond the class experience. Students raise questions that are appealing and familiar to them, activities arise which improve reasoning and decision-making. Cooperative learning becomes the primary grouping strategy. Cooperative learning is done as a cohesive group in which ideas and strengths are shared (Sherman, Richardson, Yard, 2005).

Science can be an exciting experience for students and teachers when it is taught as an active hands-on subject. Connecting with other disciplines can provide many opportunities for integration with other subjects. Teachers need subject matter knowledge that is broad and deep enough to work with second language learners and others who may have difficulty with their school work. This often requires improving language and broad-based literacy development possibilities to get at content. It may take some effort to gain insights into others' experiences and ways they may be oppressed.

To understand and use science today requires an awareness of how science connects language and technology domains and how it relates to our culture and our lives. Good science teachers are usually those who have built up their science knowledge base and developed a repertoire of current pedagogical techniques. By focusing on real investigations and participatory learning teachers move children from the concrete to the abstract as they explore themes that connect science, language arts, math and technology.

Teaching strategies include many participatory experiences and opportunities for students to explore science in their lives. The emphasis on inquiry involves posing questions, making observations, reading, planning, conducting investigations, experimenting, providing explanations, and communicating the results. Students develop effective interpersonal skills as they work together, pose questions and critically examining data. This often means designing and conducting real experiments that carry their thinking beyond the classroom. As instruction becomes more connected to children's lives, enriching possibilities arise from inquiring about real world concerns.

Science education can help students develop an understanding of scientific processes and ways of thinking. Such an understanding is essential for all literate citizens. More specifically, scientific literacy is based on knowledge and understanding of the scientific concepts and principles required for personal decision-making. This includes understanding the important ideas and rules of science and recognizing some of the important ways science and technology depend on each other. There are at least two sides to these coins. Students need to realize that science and technology are prone to the same strengths and weaknesses as any other human enterprise (Esler, W. & Esler, M., 2001).

All students can learn science, and should have the chance to become scientifically literate. This was one of the themes in the National Science Education Standards (National Research Council, NRC, 1995) The standards emphasize the processes of science and give a great deal of attention to cognitive abilities such as logic, evidence, and extending their knowledge to construct explanations of natural phenomena. Scientific literacy should begin in the early grades, where students are naturally curious and eager to explore. Another theme in the standards is that science is an active process. Getting students actively involved in the process or the *doing* of science moves students along the road to scientific awareness.

Getting in Touch with the National Science Education Standards

The National Standards for science education are based on the following fundamental truths:

- Science is for all students.
- Science is an active learning process.
- School science reflects the intellectual and cultural traditions of contemporary science.

The Science Content Standards

The content standards clearly articulate what students should know, understand, and be able to do. Students should be able to:

- Understand the basic concepts and processes in science
- Use the process of inquiry when doing science
- Apply the properties of physical science, life science, earth and space science when doing activity-based learning.
- Understand the relationship of science and technology
- Connect science to personal and social perspectives
- Identify with the history and nature of science through readings, discussions, observations and oral and written communications.

The science education standards also includes program standards. The content standards outlines what should be taught, the teaching and program standards call for the inclusion of all content standards and state that the program should:

- Be consistent across grade levels.
- Coordinate the science and mathematics programs.
- Provide sufficient resources and opportunities for all students.
- Develop communities that support, sustain and encourage teachers.

The standards provide a map that charts the way to scientific literacy. As teachers implement the standards, they will engage students by actively involving them in scientific inquiry.

Developing Inquiry

The process of inquiry helps the inquirer grow in content knowledge and in the processes and skills of the search. It also invites learners to explore anything that interests them. Whatever the problem, subject, or issue, any inquiry that is done with enthusiasm and with care will use some of the same thinking processes that are used by scholars who are searching for new knowledge in their field of study (Rohrich Ansberry, K. & Morgan, E., 2004). The intellectual tools of science can be used to explore the physical and biological universe in a manner that sparks curiosity, interest, knowledge, and action.

As children sharpen their powers of observation, they become capable of noticing things that they hadn't noticed or thought of before. In school this might mean participating in project constructions that build on the physical principles being studied. Out of school, students might act as "nature detectives" to explore a city park or wet places (like ponds) looking for plants and animals they might not have noticed before. They can record their observations like scientists. Whether inside or outside, when you teach science with active inquiry and problem-solving methods, you can't help but get closer to the standards and goals of science education.

The National Science Education Standards are having an impact. For example, until recently teaching individual students the science process skills was considered essential. The standards suggest that we should put less emphasis on the individual process skills and put more emphasis on using multiple process skills with a purpose in mind. Teachers around the country are now giving students more opportunities to explore skills like observing, sorting, describing, recording and experimenting simultaneously. The standards stress that science is an active process where students work together to ask scientific questions, investigate aspects of the world around them, and use their observations to construct reasonable explanations in an attempt to answer the questions asked. In the process they learn skills such as inference, experimentation, and continually develop their science knowledge. Through the inquiry process, students learn how to communicate about their investigations and explanations (Pearce, C. R., 1999).

The Inquiry Process Skills

Students need to be exposed to a basic body of knowledge, attitudes and skills that will build a foundation for future discoveries. Being able to use the knowledge and process skills in a meaningful way is probably the most important objective for students in their learning process. Meaningful learning implies active student control over the content learned as well as being able to practically use the knowledge in a personal way. Manipulating, adapting ideas, learning through experience, creating knowledge, and enhancing appreciation for the laws and principles that guide learners are part of the inquiry process.

Teachers should include each of the process skills in their curriculum. To effectively do that, the learning skills must be given attention to ensure that lessons are built on the curiosity of children as well as on curriculum content. As learners construct knowledge (or process, as Piaget explains it) rather than accumulate it, they make the content relevant and personal. Teachers should introduce and plan class investigations, discussions, and activities that cover each skill.

Engaging Students with the Learning Processes

Helping children develop and apply process skills across the curriculum can also help them acquire the greatest understanding of concepts and facts. Inquiry learning requires practice in one or more of the process skills.

Key Process Skills

Discovering	Communicating	Exploring
observing	valuing	predicting
inferring	recording	estimating
classifying	gathering data	experimenting
measuring	using language	investigating
comparing	nonverbal	
sequencing	graphing, charts	
	pictorial representations	
	sharing with others	

The Discovering Processes

Discovering examines how students connect and interact with their world; how they make sense or bring order to things around them. It implies direct contacts and manipulation of those contacts into recognizable patterns and structures for interpreting new information. Discovering is based on children's natural curiosity about their environment. Constructivists contend that learners build personal senses of reality as a result of their life experiences. Children have a natural need to know about how things work, survive, or are unique. The process skills of observing, inferring, classifying and measuring that support these learning processes are discussed here.

Observe, Learn, Describe, Interact

The most important tool for young children is observation. Wanting to find out about the natural world makes students eager to explore and ask questions. Observing involves using all of the senses — seeing, hearing, tasting, smelling, and feeling. Students learn about objects by grouping and ordering them, which relies primarily on observation. *Comparing, sequencing, and using space-time relationships* assists in understanding the nature of science as inquiry and helps bring order to the content standards. Once children learn to observe and describe objects, they soon begin to compare two or more objects. Teachers should offer a variety of activities that allow children to use all of their senses, to group objects in many ways, to interact with others, and to communicate their findings as they become independent inquirers about the natural world. It is almost impossible to show children an example of a science concept without having them compare it or show a relationship to something else. It is critical that we get students to be active mentally, to reflect on things presented in class. That is the way that the mind can construct a relationship (Van de Walle, 1997).

At the middle elementary level, students are able to master skills of a good inquirer. Many students make measurements using different tools — rulers, thermometers, scales, clocks, and so on. Active experiences in both science and the language arts provide opportunities to describe and compare in terms of quantity. Young children automatically use descriptive language when comparing quantities (one child is taller than another, one book is heavier, one ball is larger, and so on).

Communicate

Whether it is listening, speaking, writing, reading, or using communications technology, language is a window into students' thinking and understanding. Oral language is one means of communication. One of the goals in the classroom is to facilitate the use of oral language and listening as a means of communication and learning. Talking is not just for the language arts classroom. Speaking, writing, and reading are just as important for scientific inquiry.

Scientific language and everyday language are interrelated. We need to get rid of the idea that scientific thinking and language are somehow removed from the everyday experiences. They overlap and reinforce one another. If students practice thinking and communicating, they will connect their day-to-day experiences and discover a wealth of new techniques.

Learning to communicate effectively makes the world of science outside of school more accessible. It also promotes interaction and investigation of ideas within the classroom as students learn in an active, verbal environment. Working with language arts and science to communicate benefits all students whether they are fluid in English or another language or are developing proficiency; children need to experience the precision of speech and writing that good science demands. Communication is most effective when students express themselves with a purpose and an audience.

The skills of data gathering, analyzing, recording, using tables, and reading graphs is as important in science as it is in other subjects. Graphing skills include constructing graphs as well as interpreting graphical information. All of these topics can be introduced in early grades. Small teams work well. The data gathered depends on student interest and maturity. The process of sharing information helps students feel more comfortable and less inhibited. It builds self confidence. By sharing their work and ideas students develop independence (Manzo & Manzo, 1997).

Experiment

Inquiry processes such as forming a hypothesis, identifying variables, or analyzing data are skills used in an experiment. Skills such as predicting, estimating and inferring are part of experimenting. The ability to make predictions is based on skillful observation, inference, quantification, and communication.

The science curriculum should include estimation so that students can explore estimation strategies, recognize when an estimation is appropriate, determine the reasonableness of results, and apply estimation in working with quantities, measurement, computation, and problem solving.

The basic ability to ask questions, investigate, and arrive at an understanding based on reasoning often involves inference. Children should therefore be encouraged to talk to one another, and to the teacher and other adults while they are engaged in observing and making inferences based on their senses and experiences.

People have always been concerned about science education and the importance of transmitting attitudes, shared values, and ways of thinking to the next generation. Today, concern about the level of scientific literacy is more critical than ever because of two trends: American students' knowledge of science is down, relative to our industrial competitors (Linn, et al., 2000) – and the level of impact is up as every part of contemporary life is bombarded by science and technology. Part of the essence of scientific literacy is clarifying attitudes, possessing certain scientific values, and making informed judgments. To reach these goals students need to cultivate scientific patterns of thinking, logical reasoning, curiosity, an openness to new ideas, and skepticism in evaluating claims and arguments. Understanding how to apply the scientific processes is an important step toward scientific literacy.

Positive attitudes towards learning science are important. Being able to understand the basic principles of science, being "numerate" in dealing with quantitative matters, thinking critically, measuring accurately, using some of the tools of science (like mathematics, calculators and computers) are all part of the scientific literacy equation. We need students who are creative, can think critically, and who can solve problems with others. This means actively involving students in manipulating the materials of science and communicating science understandings both orally, and in writing.

The Changing Science Curriculum

The past quarter century has seen many pressures to reinvent goals and effect change for school science. Many changes are taking place in the culture and practices of science as well as in our economy of how people live and work. In an effort to respond to these conditions new science standards have been identified to update the traditional concepts and principles of science the disciplines (biology, chemistry, earth science, and physics).

Do these changes represent a reinvention of goals or curricula? The most important change in science education is in the nature of science itself. Research in the sciences today is concerned with finding solutions to personal and social problems, rather than focusing on theories related to the natural world. The school problems we face today are more difficult and involved than ever before. We need to recognize that a new culture is emerging. Today's culture is defined by a global economy, an information era, differing family structures, a society that is knowledge intensive effecting a new world of work, and new developments in how we think about learning (Howe, 2002).

An active curriculum for the twenty-first century should have the power to make a difference in the lives of students and in the society where they live.

Curriculum Qualities

The science curriculum for the new century has:

1. Greater depth and less superficial coverage
2. Focuses on problem solving
3. Emphasizes skills and knowledge of the subject
4. Provides for individual differences
5. Contains a common core of subject matter
6. Is closely coordinated to related subjects such as mathematics
7. Is part of an integrated curriculum
8. Is attuned to personal relevance (ASCD Yearbook, 2000)

One of the changes from the traditional curriculum is adding greater depth and less superficial coverage to the content of the science curriculum. Focusing in depth on a smaller number of skills and concepts leads to greater understanding and retention. Since the 1980's evidence has been mounting that "less is more"; reduced content stressing skills, and active hands on learning produces results (Kahle, 1997).

The core of the curriculum focuses on problem solving. Solving meaningful complex problems requires using learning strategies. Research suggests that learning strategies are most effective when they are taught in problem-solving units dealing with complex meaningful problems (Cotton & Northwest Regional Laboratory, 1999).

Both skills and science knowledge are emphasized. Students can solve complex problems in science only when they are given the opportunity to acquire the knowledge used in solving meaningful problems.

The new curriculum also provides for individual differences. There should be many ways of displaying and transferring knowledge. Most curriculum organizers stress verbal modes, many effective teachers add visual representations such as a directional chart (like a road map or web diagram). Teachers should provide a scaffolding structure at the beginning of the year; this includes offering suggestions, cues, and explanations. As the year progresses, students are able to solve problems on their own. This scaffolding approach recognizes multiple intelligences and is designed to accommodate for individual differences.

The new curriculum offers a common core of subject matter. A common curriculum for all students draws students together. A fragmented curriculum such as tracking separates students based on ability or career goals. The traditional curriculum tracked and dispersed students in different directions. In responding to individual differences, the common curriculum for all students leads to unity, and builds character among students.

Another characteristic is that the science curriculum is closely coordinated to related subjects such as mathematics. The mathematics curriculum supports and closely relates to the science curriculum. The various developmental levels of the subject should also be coordinated so the 3rd grade science content builds on the 2nd grade content and leads to the 4th grade science curriculum.

Instead of separate subjects, now elementary science is part of an integrated curriculum. Selected integration results in better achievement and improved attitudes (Glatthorn, 1998). The focus of the curriculum on active learning emphasizes results. This means improved learning for all students. A quality learning curriculum is teacher friendly, with clear objectives and less attention given to mindless activities. The new curriculum is also attuned to personal relevance. This includes technology amid the various disciplines, giving students the tools they need to improve society (ASCD Yearbook, 2000).

What Does the New Curriculum Look Like?

The science curriculum for the new millennium is meaningful, involving students in real life situations. It has a sense of unity and celebrates diversity. Active science learning makes connections; connecting students with the past, present and the rest of the world. The new curriculum reflects human values, and emphasizes responsibility. Students understand that they are part of a global community.

The reform now going on is searching for a science curriculum focusing on responsible citizenship and self-understanding. Goals include using scientific knowledge in making wise decisions and solving difficult problems related to life and living. Science is becoming more interdisciplinary; for example, some of the new research fields emerging include biochemistry, biophysics, plant engineering, terrestrial biology, and neurobiology to name a few. Today, science has dimensions that extend to the social sciences as well as ethics, values and law (Greene, 2003).

Meeting the needs of students requires finding relationships between science, technology and students' life experiences. Suggestions are needed for meeting the adaptive needs of students in a changing world. From the beginning of the reform movement, educators have recognized that the time has come to develop curricula in a way that no longer isolates science from human welfare and social and economic progress. "Learning to learn" is essential for preparing students for the world in which they will live (National Research Council, 1999).

Science Activities for the Twenty-First Century Curriculum

To enliven the curriculum, the authors introduced their preservice teachers to integrating curriculum content by using the National Science Education Standards. The preservice teachers were to design a science lesson based on the standards and the qualities of the twenty-first century curriculum.

Activity 1. Soap Drops Derby
Jennifer Lim

Students will develop an understanding that technological solutions to problems, such as phosphate-containing detergents, have intended benefits and may have unintended consequences.

Science Standards: science as inquiry, earth science, science and technology, technology-based problem solving

New Curriculum Qualities: depth of coverage, problems, skills and knowledge, coordination, integration, personal relevance

Objective:

Students apply their knowledge of surface tension. This experiment shows how water acts like it has a stretchy skin because water molecules are strongly attracted to each other. Students will also be able to watch how soap molecules squeeze between the water molecules, pushing them apart and reducing the water's surface tension.

Background information:

Milk, which is mostly water, has surface tension. When the surface of milk is touched with a drop of soap, the surface tension of the milk is reduced at that spot. Since the surface tension of the milk at the soapy spot is much weaker than it is in the rest of the milk, the water molecules elsewhere in the bowl pull water molecules away from the soapy spot. The movement of the food coloring reveals these currents in the milk.

Materials:

milk (only whole or 2% will work), newspapers, a shallow container, food coloring, dish washing soap, a saucer or a plastic lid, toothpicks

Procedures:

1. Take the milk out of the refrigerator 1/2 hour before the experiment starts.
2. Place the dish on the newspaper and pour about 1/2 inch of milk into the dish.
3. Let the milk sit for a minute or two.
4. Near the side of the dish, put one drop of food coloring in the milk. Place a few colored drops in a pattern around the dish. What happened?

5. Pour some dish washing soap into the plastic lid. Dip the end of the toothpick into the soap, and touch it to the center of the milk. What happened?
6. Dip the toothpick into the soap again, and touch it to a blob of color. What happened?
7. Rub soap over the bottom half of a food coloring bottle. Stand the bottle in the middle of the dish. What happened?
8. The colors can move for about 20 minutes when students keep dipping the toothpick into the soap and touching the colored drops.

Follow up Evaluation:

Students will discuss their findings and share their outcomes with other groups.

Activity 2. Geodesic Gumdrops
(From the Exploratorium Website)
Celeste Dizon

Students should develop understandings of how the mathematics curriculum supports and closely relates to the science curriculum. Problem solving is emphasized.

Science standards: science inquiry, physical science, science and technology, math and science coordination, problem solving

New Curriculum Qualities: depth of coverage, problems, skills and knowledge, coordination with mathematics, integration, personal relevance

Materials:

1. A bag of gumdrops (if gumdrops aren't available, try mini marshmallows, clay or larger jellied candy, cut-up, be creative).
2. A box of round toothpicks.

Basic Science Principles:

Even though the gumdrop structures are standing absolutely still, their parts are constantly pulling and pushing on each other. Structures, even large ones, remain standing because some parts are being pulled or stretched while other parts are being pushed or squashed. The parts being pulled are in *tension*. The parts being squashed are in *compression*. Things that don't squash easily are strong in compression. Things that don't break when stretched are strong in tension. Some materials are strong in both tension and compression.

Another principle that helps explain standing structures are the shapes used. Students may have noticed that squares collapse easily under compression but triangles don't. Ask students if they know why this is so. It's because a square changes shape under compression into a diamond. The only way to change a triangle shape under compression is to break one of the sides.

Have students explore these principles by building the following structures:

Making Squares and Cubes:

1. Start with 4 toothpicks and 4 gumdrops. Poke the toothpicks into the gumdrops to make a square with a gumdrop at each corner.

2. Put another toothpick into the top of each toothpick/gumdrop corner. Connect the gumdrops with toothpicks to make a cube.
3. Use more toothpicks and gumdrops to keep building squares onto the sides of the cube. When your structure is about 6 inches wide, try wiggling it from side to side. Does it feel solid, or is it kind of shaky?

Making Triangles and Pyramids:

1. Start with 3 gumdrops and 3 toothpicks. Poke the toothpicks into the gumdrops to make a triangle with a gumdrop at each point.
2. Poke another toothpick into the top of each gumdrop. Bend those three toothpicks toward the center. Poke all 3 toothpicks into one gumdrop to make a three-sided pyramid. (A three-sided pyramid has a triangle on each side. It takes 4 gumdrops and 6 toothpicks.)
3. Use more toothpicks and gumdrops to keep building triangles onto the sides of your pyramid. When your structure is about 6 inches wide, try wiggling it from side to side. Does it feel solid, or is it kind of shaky?

Making 4-sided Pyramids:

A big structure can be made out of squares and cubes, but it will be wiggly and probably fall down. If a structure is made out of only triangles and pyramids, it won't be wiggly. A four-sided pyramid has a square bottom and triangles on all four sides. When a structure is built that uses both triangles and squares the big structure will be more solid.

1. Build a square, then poke a toothpick into the top of each corner.
2. Bend all 4 toothpicks into the center and connect them with one gumdrop to make a four-sided pyramid.
3. What other ways can you use squares and triangles together?
4. The students can continue their exploration by building structures which combine triangles and squares and by looking at structures they encounter that used squares and triangles.

Activity 3. Experimenting With Paper Airplanes
M.J. Moore, SFSU Student (adapted from Blackburn & Lammers, 1996)

Description:

Teachers can turn classroom distractions into a project of design and discovery. In this activity students will discover that there's more than just folding and tossing paper. As they work on perfecting design plans, they will learn to hypothesize, experiment, and draw conclusions. Students will work in small groups to design a paper airplane of any size using any or all of the materials provided. Their challenge: to design a plane that will fly farther and straighter than the planes built by the other groups. The process skills of predicting, estimating, experimenting (forming hypotheses, identifying variables, collecting data, analyzing, and explaining outcomes) are applied. Students should develop understandings of how the learning processes such as forming a hypothesis, identifying and analyzing data are closely relates to the science curriculum. Problem solving is emphasized.

Science Standards: science inquiry, physical science, science and technology, math and science coordination, problem solving

New Curriculum Qualities: depth of coverage, problems, skills and knowledge, co-ordination with mathematics, integration, personal relevance

Materials:

1. 6–7 grades of paper: typing, onion skin, computer paper, construction paper, paper towels, cardboard, milk cartons
2. paper clips in various sizes, staples, tape
3. directions for designing paper airplanes

Objectives:

1. Students will design a plan for their airplane.
2. Students will formulate a hypothesis describing their design, and their projection of a successful flight pattern.
3. Students will experiment with the materials and modify or alter their design.
4. Students will identify the variables that influenced the outcome of their investigation and record their efforts.
5. Students will carry out the investigation and generate data.
6. Students will communicate their data through written procedures.
7. Students will actively participate in the plane throwing contest.

Procedures:

1. Give each group a copy of the paper airplane directions and at least 3 sheets of paper.
2. Introduce the class to some factors that can affect the performance of paper airplanes.

Folding:

Symmetry and sharp folds are crucial in designing the plane.

Adding weight:

A paper airplane needs weight at the front tip (nose). In many cases, the folded paper provides the weight, but if the nose isn't heavy enough, the plane will rise up in front, then fall straight down. Paper clips, staples, tape, or additional folds can add weight.

If a plane is too heavy it'll dive to the ground. To give it more lift, cut and fold flaps on the backs of the wings. If the flaps are folded at 90-degree angles, the plane will fly differently than if they're only slightly turned up.

3. Encourage students to experiment as they adjust the variables. They'll learn a lot about trial and error as well as making and testing hypotheses.
4. Next groups will test their designs and try out their model experiment. Allow lots of time for practice.
5. Before the contest begins the class may wish to design posters (stating their purpose and the skills involved) and invite other classes to watch their science and math airplane contest.
6. As a class, conduct the airplane contest. Airplanes will be judged on how far they flew and how long they stay in the air (use a stop watch). If students create designs that loop in flight, students may also want to judge the number of circles. The best

place to hold the contest is in the school auditorium (no wind, plenty of space). Allow each group to fly their model 2 or 3 times, then take the best score.

7. Groups should present their model explaining their hypotheses and how it was assembled.

Evaluation:

Students will have the opportunity to ask questions, share designs and launching tips with their classmates. Students will write their reflections and feelings about the project (frustration, satisfaction) in their notebook or portfolio.

Activity 4. Recyclable Materials Construction
Sally Morey, SFSU Student

Science Standards: science inquiry, physical science, science and technology, math and science coordination, problem solving

New Ccurriculum Qualities: depth of coverage, problems, skills and knowledge, coordination with mathematics, integration, personal relevance

Description:

"Hands-on technology" is the exciting things that happen during technological problem solving when students develop and construct their own "best" solution. This middle school activity moves beyond conducting experiments or finding solutions to word problems (all students doing the same task at the same time). In "hands-on technology" students are not shown a solution. Typically, this results in some very creative designs.

Using the tools and materials found in a normal middle school technology education laboratory, students design and construct solutions that allow them to apply the process skills. The products they create and engineer in the technology lab often use a wide range of materials such as plastics, woods, electrical supplies, etc. During the course of solving their problem students are forced to test hypotheses and frequently generate new questions (Hamm & Adams, 1998). This involves a lot of scientific investigation and mathematical problem solving, but it is quite different from the routine classroom tasks. In this activity a problem is introduced to the class. Working in small groups of four or five students their challenge is to plan a way of coming up with a solution. Students are to document the steps they used along the way. Some suggestions: brainstorm, discuss with friends, draw pictures, show design ideas, use mathematics, present technical drawings, work together, consult with experts.

Background Information:

The best construction materials are strong, yet lightweight. Wood is unexpectedly strong for its weight, and therefore well suited for many structures. Larger buildings often use steel reinforced concrete beams, rather than wood, in their construction. However steel and concrete are both heavy, presenting problems in construction. A lighter material would be a great alternative and a best seller in the construction industry. This could be done by reinforcing the beam with a material other than steel — ideally, a recyclable material.

The Problem:

Design the lightest and strongest beam possible by reinforcing concrete with one or more recyclable materials: aluminum cans, plastic milk jugs, plastic soda bottles, and/or newspaper. Students must follow the construction constraints. The beam will be weighed. Then it will be tested by supporting it at each end, and a load will be applied to the middle. The load will be increased until the beam breaks. The load divided by the beam weight will give the load-to-weight ratio. The designer of the beam with the highest load-to-weight ratio will be awarded the contract.

Construction Limits:

The solution must:
1. be made into a reusable mold that the student designs.
2. result in a 40 cm (approx. 16 in.) long beam that fits within a volume of 1050 cubic centimeters (approx. 64 cubic inches).
3. be made from concrete and recyclable materials.

Objectives:

1. Groups of students will plan and design their beam.
2. Groups will work on their construction plans.
3. Students will design and construct their beam.
4. Students will gather information from a variety of resources and make sketches of all the possibilities they considered.
5. Students will record the science,mathematics, and technology principals used.

Procedures:

1. Divide students into small groups of 3 or 4 students.
2. Present the problem to the class.
4. Students will discuss and draw out plans for how to construct a beam.
5. Students will design a concrete beam reinforced with recycled materials.
6. Students will work together to construct, measure and test the beam.
7. Students will present their invention to the class.

Evaluation:

Students will document their work in a portfolio that includes:
1. sketches of all he possibilities their group considered
2. a graphic showing how your invention performed.
3. descriptions of the process skills used in your solution.
4. information and notes gathered from resources.
5. thoughts and reflections about this project.

Activity 5: An Icy Discovery with Scientific Inquiry
Sarah Peterson, SFSU student

Science Standards: science inquiry, physical science, science and technology, problem solving

New Curriculum Qualities: depth of coverage, problems, skills and knowledge, integration, personal relevance

Objectives:

To introduce the scientific inquiry process in a collaborative setting.
To ask questions, make predictions, and find answers through experimentation.
To develop observation, communication, and cooperative group skills.

Materials:

Balloons, flashlights, magnifying glasses, salt, sugar, food coloring, containers to hold the ice, and 6-inch balls of ice for groups of three or four students.

Introduction:

Ask students what they know about ice – either in groups or with the whole class. How does water freeze, melt, and how does ice get used. Students can act like scientists and conduct scientific experiments and try different things with ice as they explore questions their small group finds interesting.

Procedures:

Put the piece of ice at the center of each group (use a small table if you can). Encourage students to touch and observe the ice, but not pick it up. The first phase is for observation. Ask the students what would happen if someone in their group shines a flashlight beam onto the ice ball. The idea is to generate some predictions and use a felt pen to put them on a large sheet of paper . . . or on the chalkboard. The next step is to give each group a flashlight and have students take turns experimenting. Have them record what they observe and decide how to communicate it.

You can follow the same procedure with salt, sugar, and food coloring – making predictions, doing experiments, and observing what they discover. You may want to have the groups rotate around so that students get to see the group differences in texture, color, clarity, and so on. Each table should end up at their original ice ball so that they can do a final drawing based on careful observation.

Evaluation:

Encourage students to relate and apply the information they learn from the ice ball activity to scientific inquiry. This includes making predictions, observations, and working collaboratively.

IMPROVING SCIENTIFIC LITERACY
IN THE NEW MILLENNIUM

The reform now going on is searching for a science curriculum focusing on responsible citizenship and self-understanding. Goals include using scientific knowledge in making wise decisions and solving difficult problems related to life and living (Abruscato, 2004). Science is becoming more interdisciplinary; for example, some of the new research fields emerging include biochemistry, biophysics, plant engineering, terrestrial biology, and neurobiology to name a few. Today, science has dimensions that extend to the social sciences as well as ethics, values and law.

Meeting the needs of students requires finding relationships between science, technology, and students' life experiences. Suggestions are needed for meeting the adaptive needs of students in a changing world. From the beginning of the reform movement, educators have recognized that the time has come to develop curricula in a way that no longer isolates science from human welfare and social and economic progress. "Learning to learn" is essential for preparing students for the world in which they will live (National Research Council, 1999).

A central role of scientific literacy is promoting intellectual processes through encounters with knowledge. Unfortunately, science, mathematics, and technological knowledge is often translated into fragmented bits and pieces rather than the essence of literate human dialogue. The richer an individual's experiences with the tools of mathematics, science and technology, the greater the prospects for living a rich life. Opportunities to gain access to the most generally useful knowledge are too frequently limited by misguided decisions with regard to grouping and tracking, maldistributed in terms of poor and minority children and youth, and overlooked by ill-prepared teachers. An emphasis today must be placed on career awareness, and awareness of opportunities in science, math and technology.

Effective teaching must be based on learning principles of research and practice. These include providing students with active hands-on experience, placing emphasis on students' curiosity and creativity and frequently using a student team approach to learning. Classrooms should be organized so that small mixed-ability groups are a forum for math/science discussions, discovery, creativity, and connections to other subjects. When students resourcefully collaborate, ask questions and explore possible answers, they can develop an energetic enthusiasm about these subjects (Wyatt, V., 2003). As mathematics and science move from their computational and factual base to a problem-solving emphasis, these subjects can come alive and stimulate students because of their immediacy. Many new strategies have emerged. Some of these include investigations, interviews, questioning techniques, journal writing, new assessment techniques such as performance assessment, portfolios, and use of multimedia. Conducting investigations gives direct experience with designing and conducting scientific experiments.

Students need to be placed in situations where they develop and create their own science understandings, connect concepts with personal meanings and put ideas together for themselves. It is important for concepts to be derived by students at all levels using thinking processes such as problem solving and research. Researching *their* questions, experimenting to find out, observing, discussing, and asking new questions are some examples of students taking responsibility for their learning.

Achieving The Goal of Scientific Literacy

> *The most beautiful thing we can experience is the mysterious.*
> *It is the source of all art and science.*
>   – Albert Einstein

To achieve the goals of scientific literacy the curricula must continue to be changed to reduce the amount of material covered and emphasize a thematic approach. There is a need to focus on the connections among the various disciplines of science, math, technology and build integrated understandings. The scientific endeavor must be presented as a social phenomenon that influences human thought and action (Cain, 2002).

It is important for teachers to open to cooperative learning practices, and to pay more attention to the collaborative links between mathematics, science and technology. For teachers the focus needs to shift to instruction, making instruction more important than curriculum. There is a need for teachers to be provided with opportunities to experience the kind of instruction they are being asked to provide. It is important to get teachers actively engaged using science so they watch themselves as learners, play with ideas, see their own minds getting involved with the topic, experience their own confusion, hesitancies, and the excitement that comes from growth in learning something as a group.

When it is taught as an active hands-on subject, science can be an exciting experience for elementary students and teachers. By connecting to other disciplines science can also provide teachers with many opportunities for integration with other subjects. Teachers need subject matter knowledge that is deep and flexible enough to work with the current influx of second-language learners and students who must face the grinding poverty found in many American cities. This often requires optimizing language and literacy possibilities to get at content.

To use and understand science today requires an awareness of how the scientific endeavor makes use of other core subject domains and how it relates to our culture and our lives. The best science teachers are usually those who have both built up their science knowledge base and developed a repertoire of current pedagogical techniques. By stressing real investigations and participatory learning teachers can move from the concrete to the abstract and vice versa.

Science educators are beginning to include many participatory experiences and opportunities for students to explore science in their lives. There is a greater emphasis on thinking skills, work teams, and inquiry. This involves posing questions, making observations, reading, planning investigations, experimenting, proposing explanations, and communicating the results.

By developing effective interpersonal skills, students can work together to frame questions and to critically examine data. This sometimes means designing and conducting real experiments that carry their thinking beyond the classroom. As language arts, mathematics, and science instruction becomes more connected to children's lives, enriching questions arise from inquiring about real-world concerns

Reconnecting With the Inquiry Process Skills

Have you ever wondered about nature, about how things work? What questions do you want to know the answer to? One question leads to many more. Like scientists who search for knowledge children are intrigued by the unknown and unexplained. Questioning is basic to societal and scientific progress. Science is still occupied with many of the questions from Aristotle's time. What makes up the universe? What constitutes matter? What and where is mind? We may now ask these questions in a more piercing way. And we may demand answers that have been rigorously tested through experiment or observation. As in the past, deeper understandings will provoke new questions we do not yet have the knowledge to ask. In the final analysis, it is the human dimension that determines the limitations and miracles of science.

Science has been portrayed to the public as the most rational of human enterprises. Yet this reasoned approach had all but been lost on the American public (Shamos, 1995). There is evidence that science is re-entering the realm of popular culture, the revolution in technology is surely a factor. The World Wide Web, e-mail, and cell phones have all been around long enough to have saturated public consciousness (Weber, B., 2000).

Scientific reasoning is more likely to become part of lifelong learning if it is frequently applied to problems encountered in life. One of the important goals in elementary science is to provide a firm foundation for linking what students are learning in science to the world of children, young adults, and citizens. As the standards point out, making what students learn about science in school relevant to their lives has all kinds of positive consequences.

One of the important goals in elementary science is to provide a firm foundation for linking what students are learning in science to the activities normally pursued by children and adults outside of school. Scientific reasoning is most likely to become a lifelong skill if it is frequently applied to problems encountered in life. When early work in science offers models that are useful in future experiences then it is more likely to be taken seriously. Making what students learn in school relevant to their lives today and tomorrow has all kinds of positive consequences.

Connecting Students to a Changing Future

The science curriculum now gives special attention to understanding what science means and how science relates to other subjects and the social system.

This includes some important historical data of science and technology. All have roots going far back into history into every part of the world. Although modern science is only a few centuries old, many scientific tools and concepts can be traced to early Egyptian, Greek, Chinese, and Arabic cultures.

A secret of science is that the easier things are usually done first. Newton, for example, conceptualized gravitational law to explain how two planetary bodies could grip each other invisibly. But he didn't have the scientific, mathematical, or technological tools to explain the mutual attraction of the earth, sun, and moon. Even with all the tools available today scientists cannot do a good job of explaining the fate of the universe or the workings of the human brain.

The messiness of the real world is sometimes ignored. Human behavior, for example, is still at odds with expert prediction. Riddles and a riot of variables means that it will be a while before there is the analog of the physics laboratory for doing experiments with social phenomena. Full answers to many questions of great complexity will have to wait and wait. But having some understanding of complex issues like human interaction and global warming is part of what it will mean to be scientifically literate in the future.

Scientific literacy is crucial in a society that is so heavily dependent on science and technology. It serves as the common ground for discussing and understanding complex issues. The media is always covering topics like the greenhouse effect, AIDS, and toxic waste dumps. Even when we buy a car we need to know something about gas mileage, horsepower, and antilock brakes. It is useful to know something about how to apply scientific processes to daily life.

Science teaching is changing and progressing as agreement is reached on *what* children need to know and as we find out more about *how* children learn. The standards give teachers some background information and informed curriculum guidance to help them reach the goal of scientific literacy for all children. The related pathways booklets delve into some of the pedagogical detail. But it is individual teachers who must continually make adaptions so that things work out in the classroom (Esler & Esler, 2001).

Goals and standards can help with accountability and improve practice without overly constraining it. As informed teachers gain more latitude, they may, for example, choose to teach certain concepts in depth. But good instructional decisions have to be based on more than whimsy. School renewal involves vision setting, inquiry, collaboration, and personal mastery. Like any other field, professional practice has to be based on what is known about subject matter content and the latest research about effective ways to teach and learn. Change is the one constant. Thus the continual professional development of teachers is interwoven with the future of schooling and the future of this nation's children.

In science the laws of the physical and biological universe are viewed as important to understanding how technological objects and systems work.

Educational technology is changing how science is taught by changing the instructional environment and providing opportunities for students to create new knowledge for themselves (Lederman, N., Lederman, J., Bell, R., 2004). The national science standards recognize technology as an important tool in inquiry-based classrooms.

As online resources for teaching and learning science become more impressive and extensive the role of the teacher is becoming more important, not less. There is simply no evidence that the Internet or any other technology can replace the critical role of teachers and peers. Technological resources for science education can help teachers and collaborative groups come closer to the goal of reaching all students with inquiry-based science. Best of all they can do it in a way that connects to good curriculum design and the technologically-intensive world of today.

Students now have the option of viewing rich visual (multimedia) presentations of relatively dry material. If they have trouble keeping good lab journals can dictate their entries with word recognition software. This list could go on. The point to be made here is that in spite of all the new digital appliances students need, more than ever, skillful teachers and cooperative classmates to learn to their full potential. A few years from now today's discussions about whether the schools should or shouldn't make use of powerful technological tools will seem as quaint as Plato's fear that the written word would implant forgetfulness in men's souls.

Schools are more than institutions of academic learning, they are complex social systems. For teachers and students to live up to their full potential ensure the social dynamics of in a school must make a positive contribution. To begin with they can make sure that administrators, bus drivers, janitors, secretaries, and everyone else understands that their job is to support learning in the classroom. Surprisingly, in some schools bus schedules and janitorial/administrative convenience trumps innovative teaching. Instead going along to get along, future educational visions should be inferences drawn from theory, the research, and today's quickly shifting environment. Whether its the culture of the school, technology, or anything else, educators must focus on what they want children to achieve and vigilant that technology serves that end.

The curriculum and instruction problems that we face today are complicated by the fact that a new global civilization is emerging. It is influenced by information age tools like the Internet, changing family structures, a literacy-intensive society, and new developments in the cognitive sciences that help us more fully recognize how we learn and use knowledge (Greene, 2004).

As educators, we know that the curricular changes we devise and implement actually foster active and collaborative inquiry in the years ahead. We also know that technology will continue to change the way we think and learn. But it is difficult to know the specific content of what children will need to know in decades to come. There are so predictable directions. For example, students will need to be literate, critical thinkers who can use technology and work with others. In addition, they will need to be lifelong learners who understand what they are learning and how it can be applied in the in the world outside of school.

Language makes us human
Literacy makes us civilized
Science and technology make us powerful
And being in community with others can make us free.

RESOURCES AND REFERENCES

Abruscato, J. (2004). *Teaching children science.* (6th ed.). Boston, MA: Pearson-Allyn & Bacon.

American Association for the Advancement of Science. (1990). *Science for all Americans.* Washington, DC: Author.

Anton, Ted. (2000). *Bold science: Seven scientists who are changing our world.* Gordonsville,VA: W.H. Freeman and Co.

Association for Supervision and Curriculum Development (ASCD) Yearbook 2000. Brandt, R. (Ed). *Education in a new era.* Alexandria, VA: Association for Supervision and Curriculum Development.

Bybee, R. W. & DeBoer, G. E. (1994). Research on goals for the science curriculum. In D. Gable (Ed.). *Handbook of research in science teaching and learning.* New York: Macmillan.

Cain, S. (2002). *Sciencing.* Upper Saddle New Jersey: Merrill-Prentice Hall.

Cotton, K., & Northwest Regional Educational Laboratory. (1999). *Research You Can Use to Improve Results.* Portland, OR: Northwest Regional Educational Laboratory.

DeHart, Hurd, P. (2000). "Science Education 2000," *NSTA Reports.* Vol. 11, No. 4. Arlington, VA: National Science Teachers Association.

Erlbach, A. (2001). *The kids invention book.* New York: Scholastic.

Esler, W, & Esler M. (2001). *Teaching elementary science.* (8th ed.) Belmont, CA: Wadsworth.

Etheredge, S., Rudnitsky, A. (2003). *Introducing students to scientific inquiry.* Boston, MA: Allyn and Bacon.

Glatthorn, A. A. (1998). *Performance assessment and standards-based curriculums.* Larchmont, NY: Eye on Education.

Glatthorn, A. & Jailall, J. (2000). "Curriculum for the new millennium" in Brandt, R. (ed.). *Education in a new era: ASCD Year book 2000.* Alexandria, VA: ASCD.

Greene, B. (2004). *The fabric of the cosmos: Space, time, and the texture of reality.* New York: Alfred A. Knopf.

Greene, B. (2003). *The elegant universe.* New York: Vintage Books.

Hamm, M. & Adams, D. (1998). *Literacy in science, technology, and the language arts. An interdisciplinary inquiry.* Westport, CT: Greenwood Publishing.

Hassard, J.(1990). *Science experiences: Cooperative learning in science.* Reading. MA: Addison Wesley.

Howe, A. (2002). *Engaging children in science.* Upper Saddle, New Jersey: Merrill-Prentice Hall.

Kayle, J. B. (1997). "Systematic reform: Challenges and changes" *Science Educator 6,* no 1 (Spring, 1997):1–6.

Lederman, N., Lederman, J., Bell, R. (2004). *Constructing science in elementary classrooms.* Boston, MA: Pearson-Allyn & Bacon.

Linn, M., Lewis, C., Tsuchida, I., Butler Songer, N. (2000). "Beyond fourth- grade science: Why do U.S. and Japanese students diverge? *Educational Researcher 29*(3) 4–14.

Manzo, A. & Manzo, U. (1997). *Content area literacy: Interactive teaching for active learning.* Columbus, OH: Merrill.

Martinello, M. & Cook, G. (1994). *Interdisciplinary inquiry in teaching and learning.* New York: Macmillan.

National Academy of Sciences. (1996). *National science education standards.* Washington, DC: National Academy Press.

National Education Goals Panel. (1999) *National Education Goals Report, 1999.* Washington, DC: National Education Goals Panel.

National Council of Teachers of English & International Reading Association. (1996). Urbana, IL & Newark, DE: Author.

National Education Goals Panel. (1999). *Building a nation of learners.* Washington, DC: Author.

National Research Council. (1999). *Global perspectives for local action: Using TIMSS to improve U.S. mathematics and science education – Professional development guide.* Washington, DC: National Academy Press.

National Science Education Standards. (1995). *National science education standards.* Washington, DC: National Academy Press.

National Science Teachers Association. (1997). *NSTA pathways to the science standards.* Arlington, VA: NSTA [Both the standards and the guidebooks can be ordered by calling 800-722-NSTA].

New York Hall of Science, Eric Marshal, director (2000). *www.TryScience.org* "Kids learn incredible things at a museum"

Pearce, C. R. (1999). *Nurturing Inquiry.* Portsmouth, NH: Heinemann.

Shamos, M. (1995). *The myth of scientific literacy.* New Brunswick, NJ: Rutgers University Press.

Sherman, H., Richardson, L., Yard, G. (2005). *Teaching children who struggle with mathematics: A systematic approach to analysis and correction.* Upper Saddle River, New Jersey: Pearson Prentic Hall.

Trowbridge, L. & Bybee, R. (1996). *Integrating mathematics and science for intermediate and middle school teachers.* Englewood Cliffs, NJ: Merrill.

Van de Walle (1997). *Elementary school mathematics: Teaching developmentally.* New York: Longman.

Weber, B. (2000). *Science finds a home onstage as two cultures meet.* June 2, New York Times, p. 4.

Wulffson, D. (2000). *Toys! Amazing stories behind some great inventions.* New York: Henry Holt.

Wyatt, V. (2003). *Inventions: Frequently asked questions.* Tonawanda, NY: Kids Can Press.

Chapter 9

INFORMED ENCOUNTERS WITH THE ARTS: KNOWLEDGE, PERFORMANCE, AND CONNECTIONS

Imagination is to break through the limits.
— Thoreau

Arts education has always taught that no part of a composition, whether in a painting or in the curriculum is independent of the whole in which it participates. As teachers work with models that explore the connection within and across disciplines they can explore the conditions with and across learners. In this way the arts act as a prism that allows students to connect with multiple dimensions and directions of focus (Miller & Drake, 1990). Whether it is visual arts, dance, music, or theater, the arts provide active entry points to subject matter and critical thinking.

Arts education is moving away from the current emphasis on performing or "doing" to a more balanced approach that includes instruction in culture, aesthetics, and how the discipline involved relates to other subjects. Integrating the arts into the curriculum can help students become better consumers (of the arts) and develop more understanding of diversity (Viadero, 1993). Besides enriching the study of the other cultures and subjects, the arts help raise student awareness of the aesthetic qualities of their surroundings. As teachers try to plug critical thinking and cooperative learning into subject matter, the arts can help with synthesis, interconnection, and generating a sense of community. Most states require some form of arts education, but the quality and emphasis vary greatly. Arts educators are developing new standards that will be bolstered by the effort to develop national student assessments in the arts. The National Assessments Governing Board plans to begin testing students' grasp of the arts through its 1996 National Assessment of Educational Progress. Even if the U.S. decides not to go through with the concept of national assessment new standards for a discipline-based arts education will bring a higher level of quality to the field.

159

Providing a Sense of Opening

Learning how visual art, dance, music, and theater interconnect with each other and other subjects is a step towards powerfully engaging students in all subjects. Since the beginnings of civilization, the arts have had a central place in ceremonies that connected cave paintings to ritual, religion, and daily life. The visual arts, dance, poetry, plays, and music have long been organizers or points of integration for a whole range of human activities. The purpose has been – and to some extent still is – to enshrine some reproduction of experience, gain some control over the process, and influence the future. It is understood that encounters with the arts also have a unique capacity to provide openings for imaginative breaks from the expected. They continue the universal human practice of making *special* certain objects, sounds, movement, or representations that have been linked with human survival for countless generations.

The arts have always provided a space, a sense of opening, a loving of the question, and a unique communal resource. Today's school reform process should not push aside such a basic aspect of social consciousness and interdisciplinary knowing. If there are no arts in a school, there are fewer alternatives to exploring subjects by the spoken and written word. The arts can open some collective doors of the mind and provide new spaces for the active construction of knowledge. What a powerful tool for countering the tendency towards standardization! At the classroom level it will take the skill of teachers to move forward and use the arts to shape the interconnected exuberance of learning – keeping light from the arts at the center of the human spirit.

Extending education in the arts with other subjects must go hand-in-hand with other new aspects of schooling and daily life. The notion that the arts can encourage wonder, inquiry, speculation, and technological literacy has for too long been lost in a morass of indifference, nostalgia, crafts, didacticism, and an already overcrowded curriculum. To dig it out requires a greater emphasis on professional development to help teachers become more familiar with the arts and discipline-based arts education. Performance and creation will continue to be important. However, arts education is becoming more focused on analysis, history and culture. In the field this is referred to as a discipline-based approach. It depends more than ever on the intellectual preparation and commitment of the teacher. Specialists can help, but it is the regular classroom teacher who will continue to be the primary source for instruction in the arts.

> *Social systems that disdain or discount beauty, form, mystery, meaning, value, and quality – whether in art or in life, are depriving their members of human requirements as fundamental as those for food, warmth and shelter.*
> – Ellen Dissanayake

Breaking Down the Disconnection Between the Arts and the People

In the "Candide" Voltaire defined blind optimism as a "mania for maintaining that all is well when things are going badly." The act of thinking that things are going well when they aren't hasn't been lost. A number of futurists (John Nesbitt (for example) predict that our culture will soon be as filled with the arts as it is with television and sports (Nesbitt, 1986). They see the arts as being central to the curriculum in the new Millennium (Eisner, 1991).

Educators and artists argue that children without knowledge of the arts are as ignorant as children without knowledge of literature or math. De Tocqueville predicted that American democracy would diminish the character of art. It took seventy years to prove him wrong – at least for a while.

In the nineties some artists are trying to break down the disconnection between the nation's establishment (including the arts, academia, and the press) and the people. Whether it's visual arts, music, or the theater, the arts have the potential to help us be receptive to new thinking and generous toward the production of something fresh. Far from being beaten down, American artistic expressions, especially film and music, have been some of our most successful exports.

Many people think of the arts as elitist, therapeutic, frivolous, impractical, or mindless entertainment. They are not always wrong, but they miss the point. The arts can provide important intellectual tools for understanding many subjects. They also build on qualities that are essential to revitalizing schooling: teamwork, analytical thinking, motivation, and self discipline. The arts provide cultural resources that people can draw on for the rest of their lives. Without attention to the substance of the discipline and concerted action, the arts more likely to be dismissed as expendable in an era of curriculum gridlock and financial difficulties. Reinvigorating American schools will depend on their skills and the perspective of art to show what thinking, learning, and life can be.

Visual Analysis and the Critical Function of the Arts

Efforts are now being made to deepen and extend education in the the arts by connecting them to critical thinking, problem solving, aesthetic analysis, technology, and new ways of working. This increasing influence of discipline-based art education (DBAE) curriculum addresses more than the traditional issues of creative expression and performance. It provides an interdisciplinary framework for connecting arts education to aesthetic criticism within a cultural, historical, and social context. In the new literature-based reading curriculum, for example, students are expected to develop the thinking skills necessary for "literary criticism." Should we expect less when it comes to the arts? A renewed emphasis on artists, criticism, aesthetic discourse, and the importance of discipline-based arts education will accompany education into the next century.

Some Selected Examples of Discipline-Based Art Education Activities (Practical Ideas for Teachers)

The following discipline-based art activities are organized around an inter-disciplinary unit theme entitled: "You and your world." This approach was selected so that critical thinking skills and interdisciplinary content could be linked and included as an integral part of classroom life.

As part of an integrated approach, it is important that children learn to be more flexible, and move freely between different communications media. To accomplish this, children need exposure to many different communication forms.

Unit Introduction Activity

Before beginning this unit, discuss with children the need all people have to communicate ideas and how there are many ways to do this. Encourage children to brainstorm all the ways people use to communicate. List the suggestions on the board, or a chart. Young children may wish to find or draw pictures which can be placed on a bulletin board. Such a chart becomes an ongoing resource for students to refer to, and additions can be incorporated throughout the year.

Unit: You and the World

When you think of how you are related to others, the thing that most people say is family. But even if you were alone in the world, you wouldn't be unrelated. The fact that you have read these words makes you a member of English speaking people. As a student you have a relationship with those who attend your school and with those who work there. The music you listen to and enjoy is enjoyed by others. Your relationships with your fellow humans are marked by the foods you think are good, the clothes you think are fashionable, the jokes you tell.

Ralph Waldo Emerson, a nineteenth-century writer saw in these relationships a basic theme of imaginative thinking. He felt that people depend on their relationships in order to understand what they read. Emerson thought, because each person is related not only to a few others, but to all people that each of us has within ourselves the sum of human history. Perhaps you have never read yourself into history. But chances are you have watched characters in movies or on television and sensed that they felt as you have felt and acted as you would have acted, that they were, in a sense related to you.

Your relationships with others are the basis of sympathy and one of the keys to imaginative thinking (Edwards, 2001).

Unit Activities

1. Make a map of significant relationships in your life. Put your name in the center of a sheet of paper. Then begin thinking of the important people in your life. As you think of them, write their names on the paper. Organize or group the names that belong together. You may wish to connect the names with lines to show the relationships.

2. Make a list of ten words you chose at random from the dictionary. Next write or make up something about you that uses all the words you have listed. It could be a paragraph in the form of a news report, a story, a creative drama, whatever works with the words you have. Just make sure you *use* the words, not just mention them.

   For example, the word *hare*.

   Use: I saw a *hare*, chewing on a carrot in my garden.
   Mention: Hare is another word for a rabbit.

   Let the words guide what you write.

3. Suppose there is a lottery in your state. A three-digit number is picked at random. For $1 you can buy a ticket picking any number from 000 to 999. If the number on your ticket matches the number on the ticket drawn you win $500. Is that a good payoff? Why or why not? How much of the money the state takes in does it keep?

4. Try reflecting on and then describing an episode from a television series that you regularly watch. Here are some questions that may help you think about the program. Jot down your answers. Then write a paragraph or two about what you've learned.

   1. For what sorts of people is the program produced?
   2. Are the main characters people like yourself? Are they people you want to be like?
   3. Are the main characters unusual in some way? If so, in what way? Are they usually attractive? Do they have special skills?
   4. If the program is a comedy, what are the jokes about? Is there a laugh track? Do you laugh as often as you hear people in the audience laughing?
   5. What kinds of problems do the characters in the program have? Are they the same sorts of problems you have?
   6. Are the characters in the program richer or poorer than you are?
   7. Describe the plot. Does it make sense? Do the characters in the program act the way real people act?

8. Does the program use background music? What sort of music? What does the music contribute to the mood of the program?
9. Try looking at the program without listening to the sound. What do you notice? Try listening to the program without watching the picture. What do you notice?
10. Do you know what is going to happen before it happens or are you surprised? How do you feel when the program ends? (Cornett, 1999)

Connecting Subject Matter with the Arts

The arts can also help get a dialogue going between disciplines that often ignore each other. When knowledge from diverse subject matter areas are brought together the result can be a new and valuable way of looking at the world. The arts and humanities have proved very useful tools for integrating curricular areas and helping students transcend narrow subject matter concerns (The College Board, 1985). Teachers at many levels have used intellectual tools from the fine arts as a thematic lens for examining diverse subjects. Some schools have even worked out an integrated school day, where interdisciplinary themes based on the fine arts add interest, meaning and function to collaboration. Mathematics, writing, science, music, art appreciation and reading can all be wrapped around central themes in the arts so that rich connections stimulate the mind and the senses.

The research suggests that using a thematic approach improves students' knowledge of subject matter and aids in transfer of the skills learned to other domains outside the school. An additional finding is that good units organized around themes can improve the students' abilities to apply their knowledge to new subjects (Sharan, 1990). In art, for example, language development flourishes when children are encouraged to discuss the materials they are using and reflect on the nature of their art work through writing. Whatever the combination, an important result of integrating various subjects around a theme results in an enhancement of thinking and learning skills – *the metacurriculum* (Wlodkowski & Jaynes, 1990).

Before we can deal with teaching the thinking process children need some solid content to think about. After that teachers need to provide continuity between activities and subjects. The thinking skills engendered in one area can serve as a connection between subjects. In making curriculum connections it's often helpful for teachers to see model lessons that include cross disciplinary suggestions and activities. The relationships established between subjects and the way teachers facilitate these relationships are important. When disciplines are integrated around a central concept students can practice the skills that they have learned from many subjects. This helps students make sense out of the world (Maeroff, 1988).

The goal of a interdisciplinary curriculum is to bring together different perspectives so that diverse intellectual tools can be applied to a common theme, issue or problem. Thematic approaches can help by providing a group experience that fosters thinking and learning skills that will serve students in the larger world. By its very definition "interdisciplinary" implies cooperation among disciplines and people. The notion that students of different abilities and backgrounds can learn from each other is a natural outgrowth of the collaborative tendency inherent in this approach. Everyone's collaborative involvement not only allows input into the planning process, but can help with self responsibility and long-term commitment to learning (Fraser, 1990).

Organizing parts of the curriculum around themes means that each subject is mutually reinforcing and connected to life-long learning. Subjects from the Greek classics to radiation theory need the historical, philosophical and aesthetic perspective afforded by interdisciplinary connections. Curriculum integration provides active linkages between areas of knowledge, consciously applies language and methods from more than one discipline to examine a central theme, issue, topic or experience. This holistic approach focuses on themes and problems and deals with them more in depth rather than memorizing facts and covering the text from cover to cover.

There is always the danger of watering down content in an attempt to cover all areas. We can, however, teach the work of Newton on one hand while paying attention to the history of the times on the other. The history of ideas, political movements, and changing relationships among people are part of the fabric of our world. We cannot narrowly train people in specialist areas and expect them to be able to deal with multifaceted nature of twenty-first century jobs.

Thematic Strategies for Connecting Subjects and People

> *Artists have the right – and possibly the obligation*
> *to reinterpret the history of our time.*
> – Oliver Stone

[Some would add they they even have the right to distort history.]

Like the arts, innovation in science can experience ups and downs and cul-de-sacs. These different ways of knowing, the arts and the sciences, do not need to grow further apart. The unity of all cultural and scientific efforts were the unwritten rule until the eighteen century. But as art and science have progressed over the last 200 years both have become more narrow, specialized and extensive.

The arts can help connect the mind and the senses – uniting the cognitive and affective dimensions of learning. Trevor Tebbs, in his seventh-grade Vermont classroom, worked with another teacher to focus on a Black History theme. Teachers assembled a list of significant events, terms, literature, and questions. Students worked in partnerships to research, discuss, and create a time line collage of visual images depicting the theme They were also responsible for written pieces, maps, and creative journal writing. Partners had to work cooperatively to complete the assignment which would be presented to their colleagues and their parents. The goal was to examine both their ethnic and human heritage – while searching for the proper balance between the two.

Tebbs explains another piece of collaborative work; an audio slide presentation based on the timeline. A small group of students was given the total responsibility of completing the assignment and making the presentation to others. In the words of the teacher involved in the project:

> *The whole enterprise was a superb success. I am of the opinion that collaborative art offers the opportunity for a really powerful and beneficial experience for our students.*
>
> – Tebbs, 1991

Whether the collaboration is in the distant past, a computer chip, or a peer sitting nearby, collaboration in art involves creating, interpreting, and connecting to others. Socially useful art requires hard thinking about the location and the intended audience in order to understand how best to engage local modes of expression and needs.

Themes can also direct the design of classroom activities by connecting classroom activities and providing them with a logical sequence and scope of instruction.

One set of steps for developing thematic concepts is to:

1. Determine what students know about a topic before beginning instruction. This is done by careful questioning and discussion.
2. Be sensitive to and capitalize on students' knowledge.
3. Use a variety of instructional techniques to help students achieve conceptual understanding.
4. Include all students in discussions and cooperative learning situations.

Thematic instruction values depth over breadth of coverage. The content should be chosen on how well it represents what is currently known in the field and its potential for dynamically making connections (Rogoff, 1990).

Thematic Units

The design of thematic units brings together a full range of disciplines in the school's curriculum: language arts, science, social studies, math, art, physical education, and music. Using a broad range of discipline-based perspectives can result in units that last an hour, a day, a few weeks or a semester.

They are not intended to replace a discipline-based approach, but act as supportive structures that foster the comprehensive study of a topic. Teachers can plan their interdisciplinary work around issues and themes that emerge from their ongoing curriculum. Deliberate steps can be taken to create a meaningful and carefully orchestrated program that is more stimulating and motivating for students and teachers. Of course shorter flexible units of study are easier to do than setting up a semester or yearlong thematic unit.

Collaborative thematic curriculum models require a change in how teachers go about their work. It takes planning and energy to create effective integrated lessons and more time is often needed for subject matter research because teachers frequently find themselves exploring and teaching new material. Thematic teaching also means planning lessons that use untraditional approaches, arranging for field trips, guest speakers, and special events. Contacting parents, staff members, community resources who can help expand the learning environment is another factor in teacher's time and planning efforts. Long-range planning and professional development for teachers are other important elements of the process.

Many middle schools have incorporated the idea of blocks or cores where language arts, reading and social studies are combined. A math-science block or humanities core are other examples. Teachers who are discipline specialists team together to teach these blocks that can include numerous combinations.

The arts have a power beyond aesthetics or making us "see." They can help us view ourselves, the environment, the future differently – even challenging our certainties about the arts themselves. In connecting the basic concerns of history, civilization, thought, and culture the arts provide spatial, kinesthetic and aesthetic skills that are the foundation to what it means to be an educated person. Such understandings do not occur spontaneously. They have to be taught.

The process of understanding or creating art is more than unguided play, self-expression, or a tonic for contentment. They can be tools for shattering stereotypes, changing behavior, building a sense of community, and as a vehicle for sociopolitical commentary. An example from the visual arts: Barbara Kruger develops popular imagery that merges words and concepts from other disciplines. Along with other post-modernist artists (like Keith Harring and Jenny Holtzman) she works outside the artistic and the aesthetic frame to harness the formative power of images to affect deep structures of personal and social belief. In a similar manner Alexis Smith combines quotes, flotsam, and jetsam that speak to the artifices and pitfalls of a mythical America. When the right object is connected to the perfect quote the result can range from the humorous to the toughest and most intriguing social observation. Moving towards music, storytelling and dance, Lori Anderson extends the edges with performance art, combining nearly every basic art form with literary references and video imagery to create theatrical performances. Like many modern artists, she releases possibilities by making use of collaborators across time, media, and subject matter.

Opening Up a Shared Sense of Wonder

There is a connection between productive citizenship, academics and the arts. For students to make these connections it will take more than a specialist in the art class for one hour a week or an inspirational theater troupe visiting the school once a year. These brief experiences can help and inspire – but it takes more sustained work in the arts to make a real difference. Quick "drive-by teaching" is the equivalent of driving a motorcycle through an art gallery, you might get some blurred notion of color but not much else. Cheating on daily arts education denies students a vital quality of life experience – expression, discovery and an understanding of the chances for human achievement (Shubert & Willis, 1991).

The arts can open up a sense of wonder and provide students with intellectual tools for engaging in a shared search. This won't occur if children are having fewer experiences with the arts at school and in their daily lives. They at least have to know enough to recognize what to notice and what to ignore. This means that some grasp of the discipline is required if the arts are going to awaken anyone to the possibilities of thoughtfulness, collaboration and life.

There are some excellent models or prototypes of art education. The Minneapolis discipline-based art program is one example. Another is in Augusta, Georgia, where the national Endowment for the Arts (NEA) has supported the development of an exemplary arts education model. This program uses the arts to improve academic achievement, the general learning environment, student self-esteem, attendance, creative thinking, and social equity among students.

Art Activities Which Encourage Reflection

Reflecting is a special kind of thinking. Reflective thinking is both active and controlled. When ideas pass aimlessly through a person's mind, or someone tells a story which triggers a memory, that is not reflecting. Reflecting means focusing attention. It means weighing, considering, choosing. Suppose you want to drive home, you get the key out of your pocket, put it in the car door and open the door. Getting into your car does not require reflection. But suppose you reached in your pocket and couldn't find the key. To get into your car requires reflection. You have to think about what you are going to do. You have to consider possibilities and imagine alternatives.

A carefully balanced combination of direct instruction, self-monitoring, and reflective thinking helps meet diverse student needs. The activities suggested here are designed to encourage higher order thinking and learning and provide a collaborative vehicle for arts education.

1. *Looking At the Familiar, Differently*
   Students are asked to empty their purses and pockets on a white sheet of paper and create a face using as few of the items as possible. For example, one case might be simply a pair of sunglasses, another a single earring representing a mouth, a third could be a profile created by a necklace forming a forehead, nose, and chin. It gives students a different way of looking at things. It's also an example of a teaching concept known as esthetic education.

2. *Collage Photo Art*
   Students at all levels can become producers as well as consumers of art. We used a videotape of David Hockney's work from *Art in America.* Hockney, one of today's important artists, spoke (on the videotape) about his work and explained his technique. Students then used cameras to explore Hockney's photo collage technique in their own environment.

   Student groups can arrange several sets of their photos differently – telling unique stories with different compositions of the same pictures. They can even add brief captions or poems to make more connections to the language arts, social studies, science, or music.

   Photographers know the meaning of their pictures depend to a large extent on the words that go with them.

   Note: teachers do need to preview any videos before they are used in the classroom because some parts may not be appropriate for elementary school children. Teachers can also select particular elements and transfer them from one VCR to another so that only the useful segments are present on the tape used in class.

3. *Painting with Water Colors and Straws*
   In this activity students simply apply a little suction to a straw which is dipped in tempera paint. Working in paints students then gently blow the paint out on a sheet of blank paper to create interesting abstract designs.

4. *Creating Paintings with Oil-Based Paints Floating on Water*
   Working in groups of three, have students put different colored oil-based paints on a flat dish of water. Apply paper. Watch it soak up the paint and water. Pull it out and let it dry.

Expanding Social and Personal Visions of the Arts

Teachers can create a space for the arts to flourish – a sense of opening – that helps free students from the predicted and the expected. Using the arts to inquire and sense openings results in what Emily Dickerson called *a slow fire lit by the imagination.* As America moves toward the new millennium we need all the imagination we can get.

Advancing the understanding, culture, art, creativity and human values has everything to do with the life and quality of this nation. Never-the-less educational decision-makers in the United States have generally not paid much attention to these issues. The art is most often found on the fringes of the American school curriculum. This is due in part to not having a long tradition of prizing artistic expression beyond the cute and the comfortable. Little is expected of our citizens or our leaders when it comes to knowledge about artistic forms. The United States spends nearly 50 billion dollars a year on science and much less than one billion on all the humanities put together (National Humanities Center, 1990). In contrast, the West Germans spend more than ten times as much on the arts as the United States (*The New York Times*, August 2, 1992).

The arts can open new horizons, enrich the spirit, and help educate students to expand an American cultural vision. An artistic perspective can color the way we see other aspects of social and educational change. When the arts are viewed as a personal luxury – and not traditionally associated with "real wage earning" occupations – developing or maintaining a good arts education program is more difficult. This is a disappointing portrait of ourselves, a reflection not of human strength and aesthetic vision, but of their absence. Restoring faith in the arts – and arts education – means expanding the margins to restore faith in ourselves as a nation.

Human societies have always depended on the arts to give insight into truths, however painful or unpopular they may be. Today, in many countries, there is wide agreement that the arts can aid children in developing creativity, becoming good citizens, and being productive workers. The basic notion is that the person and the world is poorer without the arts.

A country's richness of knowledge, enlightenment, and enduring resources for thoughtfulness also benefit from artistic endeavors. From Asia to Europe, serious arts education is one of the integrating features of the school curriculum. Such an investment of the arts is seen as an investment in the community – and vice versa. Americans are beginning to take notice.

Inventing the future of arts education means expanding the links within the arts, community, and the schools. There is a world out there that students must explore with the arts if they are to be broadly educated – to say nothing of developing self-examination, critical thinking, and problem-solving skills. All of these qualities can be taught and reinforced through the arts. They can also help children integrate thinking skills by such activities as producing critiques, reflecting on aesthetic concerns, and dealing with the nature of our humanity.

Children frequently have the innate ability to do creative work in the arts. What's frequently missing are basic artistic understandings and the opportunity for expression and analysis. When students do have the chance to express themselves there is the excitement of producing in their own way – conveying their personal aesthetic experience through the use of figurative language (metaphors, similes, etc.) in their writing and symbolism in their painting. The challenge is to provide the necessary background and opening doors so that meaningful concepts and images will emerge (Starr, 2004).

Including Art Education in School Reform

In an effort to make arts education part of the national curriculum reform a series of *Discipline Based Art Education* reports has been put forward by the Getty Foundation (1990). These reports encouraged the schools to help students go beyond crafts to art criticism, history and aesthetics. In some of the small scale projects art educators, historians, philosophy professors and local teachers gathered to collaborate in making aesthetics less mysterious for children and young adults. It was felt that even at early levels students need to be grounded in the ability to reflect on art, study the discipline, test out the skills involved in production.

In 1992, the National Endowment for the Arts (N.E.A) entered into an agreement with the U.S. Office of Education to create an "in-depth arts-in education program" that could be part of the effort to "reinvent" American schools. The arts were recognized as representing a body of knowledge – as well as a practical study of technique. Isolated school experiments are proving that there are a number of ways of doing this beautifully on a small scale. The question is whether the call for "world-class standards" in the arts will mean real change for a significant numbers of schools (National Art Education Associates, 1992).

Although the connection to a rich artistic tradition is important, no response should be considered *the* "right" one. In fact, seeking the rewards of what some adults see as good creative products, often makes their appearance less likely. Instead, teachers can mix modeling intellectual stimulation with the natural rapport and creative production that is such an important part of the mysterious art of good teaching (Fowler, 1992).

Art criticism, history, and aesthetics contribute to production and a child's ability to draw inferences and interpret the powerful ideas. Art (like television, reading or mathematics) makes use of certain conventions and symbol systems to express figurative meaning. In the visual arts, for example, this may include symbols in its expression through style (the fine detail), composition (arrangement of elements) and by creating the possibility for multiple meanings. "Reading" an artist's symbols is as much of a skill as reading print or video images.

Art means going beyond the transient messages that are often overvalued by the culture. In a multicultural society like the United States it also means weaving artistic material (visual arts, movement and music) from other cultures into the curriculum enabling students to creatively confirm the truth and beauty of their heritage. Art is not limited to specific times or cultures. Greek art learned from Egypt. Christian art was shaped by ideas from Greece and the East. African, Chinese, Egyptian and Mexican art have influenced Modernism. A high quality national culture can provide a unifying frame for a rich multiplicity of cultural influences (Gelineau, 2004).

Exposing children to a variety of artistic forms and materials will make it easier to locate areas of strength and weakness. All students may have a similar range of choices, but it is how these choices are made that count. Choosing from a variety of artistic and intellectual possibilities is beneficial for building both the strength of creativity and basic skills. In addition, the arts can also help to get a dialogue going between groups or disciplines that often ignore each other. When knowledge from diverse subject matter areas are brought together through art, the result can be a new and valuable way of looking at the world.

Children can be involved in artistic interdisciplinary projects – ranging from illustrating their own books to designing movement, to poetry, to producing videos with camcorders. Process, production, and critical dimensions are all important. To understand literature, for example, children must function as critics. With art experiences critical analysis is equally important.

The creative effect of questioning, challenging, and aesthetic reflection all contribute to creative habits of mind and set up possibilities for action. It is also important for students to see how the arts can set up possibilities for positive action and take on our world concerns. In the Los Angeles riots of 1992, for example, one of the first requests from the headquarters of "Rebuild Los Angeles" (a nonprofit group established to tackle the problems of inner-city life) was to the Design Arts Institute. The Art Institute was asked to provide design concepts and tools to help solve problems, like affordable housing, attractive parks, small shopping centers, and make the community more esthetically pleasing.

Creating Possibilities

Some Ideas for Incorporating Art Expressions Across Subject Areas. What if? These are magic words. They add exciting new possibilities to our world and the world of the child. "What if I would drop a rock into this tub of water? "What if I would make a ship for the rock out of tin foil – would the rock float instead of sink?" Since the beginning of time people have grappled with similar types of questions. An Italian sailor asked his colleagues "what if I sailed west across the unknown ocean? That sailor discovered America. The sixteen-year-old German schoolboy asked himself what would happen if he sent out a beam of light and could keep up with it? That boy was Albert Einstein, ten years later, his "what if" led him to create the theory of relativity.

In music, a frequent way of creating new possibilities is to vary a theme. Composers may start with a musical theme and then invent variations by changing it. Sometimes the melody is speeded up, sometimes slowed down, many times musicians shift keys, change notes, or add harmony. Jazz, for example, is often based on playing variations on a theme. Music is not the only area where variations are invented. You can start with anything. For instance teachers can vary a theme in their science, math, music, literature, history, social science class. The way to find variations is easy, and is much the same whether you are working with music, poetry, or mathematical equations. You rearrange the parts of what you began with, looking for new arrangements (Pinker, 2002).

Strategies for Change

Active collaboration around a thematic approach requires a depth of planning, a redefinition of testing, and cooperative classroom management skills (Albert, 1990). Cooperative learning values differences of abilities, talents, and background knowledge. Within a cooperative learning classroom many conventionally defined "disabilities" integrate naturally into the heterogeneity of expected and anticipated differences among all students.

Organizing an interdisciplinary lesson around a theme can excite and motivate all students to actively carry out projects and tasks in their group. "Disabilities" and "differences" come to constitute part of the fabric of diversity that is celebrated and cherished within cooperative groups. In such an educational climate, no individual is singled out as being difficult and no one student presents an insurmountable challenge to the teacher when it comes to accommodating a student with special needs.

In a cooperative learning classroom, no student needs to be stereotyped by others when they realize that there are many and varied "differences" among students. It is easier for the student with special needs to fit in. For some pupils "differences" may in fact constitute a "disability," defined as the inability to do a certain life or school-related task. Such a difference, however, need not constitute a handicap as cooperative learning is a joint enterprise. Some may have a disability or special talent, but all have information and skills to contribute to the learning of others.

The central question is how do individual classroom teachers, already overwhelmed with tasks, find ways to: adapt collaborative techniques, plan thematically, and modify approaches for successfully accommodating all students within their classrooms? The problem is much broader than adapting techniques or modifying current methods. It involves rethinking the structure of the curriculum and seeking different approaches for teaching all students in a way that builds on their unique human qualities.

Art flourishes where there is a sense of adventure.
                                   – Alfred North Whitehead

Using the Arts to Provide Access to Events

The arts can provide openings to other subjects by opening the imagination to other areas of understanding. They fit naturally into the "Whole Language" (literature-based) movement in reading. Literature has always connected directly to the arts. So has Social Studies and the concern about understanding cultural differences. Ethnic background images must be made available in schools. But good choices are harder to come by. The typical painting of Native Americans, for example, represent a romantic vision of Indian life that obscures the damage done (to them) and the hard realities of their lives. If teachers aren't careful they will simply add to the mound of sentimental cliches tying non-European cultures to the "cute-sy" in American life.

Aesthetic creativity seems to be deeply rooted in how a child's early symbolic products convey the meaning of their world. Even very young children can describe, interpret and evaluate their visual and auditory perceptions. Adult creative effort often draws on such early efforts in the arts. Creativity in any realm rarely occurs from scratch. Most often it is a combination of choices within a particular area. Prizing imaginative insight and artistic expression in children should be viewed as essential to cognitive competence and effective citizenship. There is an aesthetic world out there that youngsters must explore if they are to be truly educated in any subject.

The arts can motivate the social, civic, cognitive, personal and aesthetic development of students. They can also provide evidence of a shared American perspective while celebrating multicultural diversity. In spite of differences we share certain common cultural values that are separate from European, Asian or African traditions. This uniquely American multicultural perspective is built upon the premise that human lives are fully real and valuable no matter how far from the engines of power and celebrity they are lived.

To see a really good play thirty years ago you had to go to New York. Now, thanks to public support (NEA) you can see world theatrical productions all over the country. Many of the poorest areas in the U.S. share one characteristic: swift and overwhelming demographic change. Schools *must* take seriously their role as multicultural communities; they are the one place young people from all these different backgrounds come together. There has to be an open dialogue to honor what the cross-section of students found in schools today. This means exhibiting student artistic expression so that their thinking is made public. Many local papers will, for example, devote an occasional section to advertisements designed by students. What an opportunity for artistic design, connection to the mass media and communication! So is using a camcorder to create a spin-off of 30 or 60 second TV commercials. Many Cable TV systems are even required to run these as part of their community access agreements.

Placing the arts closer to the heart of school reform is important to civic values and the full functioning of the human mind. They can help convey the notion that we are all one humane world where the arts can't be separated from thinking, dreaming and social change. There is danger in the belief that the isolated self is the center of the universe and that getting in touch with one's feelings is more important than rational discourse. When it becomes more important to focus on your own problems than on larger social issues bad things start to happen. The arts are particularly effective in reducing insecurity. By sharing a commitment to each other and honoring what each individual brings to the process gives students many access points to the arts, other subjects, and the world. Solid intercultural friendships and a broad consensus that doesn't accept bigotry can reduce the display of intentional bias and inadvertent discriminatory behavior. Arts programs can help the early formation of strong multicultural relationships that can make a major contribution to intergroup understanding.

The Power to Define, Challenge and Explore

Even the Eurocentric tradition of art has borrowed from others and the geopolitical circumstances of its time. Influences fly in every direction. Octavio Paz has observed that *"every Latin American work is a prolongation and a transgression of the Western tradition."* The arts are both an end in themselves and a means to achieve other ends. They have the power to define us, challenge us and help us explore the frontiers of human existence. The effect goes well beyond the art room or performance space to connect to other domains.

A teacher has to examine his/her own thinking about which of the arts is worthy of attention. Why, for example, do I dislike most Rap music? Is it age, class, race, sex, educational level, cultural background, the limitations of spoken "music" or what? Is Rap racist, sexist, divisive, or therapeutic? Oakland rapper 2Pac, whose real name is Tupac Shakur, characterizes America's failed dream as a:

> *Nightmare. That's what I am*
> *America's nightmare.*
> *I am what you made me.*
> *The hate and the evil that you gave me . . .*
> *America, reap what you sow.*
> — Tupac Shakur

His raps send confidences to those living in similar circumstances and open windows on the inner-city for others.

Rap music captures the experience of a generation that feels shut out of mainstream culture and trapped in an environment that forces them to seek other routes to success. The art form is used to express political messages that go much deeper than the swearing and violence of some hard-core rappers — presenting a point of view that is at odds with middle-class American society.

Young white fans usually focus more on the art than the message. But with white youngsters making up much of the audience at some concerts the elders are getting concerned – much like they were with rock music in the fifties and sixties. Like reggae and some other forms of black music the theme of black anger has until recently, gone largely unnoticed by much of white society. It can generate and channel the energy of a mass of people much like rock music in the late 1960s or the way opera helped generate Italian nationalism in the 1860s. By its very nature art is critical and nothing is more deadly dull than a sanitized government style of art.

Herbert Reed once said that the goal of education is the creation of "artists" – people who can creatively make things with potential social impact. Good art participates in the creation of culture. Malcome Muggeridge recently described this process as

> *. . . a natural cafe of the mind, in which we are all the clientele; a meeting place which can be raucous at times both political assembly and place of entertainment, dance floor and theater with all kinds of rooms off it.*

In one sense even science in the context of invention, is seen as an art form. Because the arts sharpen the imagination, providing openings to the untried. Jerry King concluded in the *Art of Mathematics* that in its purest form mathematics produces an esthetic experience. He goes on to propose a "math-world" (comparable to the "art-world") comprising mathematicians' works and a public prepared to at least partially understand some of the ideas presented to them. When connected to history and innovation this "math public" can learn to view the world in new ways. In King's imaginary "math-world" good teachers play a key role in preparing the public for difficult concepts, in much the same way art critics prepared the public for nonrealistic art. To generate ideas perhaps we do 'need a rowdy natural cafe of the mind where you can find every discipline, a band, and a dance floor.

Connecting to Models Outside of School

Fostering creativity in the arts means encouraging students to think for themselves, coming up with different solutions to problems by linking arts education to their own personal experience. Just as it is in life outside of school creativity involves innovative answers to questions that can sometimes change the very nature of the question itself.

Some schools are experimenting with residencies by area artists. Others have connected to adult models by sponsoring projects on sites (an art gallery, symphony hall, the ballet company). In-depth thematic units can be developed that allow students to work on-site to solve real-world and complex problems, understand subject matter in depth, and make connections across disciplines. Recently "expeditionary learning" schools have been developed in

Portland, Maine, Boston, Decatur, Georgia, and Douglas County, Colorado. In these model schools expedition advisors, teachers and principals work on school initiated curriculum in teams. Creating an educational renaissance will require all the community resources educators can connect with.

Getting students interested in a topic or problem and interacting with others in an environment that allows thoughtful and creative expression are objectives that few educators will disagree with. Yet how, with today's already cluttered curriculum, testing requirements, and red tape does a teacher find time to unearth art topics of interdisciplinary interest? Team training can help to share the load and community resources can free up some teacher time. but to keep reform going we are going to have to change organizational structures and protect teachers from bureaucratic requirements.

Teachers can supply classroom vignettes about effective teaching: the butterfly that "hatched" from a chrysalis in their classroom, students' creative language experience stories, movement (dance), creative dramatics and painting murals. Other teachers might recall the newscast of the whale trapped in the ice which spawned an array of activities: research on whales, letters to elected representatives, a bulletin board charting bird migration patterns, and an attitude survey graph. Good teachers know that to be really excited about a subject they must really care about it.

The social forces surrounding a field of study and individual talent are important factors in generating (or inhibiting) creativity. As far as arts education is concerned this means: legitimizing its goals by becoming an active force in educational change, assuming a more aggressive role with "at-risk" students, and focusing on the potential of the arts to foster thinking skills and problem-solving abilities.

All social and educational institutions convey messages that can affect creativity and artistic development. Deep questions of value are involved in the kind of models we set and our methods for evaluating artistic products. Art may belong to everyone, but being literate in the subject means being able to understand, critique, and create in a whole array of symbol systems. It's best to get high quality instructional experiences and training early on. As children gain more aesthetic understanding teachers can think of them as participants in the artistic process. As students paint their own paintings, compose music, and collaborate in arranging their own dances they come to experience the inner nature of how aesthetic creativity develops.

Classroom Activities that Invite Thoughtfulness:
Ideas for Teachers

Create Writing Partnerships. A common collaborative learning strategy is to divide the partnership into a "thinker" and a "writer." One partner reads a short concept or question out loud and tells what he or she thinks the answer should be. The writer writes it down if they agree. If not, they try to convince the "thinker" that there is a better answer. If agreement cannot be reached they write two answers and initial one.

Literature and Movement. Some poems, stories, myths, and ballads are particularly suited to interpretation through movement. Choose one or two students to read while the others respond to the reading with creative movements. Create a magical atmosphere with poetry. Use penlights in a darkened classroom or use colorful ribbons for creative movement that requires group effort and harmony. While the teacher or one of the children reads, have the other children reflect or enact the poem in movement. Each child can hold a penlight or ribbon to help create an effect.

Improvise Short Original Music Pieces. Students can improvise music pieces and variations on existing pieces, using voices or instruments (e.g., traditional, nontraditional, jazz, rock, electronic).

Working With a Partner in the Art Museum. In an art museum, students might focus on a few paintings or pieces of sculpture. Have students make up a question or two about some aspect of the art they wish to explore further – and respond to five or six questions from the list in a notebook or writing pad they take with them.

Possible Questions for Reflection

- Compare and contrast technology and art as ways for viewing the past, present, or future differently.
- How is the art work put together?
- How are pictures, pottery, and music used to communicate?
- How did the creator of the visual art image expect the viewer to react or respond? Is the content or subject of the artwork the most important part of it? What else might the artist have wished to produce?
- How does your background affect how you view the message?
- Visuals are authored in much the way print communication is authored. How does the author of a picture or piece of sculpture guide the viewer through such things as point of view, size, distortion or lighting?
- What are the largest or smallest artistic designs of the work?
- What is the main idea, mood, or feeling of the work?
- When you close your eyes and think about the visual, what pictures do you see? What sounds do you hear? Does it remind you of anything – a book, a dream, TV, something from your life?
- How successful is the sculpture or artwork? What is your response to it?
- Where did the artist place important ideas?

- How do combinations or organization of things make you feel?
- Does the artwork tell us about big ideas such as courage, freedom, or war?
- How does it fit in with the history of art?
- What does the work say about present conflicts concerning art standards, multiculturalism and American culture?
- How did the work make you feel inside?
- Was the artistic work easy or hard to understand?
- Why do you think it was made? What would you like to change about it?

Productive Creativity

Creativity is more than originality. There is a strong connection between creativity (including originality and novelty) and basic academic skills. The two feed on each other. Developing a unique clarity, style and focus is essential as any skill area. The rote drill approach of educational fundamentalists represent narrow thinking patterns that can hinder comprehension and creativity. To flesh out dry facts with substance it is necessary to build on elements of basic skills to open up a multiplicity of images which can be creatively tapped and explored (Thousand, Villa, Nevin, 2002).

The traditional notion of educators is that if fluency, flexibility, and originality were systematically taught, true creativity would follow. Unfortunately, it isn't that simple. To begin with, teachers didn't know how to teach it or model these concepts. Secondly, fluency doesn't count for much if all the ideas generated are simply novel or trivial. Worse yet, if flexibility clouds issues or discourages student decision-making it can impede learning. Even "originality" as it's understood in this context, is sometimes simple social accommodation, rather than either intuitive boundary-pushing or barrier breaking.

Traditionally, common school practice encouraged children to be plodders who saw the rules as conduits for action, rather than as springboards for changing realities. In the real world we learn a lot about creativity from our failures, accidents, and the personal restructuring of our reality in the face of uncertainty. Taking risks, dealing with failure, the desire to be surprised, and enjoying ambiguity are all essential elements in creative behavior. All are difficult for teachers to teach and model *and* for many students to accept. However, both students and teachers profit from undergoing the fatigue of figuring things out for themselves.

The research suggests one way to fuse creative thinking to basic skills is to provide a rich arts environment and enough structure for a student to search out interesting material (Fuhrman, et al. 1989). Skillful teachers then examine the quality of the thought that has gone into student productions and helps with critical analysis and self cultivation.

Some American education institutions have proven that they can design learning experiences that in the arts are optimal for a diversity of learning styles and student dispositions. They do this by assisting students in developing both disciplined basic skills and genuine creativity thus providing multiple paths for student development (Gardner, 1990). Gaining creative observational skills seems to help students develop distinctive styles and gain familiarity with a wide range of artistic approaches.

Without the arts students would be denied the opportunity to develop the mental skills that makes art possible. Art is more than some abstract notion of beauty. Good art helps us rethink our conception of reality and alters our perspective. The creativity engendered can be a catalyst for information, change and the enrichment of our intellectual, cultural and civic life.

Artistic production, particularly for younger children, can play an important role as students produce in different artistic media. But even at early levels students need to be grounded in the ability to reflect on art and be able to think about the thinking skills involved. Seeking the rewards of what adults see as good creative products makes their appearance less likely. No student response should be considered the "right" one. The mix of modeling intellectual stimulation and natural rapport is part of the mysterious art of good teaching. Criticism, history, and aesthetics all contribute to production and a student's ability to draw inferences and interpret the powerful ideas. The arts make use of certain conventions and symbol systems to express figurative meaning. This can include symbols in its expression through style (the fine detail), composition (arrangement of elements) and by creating the possibility for multiple meanings. "Reading" an artist's symbols is as much of a skill as reading print. This means going beyond the transient messages that may be overvalued by the culture.

The playful invention of a young child may be closer to the way an innovative scientist or an artist works than a more "sophisticated" older student. Both good artists and good scientists have a highly developed sense of wonder and skepticism. They share a world of complex options and multiple paths that require flexibility and energy to negotiate. Neither the art or the science world is well understood by many Americans. Even the well educated have barely enough understanding of art, science, or politics to act effectively on aesthetic, scientific, or political matters that they encounter in their personal, professional, or civic lives.

Establishing a Collaborative Arts Community

Valuing a range of contributions within a supportive and collaborative community can make the difference between a competent self image and the devastating belief that nothing can be done "right." Recasting the teacher's role from authority figure dispensing knowledge to that of a collaborative team leader (coaching mixed ability teams) is a major ingredient of cooperative learning. This process is particularly important with new media – like video –

because it takes a small group to do much of the production. Making students active participants in deciding what and how they should learn doesn't diminish the need for informed decision-makers. But without these – and other changes – in the power relationships within schools and within the schoolroom educational reform will be stymied.

In a collaborative setting the teacher helps students gain confidence in their ability and the group's ability to work through problems and consequently rely less on the teacher for validating their thinking. This involves a conceptual reexamination of today's student population, the learning process, decision-making relationships, and classroom organizational structure. Challenges for the professional teacher in this new environment:

– taking a more active role in serving students of multicultural backgrounds and "at risk" students. In many cases this means addressing non-Western artistic formats.
– focusing and taking advantage of cooperative learning teams to foster students' thinking, reasoning and problem-solving abilities.
– making use of cooperative learning strategies, peer tutoring and new technology to reach a range of learners and learning styles.
– working to professionalize arts education and legitimatize the arts in the schools. This includes assessment of student knowledge, ability and performance.
– developing exemplary materials supportive of cooperative learning. This development will have to be done with particular attention to: the promotion of thinking skills, the needs of "at risk" students, the needs of teacher professionalism, assessment, accountability, and the advent of new technologies.

Although children are capable of both imitation and figuring out structure on their own, they can use mechanisms for thinking and digging deeply into subject matter and themselves. They also need structures for analyzing works of art, music, dance, and drama; frameworks for sorting out what is real in the environment. Children have widely divergent talents and interpretations that they derive from their own perceptions and ways they filter the world. For those who believe in educating as many "intelligences" (a la Howard Gardner) as possible, the arts have the potential to strongly influence educational thought and policies.

> *Communication is a process of sharing experience till it becomes a common possession. It modifies the disposition of both parties who partake in it.*
>
> — John Dewey

It is difficult to consider products of the imagination apart from the system of values brought to it. Good exercises in art education involve students in altering familiar or unfamiliar images along lines they feel are promising. Students need the chance to try things out, reflect on what they have done, and try again. Most teachers know how to encourage or reorient students if they are getting nowhere. They also believe all children will learn and recognize the need for high expectations as they strive to reach every individual. Good teachers are also able to facilitate, probe, and draw on additional information, examples, and alternative approaches for those students who were unable to connect with the information initially. To achieve this it is important for teachers to know the subject well enough to feel comfortable with it.

Children possess the capacity to absorb knowledge – but it takes intelligent teaching to use that knowledge to reason effectively. Curriculum development requires staff development. It is often adult models (like teachers) and family support that make the difference between a commitment to the arts or dismissing them as irrelevant.

Effective teachers strive to ensure what's being learned is a center of interest for students. This often means walking a fine line as they engage students as active thinkers – without interfering when children are working well on their own. Creative experiences in the arts are a blend of informed adult encouragement and opportunities for creative exploration. A flexible arts curriculum requires not only knowledge about each child but judgment about when to intervene, recognizing (like Emerson) that sometimes it is best to "let the bird sing without deciphering the song."

A Collaborative Arts Curriculum Means

1. Active Learning

Students exchange ideas when they are involved in well organized tasks, with materials they can manipulate. Active learning is enhanced when students can collaboratively make predictions, find patterns, explore and construct ideas, models, and stories.

2. Interesting Activities

Lessons should include activities that are designed to develop higher thinking skills, rather than quick right answers. Problems on diverse topics, which encourage speculation or estimation are more likely to motivate and encourage students to work together on the lesson.

3. Chances for Student Interaction

Students need to develop the ability to work together, to become sensitive and responsive to group members and group needs. There is a need for activities that involve all group members as well as a need to sensitize the group to include all members in active involvement.

4. Opportunities for Thinking

Students should be given opportunities to explore diverse ideas emphasizing concepts and relationships. Challenging tasks and opportunities for interaction with peers can lead to more advanced thinking and creative discussions.

5. Teachers as Advisors and Curriculum Developers

Textbooks and teacher's manuals need to be altered or replaced by teacher ideas, materials, and activities that arouse student interest and encourage cooperation. The teacher's role becomes that of a consultant, advisor, and learner who interacts with teaching peers.

6. Lesson Structure and Accountability

Opportunities should be provided for group or teacher-led summaries of important aspects of the tasks. Students need to discuss what they have learned with the teacher and other students in order to understand and explain the activities they have worked on.

Students are encouraged to take an active role in planning what they will study and how they will do it. One way to divide the class is to have students self select into cooperative groups based on common interests in a topic. Students decide on what specifically they wish to find out, divide up the work among themselves, summarize, and present their findings to the class. There is much freer communication and greater involvement when students share in the planning and decision-making and carry out *their* plan. Students achieve more through discussing, investigating and working in mixed ability groups than if working alone (Brown, & Pleydell, 1999).

A broad perspective can amplify basic subject matter and help students and teachers become better cooperative thinkers and decision-makers. The integration of diverse subjects has advantages sufficient to encourage the examination of what content best lends itself to this approach. Like any concept for organizing learning, the value of interdisciplinary curriculum lies in the quality of the implementation. It always comes back to teachers and their knowledge of their discipline – *the characteristics of effective instruction.* Like E. B. White, who wrote that he wanted to keep the notes of his own meeting, teachers must learn to script their own lesson plans.

Fostering Creativity in the Arts

Mass media, social and educational institutions convey messages that can affect creativity and artistic development. Deep questions of value are involved in the kind of models we set and our methods for evaluating artistic products. The arts may belong to everyone, but being literate means being able to understand, critique, and create in a whole array of symbol systems. It seems desirable to have some basic skill training early on. Art without imagination may be sterile – but art without at least some technical skill aborts its image. As children gain more aesthetic understanding it makes sense to think of them as participants in the artistic process. Children can paint their own paintings, jointly compose music, and collaborate in making the video and arranging their own dances. This way they can experience the nature and construct of aesthetic creativity.

With dozens of subjects to teach at the elementary level, we are fortunate to have teachers with enough artistic knowledge and skill to teach painting, pottery, music, movement, and video production. Exploring the broad philosophical dimensions of art will have to be the next step. Teaching expanded lists of facts and bits of knowledge are of little use unless they're integrated into a larger whole. In this process it is just as important to understand something about the arts as to worry about performance or the end product. With inspired teaching and hard work students can develop artistic sensitivity and reasoning skill that touches other subjects.

Distinctive modes of human intelligence can manifest themselves in surprising circumstances. The arts are natural to the way children learn. Making schools really responsible to the different ways students learn involves changing institutional structure like increasing school autonomy from bureaucratic and other outside interference. School reform requires a change in the power relationships at all levels. To produce graduates who are confident and competent means that every child should have access to a rigorous arts curriculum in a climate of reasoned thoughtfulness and high expectations. Tomorrow's arts education will be discipline-based and aimed more at developing sophisticated consumers (Zuma, Kukis, Kline, 2004).

Improving education has as much to do with improving cultural quality as it does with increasing productivity. Much of what students have to do in the world outside of school involves the ability to work in groups, self-regulate, plan, execute and complete various kinds of projects. Real-life creativity involves innovative answers to questions and sometimes even changing the nature of the question itself. To paraphrase Charles Kettering, a problem well stated is a problem half solved. Creativity is an ability to make something original, pose significant questions, and solve problems of consequence. Fostering creativity in the arts – or anything else – means encouraging students to think for themselves so that they can come up with different solutions to problems as they link arts and education to their own personal experience.

> *Creativity involves breaking out of established patterns in order to look at things in a different way.*
> — Edward de Bono

Arts Education Heightens Students' Powers

As an integral part of perception, expression, problem solving, thought and action, the arts offer insights into the educational process. At the same time, they enrich and burnish learning with wisdom. As Marten Heidegger has suggested, the arts help us see beyond what *is* – to open spaces. This clearing can help us reach beyond the mundane to something new (Rogoff, 1990). It also means shifting from an emphasis on "making art" to equal time on analysis, history and culture – known in the field as discipline based arts education.

Arts education has a role in creating an education renaissance – as an agent of social change in general and education in particular. If artwork, music, dance and drama are not found in the public schools then the chances for thoughtfulness, self expression and aesthetic appreciation are bound to be diminished. On a broader plane, the arts can help counter the tendency for standardization in the school reform process. The possibilities the arts offer for a unique opening up of new spaces will be sorely missed if they are relegated to the margins of the educational restructuring debate.

Learning how to interpret works of art – and creating their own – means more time for instruction in the arts – currently among the least taught "core subjects." The current efforts to enlarge arts education is partly the result of adding the arts to the national educational goals that call for American students to meet world class standards in core academic areas. As new standards are developed for the arts, it's important to maintain the integrity of the individual disciplines (visual art, dance, music, and theater) and show students how these disciplines interconnect.

The arts work invisibly
to widen and deepen the imagination.
– Van Duyn, 1993

RESOURCES AND REFERENCES

Albert, F. (1990). The Latin American State. *Journal of Economic Perspectives.* University of Connecticut: American Economic Association, vol. *4*(3), 61–74.

Association for Supervision and Curriculum Development. (1994). ASCD Conference Report, Fowler ASCD Update. Author.

Brown, V. & Pleydell, S. (1999). *The dramatic difference.* Portsmouth, NH: Heinemann.

Brown & Pleydell. (1999). Their own language: The language of make believe. Portsmith, NH: Heinemann.

Calkins, L. (1991). *Living between the lines.* Portsmouth, NH: Heineman.

The College Board.(1985). *Academic preparation in the arts: Teaching for transition from high school to college.* New York.

Cornett, C. (1999). *The arts as meaning makers: Integrating literature and the arts.* New Jersey: Prentice Hall.

Dissanayake, E. (1992). *HomoAestheticus.* New York: Free Press.

Eisner, E. (1991). *The enlightened eye.* New York: Macmillan.

Edwards, L. (2001). *The creative arts: A process approach for teachers and children.* (3rd Ed.), New Jersey: Prentice Hall.

Fowler, C. (1992). *Understanding how the arts contribute to excellent education.* A study prepared for the NEA.

Fraser, J.T. (1990). *Of time, passion and knowledge.* Princeton, NJ: Princeton University Press.

Fuhrman, J. K., McCallum, K. & Davis, A. A. (1989). *Nature, 356,* 148–149.

Gardner, H. (1983). *Frames of mind.* New York: Basic Books.

Gardner, H. (1990). *To open minds.* New York: Basic Books.

Gardner, H. (1993). *Creating minds.* New York, NY: Basic Books.

Gelineau, R. P. (2004). *Integrating the arts across the curriculum.* Belmont, CA: Wadsworth/Thompson Learning.

Getty Center for Education In the Arts. (1989). *Education in art: Future building.*

Goldberg, M. (2001). *Arts and learning: An integrated approach to teaching and learning in multicultural & multilingual settings.* (2nd Ed.). New York: Longman.

Kaagan, S. (1990). *Aesthetic persuasion: Pressing the cause of arts education in American schools.* A Monograph for the Getty Center for Education in the Arts.

Maeroff, G. (1988). *The empowerment of teachers.* New York: Teachers College Press.

Miller, B. C. & Drake, S. (1990). *Holostic learming: A teacher's guide to integrated studies.* Toronto: OSICE Press.

National Art Education Associates. (1992). *Elementary art programs: A guide for administrators.* Reston, VA: National Art Education Association.

National Standards for Education in the Arts (1994). *The Arts and Education Reform Goals 2000.* Washington, D.C.: U.S. Office of Education.

National Standards for Arts Education. (1994). *What every young American should know and be able to do in the Arts.* Reston, VA: Developed by the Consortium of National Arts Education Associations.

Nesbitt, J. (1986). *International directory of recreation-oriented assistance.* Venice, CA: Lifeboat Press.

Pinker, S. (2002). *The blank slate: The modern denial of human nature.* New York: Viking Press.

Rogoff, B. (1990). *Apprentices in thinking: Children's guided participation in culture.* New York: Oxford University Press.

Sampson, M., Rasinski, J., Sampson, M. (2003). *Total Literacy* (3rd ed.) Belmont, CA: Wadsworth/Thomson Learning.

Schubert, W. & Willis, G. (1991). *Understanding curricula and teaching through the arts.* New York: SUNY Press.

Sharan, S. (1990). *Cooperative learning: Theory and research.* Westport, CT: Bergin & Garvey and Praeger Publishing.

Smith, R., (Ed.). (1990). *Discipline-based art education: Origins, meaning and development.* Champagne, IL: University of Illinois Press.

Spacks, P. M. (1990). Books by Fellows of the National Humanities Center. Chapel Hill, NC: University of North Carolina Press.

Starr, P. (2004). *The creation of the media: Political origins of modern communications.* Cambridge, MA: Basic Books.

Tebbs, T. (1991), Unpublished paper dealing with art, collaboration, and gifted education. (1994).

Thousand, J., Villa, R., Nevin, A. (2002). *Creativity and collaborative learning: The practical guide to empowering students, teachers, and families.* (2nd ed.). Baltimore, MD: Brookes Publishing

Viadero, D. (1993). *Draft standards for arts education: Knowledge, performance, and discipline based learners.* Washington D.C.: U.S. Education Department, the National Endowment for the Arts, and the National Endowment for the Humanities. National Panel for the Development of Standards for Arts Education.

Whitehead, A, N. (1933). *Adventures of ideas.* London: Collier Macmillan.

Wlodkowski, R. & Jaynes, J. (1990). *Eager to learn.* San Francisco, CA: Jossey-Bass.

Zmuda, A., Kuklis, R., Kline, E. (2004). *Transforming schools: Creating a culture of continuous improvement.* Alexandria, VA: Association for Supervision and Curriculum Development.

Zuma, K. et al. (2004). *Who invects whom?* Luri, MN: Lippincott, Williams & Wilkins, Inc.

Chapter 10

INVENTING THE CIVIC FUTURE: SOCIAL RESPONSIBILITY AND CITIZENSHIP EDUCATION

In practice, the development of deliberative character is essential to realizing the ideal of a democratically sovereign society. . . . The willingness and ability to deliberate set socially serious people apart from both sophists, who use clever argument to elevate their own interests into self-righteous causes. . . . Citizens therefore have good reason to wonder how deliberative or democratic character can be developed in children, and who can develop it.

– Amy Gutmann

Disturbing signs of civic ignorance are reflected in the steady decline in the percentage of young adults who vote. According to a poll by People for the American Way, only 12% of 18 to 24-year-olds believe that voting is an important part of citizenship (Democracy's Next Generation, November, 1989). The results of the nation's first examination of "legal literacy" show that a majority of students didn't know what the Bill of Rights was. Many Americans were even surprised to find out that the American legal system assumes innocence until guilt is proven (Carroll, J.D. et al., 1987).

Are the schools to blame for the decline of knowledge about democratic institutions and the increase in apathy when it comes to participation? By the 1980s the schools had almost stopped trying to inculcate civic virtues and the ability to participate in the broader community (Boyer, 1991). But whether it's a national poll, educational survey, or legal study, the results point to institutions sharing in the responsibility for fewer citizens than ever understanding the fundamental social rights and responsibilities of citizenship. There is enough blame to go around.

More than most cultures, Americans have reinvented history – as they went along – from half remembered scraps of folklore (television sound bites) that

188

put sentimentalized visions in the way of the truth. "Out here," as John Wayne said, "due process is a bullet . . . ." As living realities get transformed into posthumous myths there is a teasing gap separating the initial event and its subsequent narration. With today's incessant electronic distortion, thinking critically and showing a high level of civic responsibility not only becomes more difficult, but more important. Like getting other aspects of a national curriculum to work, citizenship education must be broadly conceived and developed as a grand cooperative educational venture.

Social Responsibility

New blueprints for reintroducing social responsibility and civics into the curriculum will require a curriculum that helps students develop the knowledge and skills needed to participate in a civil society – open-mindedness, willingness to compromise, a tolerance of diversity, and a general civility.

Teachers contribute to social responsibility when they teach important social skills like cooperation, effective group communication, and a sense of responsibility for living in the community with others. Citizenship skills include steps for social problem solving, handling conflict, and ways of saying "no" to negative influences. Social and civic responsibility means going beyond self to taking a degree of responsibility for the various groups than one is part of. As the new framework for national civic education points out, a major goal is to encourage students to "participate in all elements of a civil society (National Council for the Social Studies, 'Civitas,' 1991)."

Teaching civics and social responsibility can begin by providing classroom practice in using social skills while establishing a classroom community of learners. Teachers and students create ground rules for treating others in the classroom that emphasize caring and respect. When students are socially responsible in their immediate group it is easier to deal with knowledge regarding social issues, institutions, policies and what it means to be a citizen in a democracy.

Beyond history, government and civics classes, social responsibility is fostered by having students explore issues of importance to them and their various "communities" – becoming active participants in planning and carrying out service projects. This approach to practicing social responsibility gets students actively engaged and teaches them about taking action to make things happen.

Developing a sense of responsibility for the world around us adds to our capacity to make a difference to the world throughout their lives. The merger of public issues with citizenship education and personal development helps young people recognize the importance of a life of contribution to the public good.

To balance intellectual challenge with deep personal involvement and open expression of ideas and feelings, a strong sense of community and trust must be created. Small-group discussions – exchanging ideas with people who have different personalities, interests, and backgrounds – helps students connect the large concepts they've contemplated with their own lives.

Implicit in the idea of civic education is the privilege to criticize, oppose, and participate in the positive shaping of public policy. To play their role in building a society with a stronger moral foundation, schools must contribute to improving the social ethic – as well as individual moral behavior. Individual responsibility by itself is simply not enough. For students to escape their feelings of powerlessness there is a need to develop their sense of community and build confidence about the possibility for making a difference in the world.

Social responsibility – that is, a personal investment in the well-being of others and of the planet – doesn't just happen. Aspects of social responsibility that are taking shape throughout the country: cooperative learning, conflict resolution, multicultural education, moral development, global education, environmental education, community service, and involvement in political/ social issues. The stance is proactive, not reactive. Involvement in social issues that affect us, can be implicit in a curriculum that connects to human values and global concerns.

Deliberation on public issues cannot be put on hold until adulthood. Students need to make sense of local community concerns and authentic problems. This can be accomplished by engaging students in deliberations concerning public problems and controversies. Such tasks as selecting a controversy from the evening news or newspaper and writing an analysis, presenting arguments for and against the issue and drawing on history to show similarities and differences serve as examples. Looking critically at issues like economic systems in turmoil, environmental problems (like the rainforest), help students recognize the interdependent, global nature of our actions.

Caught Between Social Disintegration and the Lack of a Powerful Vision

As we begin to look at our own shortcomings – we must judge ourselves by the norms of a decent and democratic society. Today, many American children are caught in a crossfire of institutional irresponsibility and violence. Social disintegration and a downward spiral of educational quality should come as no surprise when schools are going bankrupt and having to close before the end of the term. You can only get the pony express to run so fast – at some point you have to move up to the telegraph. Keeping them open – and improving the quality is a question of will.

There is general agreement in the United States today that old models of schooling are not working. The entertainment-driven late twentieth century American society has developed a short attention span. Symbolic issues are highlighted, genuine civic debate short-circuited, and citizens find few real outlets for their concerns. Issues are dealt with in a fast and symbolic manner, with little thought of the big picture or root causes. The flag, death penalty, and racial issues are great for stirring people up, but they can get in the way of civic education and a desire to participate. Both our political and our educational failings cry out for sustained intelligent interest and the participation of the public, not convenient avoidance or private answers to public problems (Sampson, M., Rasinski, T., Sampson, M., 2003).

Quality education is caught between social disintegration and the lack of a powerful moral vision. To help students assume the role of responsible citizens, civic education must be strengthened. Helping students learn to think critically, exercise natural curiosity and develop a civic consciousness can buttress educational and democratic values. A preoccupation with the economic impact of education needs to be balanced with the advancement of citizenship. It's important to recognize the fact that even a successful economic or system will fail unless its people become competent and caring citizens.

At the very time social consciousness and democracy are growing around the globe, there are indications that many American students leave school without knowledge of democracy and understanding of responsible citizenship. It is only through a knowledge of civic issues and an appreciation of citizenship that our students will gain the capacity to live responsibly. The moral test of any society is how it provides appropriate models that can help students see beyond themselves.

> *It would be the ultimate irony of modern history if Americans*
> *gave themselves up to self-indulgence, corruptions, apathy, or greed*
> *just as the rest of the world was clamoring for democracy and*
> *freedom in the idioms of Jefferson, Madison, and Lincoln.*
> – "Civitas," Report from the National Council of the Social Studies

The Central Role of Civic Education

Civic education is a broad view of citizenship that encompasses knowledge and skills required for full participation in a democratic society and the civic values such as open-mindedness, willingness to compromise, and tolerance for diversity. To develop the skills for informed democratic participation requires a civic knowledge and an understanding of how to act on ethical issues. Just what is civic education?

- *Communication*
  Democracy is built on thoughtful discourse. This means teaching students to think critically, listen, and communicate effectively.

- *Active Participation*
  Students need to be actively involved in learning and in the decision-making process. Rather than textbooks and worksheets, students need to

work on group projects, write about issues and ideas important in their lives, discuss, research important questions, debate, and work cooperatively.

- *Core of basic knowledge reflecting the democratic perspective*
  This includes a knowledge of history and government as well as social issues and problems.
- *Thoughtful debate*
  Dealing with sensitive, often controversial social issues, conflict and consensus concerning the common good. Giving students opportunities to think carefully about life's most important concerns.
- *Responsible school and community behavior*
  Students need to recognize their role as part of the school community, work and participate in decisions that affect their lives.
- *Help Students make connections between learning and life*
  Too many students feel disconnected and rejected. Students need to understand that learning is connected to living. This means developing decision-making skills, forming convictions, and acting boldly on values held (Ernest Boyer, Carnegie Foundation, 1991).

Being informed and active in the community are part of civic competence. Many teachers are afraid to teach values because they ask "whose values?" When it comes to American civic values we get even more specific: democracy functions by the sustained involvement of its people, and concepts of intellectual freedom, tolerance, equity and due process are all important for students to understand. A balance between participation, knowledge, and moral development is a key to the social consciousness. Schools can decide to focus on the cognitive skills and knowledge related to civics – while arranging for students to learn participation skills through community service projects or internships.

Future Learning Communities

> *Has democracy been reduced to a kind of state (electronic) fair for kids and suckers, while the real decisions are made behind tightly closed doors?*
> — Scott Spencer

School is not just a place to study formal civic structures. It is "also a place to examine the way things work *behind* closed doors.". Students can study ideas and work out the impact of those ideas on society. Schooling also means more than setting goals or striving for higher levels of academic achievement. Creating a caring learning culture is just as important. When each child has the time and space to play a meaningful role in the classroom, the result is a more genuine community. The '90s show promise of developing a new moral density that includes an awareness of consequences and time. This means reaching beyond a narrow view of academic knowledge to helping students achieve socially responsible and fulfilling lives. What students think about, talk about, and the civic values they act on are all important. Creative teachers are sensitive to these needs and are inventing diverse ways of helping students succeed (Stronge, 2002).

Learning is the result of personal efforts to construct meaning. The best teachers don't try to perform like surgeons, rather they try to help children become active learners who can "operate" on themselves. By taking some power over their immediate situation students can feel more empowered when it comes to dealing with broader social issues. The central idea here is that learning is most effective when it is personal, purposeful, and intrinsically motivated. Building on the dynamic of self-actualization means looking at what stimulates the responsibilities of citizenship and what constrains it.

Learning about social responsibility and democratic principles is a social process of actively constructing meaning from experience – including a broad range of print and visual imagery. Collaborators: peers, teachers, and parents can assist by helping to define social problems, present possible solutions, and provide a supportive frame of reference. The sense of a learning community can help children become literate enough to comprehend an extremely complex world. Quite simply, the reason for including ethics and civics is to produce better citizens. And these concepts must receive greater attention as we construct new national education reform efforts. Lip service to civics education just won't get it done.

> *Learning involves an active reconstruction of the knowledge of skill that is presented, on the basis of the learner's existing internal model of the world. The process is therefore interactional in nature, both within the learner and between the learner and the teacher, and calls for negotiation of meaning, not its unidirectional transmission.*
> – Gorden Wells, The Meaning Makers

A major direction for the twenty-first century is to create classrooms that recognize students and teachers as active thinkers, doers, investigators, and cooperative problem solvers. Future lessons will include meaning-centered explorations where learning how to think is just as important as any set curriculum. Many models and different experimental schools are needed to reach all of our children. As the research literature develops, directions in teaching are bound to change – along with the technological base. Keeping these developments in contact with practice is a major challenge. Teachers must be inspired to be lifetime learners and responsible participants in social change.

In the future students will spend more time working together on projects. Classrooms will be arranged for cooperative learning with clustered desks (or tables) and plenty of resource materials. Teachers will guide explorations and spend less time lecturing to entire classrooms of children. As children form active learning teams and communicate more freely, they teach one another. Learning responsibility in a small group can then be extended to understanding the nature of social responsibility.

> *Prejudice . . . may be reduced by equal status contact between majority and minority groups in the pursuit of common goals. The effect is greatly enhanced if this contact is sanctioned by institutional supports . . . and provided it is of the sort that leads to the perception of common interests and common humanity between members of the two groups.*
> – Gordon W. Allport

Central to a vigorous campaign against ineffective education is a change of orientation towards the common good – with less room for egocentrism and special interests. It is time to attend to our common interests (as opposed to our differences) and help students develop a framework that allows us to come together. Instruction in the future will help students understand both fundamental access of knowledge and the knowledge that is essential to be a citizen in a democratic society. This includes understanding how a democratic society works – and what can be done to make it better. These civic and citizenship agendas are inherent in any school reform efforts.

Highly educated people and fresh ideas are needed to overcome the American tendency for talk (grand objectives) and taking little action. In the 1980s grim reality was often powdered over with the current version of unreality that the public had been induced to buy. Fortunately, buying does not automatically imply belief. Rather it is often simply a sign that no institutional alternative exists. In recent years Americans have been obsessed with symbolism. As we prepare to enter the twenty-first century we can no longer rely on pretense, myth, and past accomplishments. Now it's time to get serious and deal with substantive issues (Ohler, 2001).

Reinventing American schooling and civic education will take more than national standards and model schools. Creating a new context for learning and the thoughtful preparation needed to equip young people for citizenship requires sustained economic, political, and public support. It is a complex task that must involve a mixture of new models and an openness to a range of approaches. One of the most important contributions that educators can make is to provide some bright tiles in the educational mosaic that schools can examine as they search to build the instructional and social future.

We would like to thank Dr. Thomassine Sellers for her ideas and contributions.

REFERENCES AND READINGS

Adams, D. & Hamm, M. (1991). *Cooperative learning: Critical yhinking and collaboration across the curriculum.* Springfield, IL: Charles C Thomas.

Boyer, E. (1991). *Ready to learn, a mandate for the nation.* Princeton, NJ: Carnegie Foundation for the Advancement of Teaching.

Boyer, E. (1990). Civic Responsibility for Responsible Citizens. *Educational Leadership 48,* (3), 5–7.

Carroll, J. D. et. al., (1987). *We the people: A review of U.S. government and civics textbooks.* Washington, DC: People for the American Way.

Democracy's Next Generation, (November, 1989). Washington, D.C.: People for the American Way. Study conducted by Peter D. Hart Research Associates.

Dionne, E. J. Jr. (1991). *Why Americans hate politics.* New York: Simon & Schuster.

Dublin, M. (1991). *Futurehype: The tyranny of prophecy.* E.P. Dutton.

Gutmann, A. (1987). *Democratic education.* Princeton, NJ: Princeton University Press.

National Council for the Social Studies. (1991). *Civitas* (Report available from National Council for the Social Studies, 3501 Newark St. N.W., Washington, D.C. 20016.

Noddings, N. (1989). Who Cares? in *Education Moral People,* pp. 216–232. M. Brabeck (Ed.) New York: Praeger.

Ohler, J. (2001). Future courses: *A compendium of thought about education, technology, and the future.* Bloomington, IN: Technos Press.

Sampson, M. B., Rasinski, T., Sampson, M. (2003). Belmont, CA: Wadsworth/ Thomson Learning.

Spencer, S. (1991). "The old man and the novel." *New York Times Magazine,* Sept. 22, 1991, Section 6, 28–31, 40, 42, 47.

Stronge, J. (2002). *Qualities of effective teachers.* Alexandria, VA: Association for Supervision and Curriculum Development.